THE ROAD TO MARGARET

A Story of Hope and Survival in the Industrial South

Lyn Stafford

EASTERN LAKE BOOKS

2015

© Copyright 2015, by Lyn C. Stafford
ISBN: 9781505724301
Layout: Cheryl Perez, www.yourepublished.com
Publisher: Eastern Lake Books, Santa Rosa Beach, FL
Cover art: Farview, Emma Stafford, oil on canvas.

For my children, Keith, Susan and Walter Johns and their families.

CONTENTS

CHARACTERS

Josiah (Johnstone Savage, bef 1780-1820), b Doddington,
    Cambridgeshire, England, m Susan Stafford, d Cambridgeshire.
Johnstone Stafford, boot and shoemaker from March, Cambridgeshire,
    England (Real name, William Savage Stafford, 1814-1906).
Elizabeth, his wife.
William Savage Stafford, Johnstone's son, born in March,
    Cambridgeshire, England, died in Birmingham, AL (Real name
    William Savage Stafford, Jr., 1835-1905).
Emma Rebecca Melsheimer (1849-1934) from Ohio, moved to
    Woodlawn, AL with William.
Frederick Stafford (1847-1912), Freddie's uncle and William's brother,
    also born in Cambridgeshire.
Will (William Marcus Stafford, 1861-1938) born in Waukegan, IL to
    William's first wife. George Timothy's half brother.
Freddie (Frederick L. Stafford, 1862-abt 1890), born in Waukegan, IL
    to William's first wife. George Timothy's half brother.
Joseph and Alma Caswell, fictional characters. Joseph's story is based
    on that of John Dean, a union organizer in Alabama in the
    1930s.
Sam, fictitious name for Big Warrior's son, mikka or chief of the
    Abhika clan, Upper Creek Nation.
Thomas Hodge (d 1860s), fictitious name for Lella's husband,
    Luchipoga clan, Upper Creek Nation..
Lella (abt 1850-1890), Sam's granddaughter and Abhika.
Lila Hodge (abt 1889-1928), Lella's granddaughter and mother of
    Gertrude, Charlie and Jerry.

Bradford (Charles Bradford, Sr. abt 1893-1974), descended from slaves in South Carolina. Farmer married to Lila Hodge. Died in West Blocton mining town in 1974. Gertrude's father.

Gertrude Bradford (1912-1983), cook and housekeeper born in Margaret, AL. Bradford and Lila's daughter.

Jerry Bradford, Bradford's oldest son.

Charlie (Charles Bradford, Jr.), Bradford's youngest son.

George Timothy Stafford (1875-1934), tile distributor, born in Eldora, IA, died in Birmingham, AL. Margot's husband.

Margot Berry, wife of George Timothy Stafford (Real name, Margaret Chapman Berry, 1875-1963).

Alice Mary Stafford (1873-1924), Edwin Grant Stafford (1870-1929) and Cyrus Black Stafford, Sr. (1878-1930) George Timothy Stafford's sisters and brothers who moved to Birmingham.

Georgie, George and Margot's son. Engineer who built Birmingham Manufacturing Company (Real name George Timothy Stafford, Jr., 1907-1991 and the author's father), born in Birmingham.

Evelyn Coffin, George's wife (and the author's mother, 1907-1986), born in Birmingham.

Cy (Cyrus Black Stafford, Jr. 1917-1945), Georgie's first cousin, Cyrus Black Stafford's son.

Tim (George Timothy Stafford, III) and Harry Coffin Stafford, the author's brothers, born in Birmingham.

Dr. Cloud fictitious name for doctor in Mountain Brook.

Henry Fairchild DeBardeleben (1840-1910), Alabama's famous industrialist and owner of more than 150,000 acres of mineral lands, as well as coal and coke companies and blast furnaces.

Charles F. DeBardeleben (1897-1979), son of Henry F. DeBardeleben. Vice-president of Alabama Fuel and Iron Company and operator of the mines in St. Clair and Jefferson Counties. The town of Margaret is named for his wife.

Karl Daly (William Daly), William's neighbor. I used William Daly's son's name to avoid confusion. Son Karl was George's friend and contemporary.

Disclaimer: The characters in this story are real people, unless otherwise indicated. The stories in this book are based on events that actually occurred. Although the author makes every attempt to quote historical persons accurately, when quotes are available from reliable resources, and to portray them in as true a light as possible, the author was not there—except in Part III. Clearly the words and actions herein are the result of the creative process and not to be taken literally.

FOREWORD

The same year the statue of Vulcan, the largest cast iron statue in the world, became a Works Progress Administration (WPA) project in 1937 in Alabama, I came into the world. According to mythology, Juno bore Jupiter a child named Vulcan, a child so ugly and deformed that Juno threw him down from heaven. Vulcan broke one of his legs in the fall, but survived. He built a fire to keep warm. As he huddled in front of that fire, he watched precious metals melt from the stone. From these metals he began to craft objects both useful and beautiful—metal chairs, pots and pans, gold and silver jewelry. The gods held his work in such high regard that they proclaimed him god of fire and the forge. Today, his statue stands on top of Red Mountain, high above the city of Birmingham, Alabama—a city with its own disfigurements to overcome.

I spent my childhood among great aunts and uncles, whose lives spanned the better part of two centuries. Their stories covered the Gold Rush, the Civil War and both World Wars. No wonder I love Southern history and spend time in musty archives trying to solve history's puzzles.

The first Birmingham mystery I tackled was a murder in a mine that took place long before I was born. My great grandfather, an English immigrant and civil engineer, was murdered in a mine. How could I not try to solve that? Another was a how my truest friend, Gertrude, lost her hand in a dynamite blast. Gertrude lived with us. I hung onto every clue, every silly anecdote, until I began to see the larger puzzle that is the South. Those anecdotes harbored the germs of real history, and the stories became *The Road to Margaret*, which made me look at the South anew.

Far more intriguing than these two mysteries were stories about the mining communities, especially Margaret, their rich and powerful operators, labor unions, industry and laws, and how they interconnected. The industrial South was both booming and full of trauma and conflict. Its written records of these events are remarkably complete given the times.

During one trip to Birmingham Public Library's Department of Archives and History, my favorite archivist, Marvin Whiting, asked me to annotate some newspaper columns written by Charles Zukoski for the *Shades Valley Sun* during the Civil Rights era. Mr. Zukoski, then mayor of Birmingham's suburb, Mountain Brook, wrote under the pen name *Button Gwinett[1]* to cover the most horrific events of the day, often using cryptic language to describe them.

In one column he spoke of "the incident of the night before," but failed to identify the event. My job was to find it: I searched the local papers only to find nothing on the front page or even the sports page. After many futile attempts, I turned to the *New York Times* and the *Washington Post* to find answers. Clearly Alabama's newspapers watered down disturbing content to keep readers happy, busy and spending money. Racial violence was often not reported at all. Ribbon-cuttings, football, charitable extravaganzas and new automobiles featuring smiling coeds were.

During another archival excursion in 1983, I stumbled upon the papers of Eugene "Bull" Connor, Birmingham's notorious police commissioner who turned fire hoses on children marching for justice. This infamous segregationist instituted a reign of terror: unchecked bombings, beatings, torture and killings of African American citizens. Many white Southerners believed if they rid themselves of Bull and his buddies—the nasty and, we hoped, short-lived Ku Klux Klan—everything would be set right.

Birmingham Public Library's Archives held letters from Connor, including directives to an unnamed judge[2] to either convict or not convict. Other correspondence in the file came from George Lincoln Rockwell, then head of the Nazi Party in the United States. One of Rockwell's letters to Connor, dated just days before the Freedom Riders' bus was due to arrive in Anniston, instructed Connor to keep his troops back to 'allow his men to do their work.' History tells us that Connor did just that: He held his troops back long enough to allow his Nazi-inspired thugs to lock the Freedom Riders inside their bus in Anniston and burn it. When the riders reached Birmingham, they were almost beaten to death. This was Zukoski's "incident of the night before." Years later, on a return trip to the Archives, to my utter dismay, I discovered that most of that correspondence was now missing from the files. All I had was my notes.

In writing the book, I faced several problems. First, everyone knows the term *nigger*, the derogatory term that was never acceptable, even to Southerners. White folks coined the term *colored* hoping to be less offensive, but that term went the way of the dodo bird, as did lower-case *negro* (pronounced *nig-rah* in the South). The capitalized version, *Negro*, came into use after the Civil War. Not until later in the 20th Century did the term *African-American* come into use. I try to use the term best suited for the times.

Another challenge was naming my characters. I chose to use real names where I knew them, but my dilemma came in distinguishing one character from another. In real life there were too many Georges, Margarets, Charleses and Williams. My grandmother's name, for instance, was Margaret, but Margaret is also the name of the mining town in St. Clair County, so my grandmother was renamed Margot for clarity's sake. Joseph Caswell's life parallels that of a real union organizer, but he and his family are fictional characters invented to tie the stories together. A cast of characters appears after the Contents, with further information sometimes in an endnote.

Whatever their names, the stories are true. I love these characters, and they have changed me forever. I hope their stories will both entertain and challenge you to think anew about the South.

PART I

TWO AMERICAN FAMILIES

Keepers of the dream will come again and again, from what humble places we do not know, to struggle against the crushing odds, leaving behind no worldly kingdom, but only a gleam in the dark hills to show how high we may climb. Already there have been many such heroes— women and men whose names we do not know, but whose words and deeds still light the path for us.

–H. G. Wenzel

1. The '49ers

Glorious summer days at sea invariably turned to nights with moaning winds and waves tossing passengers about. On those chilly nights, Johnstone and the other male passengers, many of them fathers, walked the decks as a way to hush the demons in their heads that told them they were requiring too much of their families. Those without families leaned against the rails smoking their pipes or cigars. Old men huddled in deck chairs covered with blankets and nodded off between sentences.

Below decks were mothers and children, and boys who thought themselves old enough to join their fathers. They ate what their mothers prepared for them, which was mostly treacle, hard biscuits and potatoes. Johnstone's family came from England, but when they ate their potatoes, they ate them slowly and with reverence for their fellow travelers from Ireland, whose relations back in Ireland were dying from lack of the very potatoes they were eating.

Mothers and maiden aunts and cousins fought off seasickness and tended those who suffered from it. They looked after the smallest passengers, especially those with childhood ailments like catarrh. So far none suffered from fevers or pox or cholera, which in 1848, hit London for the second time.

Cholera was not the main reason Johnstone left England. If he were not working, he found his hands balled up into tight fists. He could not shake the tensions. Elizabeth knew this, but her fears were for her children. So she kept them close and made them warm woolen clothing. As the ship rose and fell, she told them stories.

Johnstone made them shoes that all but shone in the dark. He and his children had a ritual each morning spit shining those shoes. The smell of leather and polish forever after reminded the children of their first home in England and their beloved father, the shoemaker of March.

William estimated that by the time he turned eleven he had polished his shoes at least three thousand times. Now he fidgeted, desperate to join the adults on deck and to command the most advantageous spot for watching the sparkle of the ship's wake in the moonlight. He wolfed down his last biscuit and finally was allowed to join his father.

William wore a waistcoat just like his father's. He stood ramrod straight, just like Johnstone.

Johnstone was only five foot eight. He wore calf-high boots—full Wellingtons but with only practical, low, two-inch heels. The men on deck noticed.

"Mr. Stafford now tell me where you got them fine shoes?" The man lit his pipe.

"Now that's my business!" Johnstone knew advertising was important in America, so he bantered with the men. "A pun for you in case you missed it."

"He's a jokester to boot," said an Irishman.

"That's enough of that!" The smoker knocked his pipe against the rail and watched the ashes blow aft. "Glad to see you ain't got none of them high heels on you. Fancy any fool trying to ride a horse with them things on. Might even get some myself when I settle in."

Johnstone's secret weapon was his crimping machine. An invention by an American named Shive,[3] the crimping machine and their uncle awaited them on land.

"You've got a good eye, Sir. I think I'll make them that way from now on!" Johnstone gave others credit when due. He asked the Irishman "Are you staying in New York?"

"I ain't about to settle in a big city. You couldn't give me a crown to. I'm going west."

"You're headed west right after we land? Are you looking for gold?" Johnstone was curious. So was William.

"Straight off the boat! I'll buy me a strong horse, climb on, and off I'll go."

"Off the horse?"

Johnstone's bantering calmed William. He had not seen this side of his father in a long, long time. Too many times his father went into a dark spot where nobody could reach him. Whatever regrets Johnstone had, whatever ate away at him, William believed America could cure it. Then, too, perhaps they would find gold. He quizzed the men on deck. Where was it? How did you get there? Had they ever really seen it?

An older man with a white beard hushed his questioning.

"Forget it, Son. I hear lots of men have died trying."

"Yer a pessimist yer are." The Irishman, undeterred, hummed invitingly until they all turned away from the rolling sea to join in singing "Coming through the Rye."

The stars disappeared. The boat rolled high alongside a giant wave, then hung briefly leeward before it came crashing down. Cases and gear slid wildly back and forth across the decks. Johnstone sent William below again, but kept William's older brother Hezekiah on deck to lend a hand.

Nobody on board ever doubted there would be such a storm; they expected at least one during the journey. They lashed down what they could, stored carts in the hold. Elizabeth was terrified; the boys thought it a great and memorable adventure.

Elizabeth pulled them close—the three youngest, barefoot and naked for the night, small cocoons in Elizabeth's woolen blankets. Caroline's legs stuck out from under her blanket, her feet still shod in shiny shoes with black straps, clicks her father made for her. Nobody could make her take them off. In spite of the rocking, Frederick and Matilda and Caroline began to nod off, but when their mother began a story, they listened.

"Your grandfather, Josiah, died long before you were born. Your father was only ten, and he loved his father very much. Father and son rode together many times through Cambridge, across its fields and fens. When his father lay dying, Johnstone promised Josiah he would take care of his mother Susan. But a terrible thing happened that your father could not prevent.

"Your grandmother Susan was very young and beautiful. She wore her long blonde hair braided around her head. She, too, loved to ride with her husband and would have gone anywhere with him. But when he died, she closed herself up in the cottage, alone with her children.

The villagers said she was 'fragile,' which was their way of saying she couldn't handle being alone with four babies. She missed her husband dreadfully. Even worse, her children grew hungry because the solicitor who controlled Josiah's estate refused to give her the money Josiah had left her. He made one excuse after another, and Susan could do little to help herself because in those days, women could not own property.

"At first, neighbors brought food and helped bathe the babies, but they had homes and children of their own to care for and grew tired of helping Susan. They whispered among themselves that it was time to let the widow fend for herself. She would be fine, they said. She had money, they told each other. They knew her husband had left her money. But as winter approached, Susan's children became sick.

"Josiah's will was clear. His will told the courts to give his money and his land to Susan after he died, but the courts would not give her control of these things because she was a woman. So the courts appointed a solicitor. As a widow, Susan had to wait for the solicitor to decide when she could receive what was rightfully hers. When Josiah's sons grew up, they would inherit everything. Meanwhile, months went by.

"Then an older man from the village came courting. Susan thought he would be a good husband and a father to her fatherless children, so she married him."

"That was a good thing, wasn't it?" asked William.

"For a while. Then Mr. Ginby—that was his name—went to the solicitor, and the solicitor gave him everything. Susan was sure Josiah would not have wanted that, but then she was also sure Mr. Ginby would take care of them. She was wrong. Mr. Ginby did not want the children around."

"Did he hate children?" William could not believe it.

"I don't know."

"Did the children hate him?" Frederick thought that likely.

"No, not when they were small. But when each boy turned thirteen, Mr. Gimby figured out a way to get rid of him."

The boat floated high on another wave and came crashing down. Elizabeth gripped the bedpost. William saw that his mother's hands were turning red.

"What happened to Father?"

"Well, Mr. Gimby sent him and his brothers away to become apprentices in other towns. Your father was sent to Leicester for seven long years." Elizabeth grew pensive. "We played together as children. We walked the meadows and climbed the stiles to reach a little brook where we sat on a rock and watched the cows graze.

"The day he turned thirteen, I went looking for him, but he was gone. I cried for days. My mother explained that he had been sent away as an apprentice to a boot and shoe maker in Leicester. I did not see him for seven long years. During those years he worked every day but Sunday for twelve hours a day."

"So that is why he looks so sad? What happened to the other children?"

"Two of them died while he was gone. But one brother managed to find a position in the United States. That is who we are going to see first—your Uncle John. He lives in New York, near Niagara.

"When your father came home, he was so thin that Susan said she could see right through him. His eyes had dark circles around them, and his clothes hung loose. His fists were clenched tight. He told Susan terrible stories of how the boys were treated and how he hated to leave them behind.

"Because of this, when your father became a master tradesman, he traveled back to Leicester to try to intervene on the boys' behalf. But the other master tradesmen would have none of it. They conspired to destroy him. It was then we decided to leave Cambridgeshire."

Well after midnight, when all the children were in bed, William saw his father come in and bend down to kiss him. Johnstone kissed each of his brothers and sisters in turn. When Elizabeth asked Johnstone if he had been listening, William heard Johnstone's answer.

"That is why I stood up for them—the apprentices. How would you like to be accused of theft? Or risk being hanged and having your body turned over to the surgeons to be dissected? That is what some of those lads thought about every day. That is why they formed their guilds and why I supported them."

"Yes, I know. And that is why all the master shoemakers wanted to run you out of town, too!"

Then Johnstone promised out loud to his sleeping children that even though he might not be with them forever, he would never ever send them away, and they would never ever have to work twelve hours a day.

"That is behind us. That will not happen in America."

William was not asleep. He took that promise to his heart.

Cousins waited for them near the docks. After they gathered their gear and the crimping machine, they piled into their uncle's waiting coach, which they rode all the way to Lockport, which was named for the locks on the Erie Canal. They saw the water flowing down to the Niagara River, and when they saw the mighty falls, they shed tears, just as they shed tears at everything they saw in this vast new country.

The city of Lockport was disappointingly small. The children arrived with expectations of good beef, treacle puddings, fresh Swedes—which Americans called turnips—and peas. No more potatoes. But the food put before them now was as strange as the country itself—smoked ham and corn, and beans sweetened with molasses. They stayed with their cousins only long enough to file the necessary immigration papers.

Johnstone wanted to find the city with the most promise. It was 1849, and everyone urged him to go farther west to the city with the most promise of all, Chicago. The very word *Chicago* called up images of tall buildings, the vast waters of Lake Michigan and the great ships that plied it. This metropolis meant everything new, inventions being made every day, promises.

They boarded the steamer *Illinois* for the final leg of their journey. When the boat arrived in Chicago to refuel, the family disembarked to see the great city. In all their dreams and in their wildest imaginations they could never have done justice to the reality that was Chicago. This busy, laughing, loud, convoluted, extravagant city might be their new home. All the romance of the sea was there, too. Lake Michigan lay before them—a vast and lovely water with waves sometimes as high as those on the Atlantic. Boat horns wailed the arrival of new cargo and new passengers. Stevedores shouted as they hauled ropes, and wives and children embraced their families with cries of joy and recognition.

But Johnstone longed for something quieter, something more like his native Cambridgeshire, with countryside where he might have horses, fresh water and lovely arched bridges. The *Illinois* passed several large shipping vessels going east, coming from a safe harbor called Little Fort. Little Fort, Johnstone discovered, was no farther from Chicago than March was from Cambridge. Little Fort was home to salmon and trout fishing, and loveliest of all, to large tracts of land where farmers could breed horses, not English horses, but hard-working Clydesdales and pretty little Shetlands.

They re-boarded the steamship. Johnstone was not ready yet to make his final stop. He would know when he reached it.

The next day, when the *Illinois* arrived at Little Fort, he instructed his boys to take all their belongings on shore. Then the family bade a final goodbye to the *Illinois*.

Greek revival homes stood along the waterfront. Beyond them, down Water Street, Johnstone could see the towers of the lighthouse and, blessing of all blessings, an arched wooden bridge just like the one back home over the

River Cam. Under the bridge, he was told, ran five mineral springs. They were home.

1850. Soon after they settled and Johnstone opened his boot and shoe shop, the town renamed itself *Waukegan*, which means "little fort" in Potawatomi. The people of Waukegan walked by the Stafford house every day, and their workshop became a kind of gathering place. Men and women alike tarried there to consider shoes for themselves or shoes for their children. Among the townspeople who came most often was a little girl named Malvinia.

Most of the neighbors grumbled about the burdens and unhappy goings on in Chicago, and their wives even moaned about Waukegan, claiming it had too few sheriffs and too few doctors. Transients, too, came through to escape the harsh conditions in Chicago's meat packing industry or worse, to run away from the law.

Blame for the town's shortcomings was rampant and fell on everybody else, especially transients and adventure seekers. But the women mostly blamed "evil rum" for all of their disappointments. No matter whether entrepreneurs bottled ale or port, the townspeople didn't differentiate: It was all evil rum.

William, twelve years old by this time, was more attuned to having lamb stew and rice pudding for supper than he was to listening to the politics and goings on in his new country. The Stafford house once again smelled of stews and cabbages. The family sang loudly because they had no close neighbors to complain. Waukegan was home to fewer than five hundred people.

Johnstone was right. His boots lasted and his shoes became famous. When the shop was open, the whole family worked. Johnstone was the clicker, the one who cut leather from a tanned hide. He refused to let the others risk injury or burns that might come from the voracious steam machine that cut and punched leather. If he were busy, he would send his restless boys out on horseback all the way to the stockyards in Chicago to look for the best leather to pound and cure. Elizabeth—and as they grew older, Matilda and Caroline—sewed the lasts.

The demand meant that Johnstone, thanking God for his good fortune, hired more shoemakers. Whenever a new lad came on, Johnstone looked him earnestly in the eye and asked him why he wanted to make shoes. Then, when he hired the fellow, he promised him fair wages and that he would not object if the boy wanted to belong to a union. When he said this, his body tensed from the memories of master tradesmen in England and the severe beatings they gave the lads from Ireland or Wales or even from as far away as China, for the slightest mistake. He was English or he might have been beaten worse.

"I was lucky to be English," he told William. "Even though we were fed poorly, the others fared worse. When I left and owned my own shop, I found myself defending those same lads from my own colleagues. Many master tradesmen had no regard for apprentices and beat them even more if they banded together.

"I was not the only one who took the boys' sides. But after the master tradesmen in Leicester formed their own powerful trades council, they began to prosecute those of us who backed the workers. They threw my friends into prison, and some died. It was so bad many of us left England."[4]

A story was circulating about a Lithuanian who was looking for a job as a shoemaker. Wherever he went, the master shoemakers asked the same question: Why did he want to make shoes?

According to the story, he gave a peculiar answer. "Well sir, I worked in the stock yards. This was bad enough, but we had a worse problem, which leads me to ask a question of you: Will I be paid in cash or check?"

The story was that the Lithuanian was always paid by check, late in the day. So late that the only place open, the only place he could cash it, was in the saloon. The employer asked why that was such an inconvenience.

"Well, Sir, they refuse to cash your check unless you buy a drink. So the saloon keeper always takes a cut."

The Cattle Butchers' Union stepped in about then, according to the man. The Lithuanian praised that organization to the sky, saying it made him feel more independent, more useful. He praised the president, an Irishman named

Mike Donnelly, who had three interpreters. He praised him because these men came from different places and the union took care of them all. This gave them all some dignity, he said. Then the union found another way for these men to cash their checks.

Then the Lithuanian added: "and I cannot be discharged unless I'm no good."[5]

At the end of the story, William looked over at his family, his own brothers and sisters. He also looked over at Malvinia, who always sat quietly on the bench next to his, to see if she was listening. He thought Malvinia might just be the girl he would marry when he was old enough to take a wife and was no longer a shoemaker. He and Malvinia had dreams.

Prospectors grew rich overnight and railroads crisscrossed the West. William was envious of strangers who slapped each other on the back when they talked about gold, men in uniforms who guarded trains and engineers who built railroads. He would make his mark. He never thought his dreams would come to an end before he even turned twenty-five.

Ever since the War of 1812, the Corps of Engineers had been building a string of forts all along the country's coastline, a bulwark against another attack from the sea. One of these, built in peace time on a man-made pile of rubble on a sand bar off the shores of Charleston, was a tiny stronghold called Fort Sumter. The fort was manned with fewer than 600 men and some officers. Of the 600, just a handful were trained well enough to man the fort's six cannons. The fort barely stocked enough powder to fire even six cannons.

The country watched in disbelief as a few Southern states elected Jefferson Davis and began to secede from the union. Lincoln tried to assure the remaining states that the Union would stand, that it could and would constitutionally defend and maintain itself. But tensions ran high.

On April 12, 1861, Southern forces stationed themselves at the four corners of land surrounding Fort Sumter. From these four excellent vantage points, they shot burning cannonballs over the walls and set the fort on fire.

When word of the attack reached Waukegan, everything changed for William and his brothers. Clouds swept in from Lake Michigan on that unforgettable day, and a foghorn wailed in the distance. A small group of uniformed soldiers led by a fife and drum corps marched through Waukegan, led by a crier who announced the news. As the drummers marched, men— hundreds of them—dropped their plows or their anvils, stopped whatever they were doing to gather on the steps of the courthouse. Work ceased in Johnstone's shop. Waukegan's men were ready to fight for their country, and Johnstone's sons were no exception, even though they had only been in their new country a few years.

Malvinia was only seventeen when she married William, and she was only eighteen when they had a baby boy named Will. She had only been six years old when she watched the Stafford family move in to the house on Gennessee Street for the first time. Now she cried as her husband and his younger brother Frederick left home for the first time in their lives to offer themselves for duty.

In those early days in Waukegan, Elizabeth often found the little girl waiting in the parlor, and she would quietly set another place for her at the table. She and Johnstone watched the bond between the two children become stronger with the years, so when Malvinia and William married, the older couple thought nothing of having them move into the house with the rest of the family.

That day, Elizabeth and Malvinia were among the masses of people who stood outside, watching fathers and brothers and cousins mill around the courthouse steps, waiting for someone to tell them what to do. Finally, a duty officer came out.

There were too many volunteers to process easily, he said. He motioned the men to move away from the steps, then he directed them to count off by ones and twos so they might be processed separately. The men then sorted themselves into groups of evens and odds.

William and Frederick counted off and were cordoned into separate groups. Both returned home as newly enlisted cavalrymen, flushed with the pride of answering the call to a cause greater than themselves.

That night, William tried to console everyone by saying he would come back. He had to because he had a wife and child. He was already an engineer and had served brief stints on the Rock Island Line. He wanted to finish attending lectures on civil engineering. He had begun attending lectures in Cincinnati, given by the great mathematician and lecturer, Professor Ormsby McKnight Mitchel.[6]

Mitchel, a West Point graduate, never appeared out of uniform. He cut his hair military style. He loved mathematics and engineering, but he loved railroads even more. His habitual scowl disappeared when he wandered off the subject of engineering and began to ramble about his years constructing the Ohio and Mississippi Railroad.

William shared the old professor's passion for trains and vowed to walk in his footsteps. His brother Frederick did, too. Frederick loved to say they would go back to England one day and join the Institute of Civil Engineers.

"We're English, Brother; we can conquer mountains," he said.

William stopped him every time. "We are Americans now. We're not going back."

Days passed, then word came. The phalanx that Frederick had been assigned to would not be going after all, but William's would muster. William kissed Malvinia and baby Will goodbye and strode into the town square with his horse to become a private in Company D of the 13th Illinois Cavalry. Those left behind did their best to equip the men of Company D: they sold all their horses to the 13th for $110 apiece. Most of their horses would haul cannon.

Frederick sat on the fence outside the house with Malvinia and her baby beside him as the newly formed regiment marched by. They watched together as William rode by on his saddle-bred Morgan, going off to war. Malvinia's pride turned to tears. She buried her face in Frederick's shoulder.

Frederick shed tears, too, but his tears were those of frustration at having been left behind with mouths to feed and no horses with which to farm. He railed at a providence that placed him in the wrong band of men on the courthouse steps and left him behind.

2. Coal in St. Clair County

Big Warrior was a Kusa Muskogee and chief of the Abhika. He lived in the years before Alabama became a state.[7] As he grew old, he appointed his friend and council leader, Opothle Yoholo, to speak for him. Big Warrior's sons did not succeed him but became *mikko* or chiefs of their own villages. They kept Big Warrior's legacy alive, and passed down his stories to their grandchildren. The mikko spoke Muscogean, and so did their children.

Sam was a mikko before the Civil War. He chose to honor and mourn the great leader by wearing a blue shirt and deerskin jacket adorned with a colorful scarf around his neck just like the one Opothle Yoholo wore in 1832, when he fought for the Creek tribesmen left in Alabama after the Trail of Tears.

Sam's family gathered to celebrate the end of the longest, most important festival of all, poskita. They celebrated poskita on their own land on the banks of the Coosa River. The United States government guaranteed Sam's family this land when it made its treaty with Yoholo, a treaty that promised 320 acres and an education to each family of the Creek nation who remained in Alabama after the others went west.[8] Sam and his children celebrated; they belonged to this new state and gathered on the banks of the Coosa to feast and watch the flatboats head south, hauling logs and timber for railroads.

When the feast was over, women gathered up remnants of boiled ham, chicken, mutton, corn and turkey to turn into stew another day. Children gathered around, sucking on juicy sugar cane as the shadows grew long. Sam found a log to sit on so he could tell his old tales in the warmth of the sun's last rays. He leaned forward and began a tale that everyone already knew by heart.

"In about 1820, two white boys—real boys, not legends—came to live in Creek territory. The government sent them. They came with their families and livestock, chickens, tools and seeds to plant. We welcomed them to what was left of our land.

"If the southern tribes had not sold us out, you know, the tribes of the Lower Creek nation would be here with us still today."[9] Sam tried to hide the bitterness in his voice.

"The boys wandered freely in our woods. We taught them our ways and loved them. Their names were Jonathan Newton Smith and Pleasant Fancher."[10] Sam stopped to let his youngest grandchild rest her head on his knee.

"Well, Jonathan and Newton decided to venture into the forest alone to hunt game. They had rifles and were afraid of nothing. They shot at everything and soon had a rucksack full of raccoons and possums and rabbits. By nightfall, their pack weighed so much they could hardly carry it.

"Winter had begun, and the wind picked up, forcing them to find shelter for the night. They found a small clearing under a cliff and stopped there beside the Big Cahaba River with the wind in their hair and the rush of water nearby. Their kill would keep in the cold.

"A few snowflakes drifted through the branches of the trees and onto their noses, an early snow." Sam digressed as he looked at his children. "First snows never last you know."

He gazed out over the valley and continued. "The boys prepared for the cold night. It was too late to gather much wood for a fire, but they found kindling and started a fire on a bed of rock. They strung their kill high in a sweet gum tree to keep panthers and bear away, and went to sleep.

"When the first birds began to call, the boys woke and brushed snow dust off their coats. The world was new and beautiful, almost magic, and their tiny fire still glowed cheerfully. Remembering what their grandfathers taught them, they beat the fire with sticks and frozen branches to quench it before breaking camp, but they could not keep it from smoldering. So they gathered more black rock and buried their fire. No matter how much rock they heaped on it, curls of smoke drifted up; the rock burned hotter than ever. Frightened, they cut their catch down, strapped their prey to their backs and began to run through the forest. One of the boys threw some lumps of the black rock into his sack.

"As it happened, they ran right through the Muskogee settlement, where they stopped just long enough to ask one of the elders about the rocks. This is how they learned about coal, and why they named that stream 'Coal Stream.' The news of their discovery spread all over the country."

Sam ended, always, by telling how Muskogee tribes to the south of them had signed away their lands with the Treaty of Indian Springs. Sam felt personally betrayed. Opothle Yoholo, he said, fought the rest of his life to declare that treaty illegal, but he never succeeded. Sam continued.

"The government didn't care. We lost our cousins and our councilors, our tribesmen and our slaves. So you see, we will never stop fighting to regain our lands."

Sam's favorite daughter was Lella. She was only ten, but she understood when Sam was talking only to her.

"Yoholo wanted women to be educated first. As you all know, land is passed down to the women in our clans from their mothers, so girls must learn to read and write. They must read documents and know what they say.

"This is Yoholo's greatest wish: that the whole Creek nation be educated; even its slaves. He sent his own son to school in Kentucky. Sadly, all the educated slaves were sent away to Arkansas, because Alabama was afraid that educated slaves might start an uprising."

Sam pulled a pine sapling up by the roots and drew a line in the sand. He marked an X on one side of the line.

"Do you know why Yoholo killed McIntosh? Yoholo told us that the Southern tribes would not have sold their land to Georgia if they had not listened to McIntosh. The southern clans did not even give the northern tribes the chance to speak. Because of that, Yoholo killed McIntosh and we have this evil line, even though Big Warrior told us to live as though we were one. Betrayal draws the bitterest of lines."

The children sat transfixed, silent. Lella could no longer be quiet. "How can we erase such a line?"

Sam just shook his head in discouragement. "It might have to start with convincing the white land owners. They want to keep us apart, to divide us. That is why they gave us different names: the Upper Towns and the Lower Towns."[11]

One of the Hodge boys spoke. He had long been trying to impress Lella.

"The Great Cahaba River and the Coosa River join with their sister Tallapoosa in Wetumpka. Together they flow into the Alabama River and run together to the sea. We are like the rivers; we will become a nation again."

Lella could not take her eyes off of Thomas Hodge. He was slight of build and quick. No cloth shirts for him; he wore his hair loose to the shoulders and let his skin burn dark in the sun. She knew she would marry him when she grew up. Thomas was growing into a practical man: He listened to Lella's grandfather and heard his dreams, but had no time for such dreams himself. He understood that white men used their papers for their own gain, but he respected Sam and kept his thoughts to himself. He spoke only in practicalities.

"We are still here, and we have land. I am told that some of our land disappeared when the government's assayers made mistakes. Some of that land is in Bibb County. Can we claim those lands? Did the Lower Creeks lose land that way, too?"

Sam took the folded map out from his vest pocket and held it high.

"Yes, some of our lands were forgotten, but see here: I have a map given me by my friend Phineas Browne, who is a white prospector. Mr. Browne took my map to Governor Clay, and the Governor certified it."

Sam once helped William Phineas Browne find the biggest coal seam in the territory, which was near the town of Montevallo and ran all the way through Shelby County and on into what would become St. Clair.[12] It was so big it took years for Browne to stake his claim, and when he did, some of his claim wound up very close to Sam's house. In turn Browne offered him a hand in sorting out titles and such. When Sam finished his story, he gave the map to Lella, for her safekeeping.

Alabama's entrepreneurs did not concern themselves much about such titles even if a parcel was not listed among the land patents. They figured these lands were theirs by right—gifts from God. They brought young tribesmen in to work their lands alongside African slaves. Sometimes, if land titles caused problems, these entrepreneurs burned the courthouse down.

Thomas watched one neighbor after another abandon his crops and his children to go work in the mines. Many of them did not survive. His neighbors knew nothing about mining and had only farm tools to work with—picks and axes, saws, bars, and shovels—none of them adequate for digging deep into coal seams. These men had no defense against collapsing overhangs or explosions from the ever-present gases in the caves.

Thomas and Lella married and built a cabin way up on a high ridge to the south of the Coosa River. When their first summer came, they took their blankets downhill to the riverbank to watch the timber haulers load their flatboats as they always had. Any day by the river was an occasion for great joy and a rare thing for Thomas and Lella.

Thomas sometimes helped cut timber for the railroads. When he did, he rode the flatboats that hauled the logs all the way down to the Creek capital of Tallassee. Tallassee was the stopover before Wewahitchka, where the river widened and poured into the Alabama. Huge ships plied the Alabama River on to Montgomery and farther—to the great ports of Pensacola and Mobile. While he was on these journeys, he listened for news from the cities.

One day in autumn while Thomas walked his dogs near the branch and waited for the flatboats to arrive from Tallassee, he noticed Sam sitting on an old stump under a water oak with his head down. Thomas called to him, but Sam did not answer. He ran over to the grandfather, who only looked sadly up at him without speaking. Thomas slung the old chief's arm around his neck and half walked, half carried Sam back to the cabin. Sam died later that day. Gently,

Thomas and Lella buried him in the ground beneath his bed, in a square pit according to custom.

Lella became the mother of the tribe. As the Confederacy came into being, she told her husband she was afraid they would take him away, that they might not survive such a war. Thomas reassured her because, at first anyway, the Confederacy only demanded all of Alabama's ore and munitions. Alabama did everything it could to keep its mines open, and it needed able-bodied men and forced as many as it could down into the mines. Thomas did not want to be one of those men.

In July and August of 1861, the Confederacy demanded more men and systematically signed up all pro-slavery Creeks between the ages of 18 and 45 as part of the First Creek Regiment.[13] Among the tribes who remained with the Confederacy was Thomas's birth tribe. Even though Thomas was now married to Lella and was part of her anti-slavery tribe, he and Lella were afraid the government of Alabama would hunt him down and take him. By September, the Confederates had taken all of his brothers and their horses, and he told Lella he was afraid he would never see them again.

"I watched them," he said. "I saw the last ones leave. My brothers were forced to march off without arms or even tents or clothing. It is terrible!"

"Perhaps the government will issue clothing later." Lella tried to console him.

"No. Even those who left in early July still have nothing. Not even pay. They are going to die."

"But Thomas, the miners and the railroad workers are not being paid either."

Thomas looked down at the ground. "I didn't know you knew. I thought I had kept it from you."

"No, but thank you for keeping it from Sam."

Opothle Yoholo refused to ally with the Confederacy, but he still lived in Alabama. By September of 1861, his plantation at Tuckabatchee overflowed with refugees who did not want to serve the Confederacy: Abhika, northern

Muskogee, freedmen and runaway slaves. Yoholo wrote President Lincoln and asked for protection, saying his people were loyal to the union and would not survive long without that protection. Lincoln wrote back, telling Yoholo to go, to leave with all the refugees and go to Fort Row in Kansas.

Only then did Yoholo agree to leave Alabama. On the way, he lost two thousand of his people, including his own daughter. He never made it to Kansas. He died in Osage County.

Thomas and Lella did not go with Yoholo but closed their cabin, took their babies and walked northward across Blount Mountain. The growing family found employment in a house in a far north corner of the county with a family named Bradford. But the Confederates found Thomas anyway. They conscripted him into the Confederate army, and he was soon a casualty of war.

Lella's six children grew up near the Bradford farm. The war raged on to its inglorious end, and time passed without Thomas. Lella herself grew old, and the time came when she wanted her children and grandchildren and great grandchildren to return to their native land. With each passing year she despaired she might never find their old cabin up on the hill.

The Bradford family helped her. They let her leave and take her belongings and her whole family with her. It was a new era, they said. They wished her well and even assigned a woods-wise young Negro, Charles Bradford, to accompany Lella and her children across the mountain.

Charles's grandfather was born a slave in South Carolina and became a free man after the War. His children grew up on Alabama's sandstone ridges, and many of them stayed on to become farmers themselves or preachers of the gospel.[14]

Free men called each other by their last names, so Bradford's grandfather became "Mr. Bradford." Because Mr. Bradford's grandson Charles was so like him, they called him "Little Bradford." He outgrew that name in a hurry and answered only to *Bradford*.

As a child, Bradford spent so many days alone in the woods, wandering through oak and sycamore groves, that he knew every tree, every stone and every dry creek. He could find cougars' dens and eagles' nests and the best places to ford a river. Above all, he knew Blount Mountain. He ran hundreds of errands across its brow before he was twelve years old.

When he swore he could find Lella's old cabin, he never doubted himself. He led the way for all the children and grandchildren and Lella, who held tight to the old map as she walked. She read:

"Find the place along the river where the bank is steepest. At the bottom is a sandy beach where three large stones lie where they fell from the rock cliff above. Cross the water here and journey along the south side of the bank westward until you see where two rivers join. Go straight south through the woods for half a day until you come to an opening surrounded by a forest of sycamore at the top of the hill. That begins our land."

They took off toward the banks of the Coosa. Lella and her children followed Bradford along the bank for what seemed forever before they came to the three stones. Lella sat there to rest. Bradford urged her on.

"No," Lella said to Bradford. "You have to sit still. You have to listen to the winds and the land while they are talking. They will tell us which way."

After a bit, she informed Bradford she was sure she knew the way. She sharpened the blade of her knife on the stone and cut a mark where she had been sitting. Then they found a boatman to take them across. Once on the other side, the little group drifted slowly downstream until they spotted a landing place. Steering clear of a long moccasin dangled from an overhanging branch, they went ashore.

Lella thanked Bradford then. "We are here; we have made it. We are near where we need to be, and you must go on home."

"I thank you, ma'am, but I'm not leaving," said Bradford.

He walked until he caught up with Lella's oldest granddaughter, Lila. Lila's gentle smile had won Bradford's heart. The family named her right when they named her "Lila," because it means "we come in peace" in Muskogee.

Bradford took it upon himself to teach her how to find her way in the woods. He showed her how to mark where they had been by cutting his own mark on outcroppings and trees. When he marked the tree stump where they once sat together, he added an extra flourish beside his mark.

The next day they cut through dense undergrowth until they came to a clearing near the top of the hill. There before them lay a square of crumbled mud in the weeds. The bark roof of the old cabin had disintegrated long ago, as had the woven vines that shored up the walls, but Lella was sure of where she was. Below the remains of the cabin, the land still bore the shape of a gathering place, a semicircle cut into the slope of the mountain. Lella sat her tired body on one of the terraces. Deep down she worried the marks on the rocks and the map in her hand might not be enough to stake her claim, but she had no money for a house and certainly no money for a survey.

She would stay. It was her home, wasn't it? She tucked the fraying map in her bosom and kept it there until she died.

3. The Man from Nowhere

One fall day many years after Lella died but only a year or so after the new century began, Lila and Bradford were tending their crops way up on the hillside in front of the new cabin Bradford built. Their boys trudged through the cornfields, gathering corn for supper and sticks for firewood; their girls toted water from the creek for their mother. Lila moved quickly among her children, emptying buckets and sorting piles of vegetables. Her long black hair hung out from under the red scarf she tied around her forehead.

In the years since Lella died, many of the old Abhika families and freedmen returned to raise cabins up near the ridge. Lila was tending a table for a pot luck. She and Bradford were part of a village now, and the whole village was coming to their pot luck.

The smallest children scuffled in the dust or played pick-up sticks. The day was so still Lila could see clouds breathe in and out. She paused for a minute to watch them, so did not see the stranger at first. When she did, she turned to Bradford to tell him that someone was approaching.

A white man appeared on the edge of the clearing, hatless and hesitant, as though he were lost. But he was not. He walked determinedly up the hill, as though he had a mission.

As the man drew closer to the cabin, Bradford told Lila the man looked more out of place than lost. He said, too, that he did not like what he saw.

The man stopped near their well. He wiped his brow and rested his foot on a stone. His dark hair was slicked down and stiff with pomade, parted down the middle of his head. He chewed slowly on a grass stalk. The most outstanding thing about him was his moustache, which drooped down over his mouth and beyond his chin so that the hair on it gyrated when he chewed. He wore leather britches and fine boots, but his deerskin jacket was stained and tattered.

Instinctively Bradford knew the man wanted something. He tensed ever so slightly. Neither man made any quick moves.

"Beautiful day for a pot luck," the man called to him from fifteen yards away.

Bradford did not respond. A slight breeze rippled through the pines, and an old hound sidled up to the stranger and began to bark. The other dogs ran towards the man, howling and barking as well, until they were all close enough to do some damage

"No!" Bradford commanded the dogs. "Be still!"

The dogs slowed their advance, but ran around in crazy, frustrated circles. They were hunters, men's dogs, unaccustomed to strangers.

The women fixed their attention solely on the man, alert even while they stirred laundry in steaming iron pots or spread blankets out on the rocks to dry. The smell of lye soap drifted clean across the yard, and the day's chores, which were well under way that amiable morning, suspended. Lila signaled the women to go back to work, to pay the man no attention.

Among the tribes, women's dogs were traditionally smaller than the ones their husbands kept, but just as feisty. Lila's little dog yapped out from the safety of the back side of her shins. The pup ran closer to the man and nipped at his trouser legs. The man's foot moved almost imperceptibly to kick the mutt, but he stayed his boot. Lila could have let the dog continue chewing away at the man, even though it was not big enough to do much damage, but she picked up her yapping pet and walked over to her husband's side.

The man held his hand loosely on his gun, but he made no move to unshoulder it. Rather, he raised both hands in salute, to indicate his peaceful intentions. When he did, Bradford saw the sweat under his arms and took it as a sign that the man was not to be trusted.

"What can I do for you, Sir?" Bradford did not let go of the pickaxe he was carrying.

The man took the grass out from between his teeth, threw it on the ground and walked near enough to Bradford to extend his hand. "Henry DeBardeleben, here. I'm turned around a little and need to get my bearings. May I sit a spell with you folks until I have enough energy to go look for the train to take me back to Birmingham?"

"Make yourself comfortable, Sir." Bradford nodded at Lila to go on about her business. Lila left to join the other women.

"Obliged," said the man.

"We have not started the evening meal, so I can't offer any." Bradford was not inclined to be hospitable, but he would not be rude. "You are welcome to sit."

The Central Railroad ran along below them in a gash cut through the trees between Jefferson County and Woodstock. Anybody could find it in no time. The village was not a destination for most people. As far as Bradford knew, the only things those cars carried were coal and maybe timber for tracks and mining equipment.

Underneath his jacket, the man wore a starched yellow shirt and a nice belt with a silver buckle. His boots betrayed him. Only powerful railroad men wore boots like that. This man would only have to wave at the train and the engineer would stop.

The afternoon passed without incident, pleasantly enough. The visitor drank his water and tousled the children's hair, complementing the family. Bradford understood he was being buttered, but he loosened up a little.

"And which one is your cabin?" asked Henry.

Bradford skirted the issue. "Just up there over the ridge and off to the east some. A small farm but plenty for us."

"You homesteading or renting?"

"No. Don't rent." He began to be uneasy again at all the questions. It occurred to him he might be telling this stranger too much, but then again what was the harm in it?

"You work in the mines?" asked Henry.

"I farm."

"Well, I'm just prospecting." Henry gazed off as though he had not a care in the world, but his words made Bradford bristle. "Looking around here and there."

"For what?"

"Ore. Coal. Well, who isn't?"

"None up here." Now that he knew what the man was after, Bradford wanted him to leave. "Just got corn and okra. Guess you'll have to move on down the mountain toward Montevallo. Browne's seam starts there." He didn't finish the sentence. He did not tell the man that Browne's seam went all the way to his ridge.

"Well, even if you ain't got ore, I like your land. I would gladly buy it from you." Henry pulled out a piece of folded paper from his jacket pocket.

"Not for sale."

"Well, it sure is pretty. I would make a beautiful place out of it. Build a mansion up on that hill. You and your family could stay on."

"Nope."

"Don't you even want to look at my offer?"

"Nope."

"Well, I'm going to leave it with you anyway." He held a letter out to Bradford, but Bradford kept his hands away.

Lila returned about then. She had been so quiet, she startled Bradford, but she stepped forward and reached out for the letter. Henry appeared reluctant to turn it over to a woman, but in the end he did.

"Guess I'll excuse myself and head on down the hill. Take a look at my offer and let me know if you change your mind." He turned to Lila. "Mighty good fry bread, Ma'am. Thanks," and without another word he headed back down the hill.

"Man wasn't much account," said Bradford to Lila.

"You mean his coat was torn?"

"That and . . . other things." He decided not to enumerate them.

"That Mr. DeBardeleben wore that tattered coat to put you off your guard," said Lila.

Bradford was always amused and impressed with the way Lila read men. She was invaluable to him for many reasons. She would read him what the man offered when he told her he was curious, but he refused to be curious. So she read it anyway.

"Says nothing about us staying on. Says he would find work for us, though."

Bradford was disgusted. Just one more white man trying to trick them. He went back into the cabin and came out with his gun. He set out down the hill.

Sycamore leaves rustled as the afternoon came and went. Henry wore his old jacket because that colored family just wasn't worth dressing up for. He planned to change into his dinner jacket when he reached Jefferson County. A lady was waiting for him there.

Bradford trailed silently along behind Henry to be sure he was gone. He never took his eyes off the man's departing backside. The ragged bits of hide on Henry's jacket blew crazily behind him like a hen ruffling its feathers, and it made Bradford grin. The man had looked more than once at Lila, and it made him even more determined to stand between his people and the poison he saw in front of him. This was his and Lila's village, and it was for Abhika families, not white men.

"Abhika," he called after the man, "means 'door shutter.'"[15] Bradford would not only shut it, he would barricade it. This time he laughed out loud.

1920. Their house was possibly the best one in the village, even stronger than the old Mt. Zion Baptist Church down the road, which he also helped build. The pastor at Mt. Zion called all the neighbors to church on Sunday mornings, where he praised those in attendance and condemned to hell those who missed.

On weekdays, the church turned into the official school. Most of the children never made it past third grade because the authorities figured those children needed to work more than they needed to learn. But on Sunday nights, while everybody else was otherwise occupied, the pastor assembled the mostly Black Indian children in the sanctuary and taught them to read and write from the Bible. Nobody dared object if children learned from the Bible. Anyway, he didn't have any school books. All he had was his sonorous voice, his passion, and his Bible.

Lila and the other mothers scavenged books wherever they could—from peddlers who came through and wanted to lighten their loads or from white folks who had finished with their books. Then two teacher women came to live in the village. They had a fire in their hearts to teach colored children. Lila thought the Lord had rewarded her for finding all those books.

The two women rented a house a few doors down from Lila, and they made sure the old church building came to life during the week. Lila found even more books for the school now, and the teachers thanked her.

Even though the newcomers only came from north Alabama, somehow word got out that those teachers were Yankees who had come south to destroy the Southern way of life. Suddenly white folks' attitude toward the school and the dedicated teachers in town began to change. Rumors were started that somebody was going to lynch the teachers, and the rumors worked. One of the teachers left; then there was only one.

The remaining teacher did what she could, once again in the evenings. She never turned a child away no matter how late it was, so Lila gave her children reasons to visit the teacher when they missed school. She sent them over with fry bread and black-eyed peas.

Alabama's constitution was the problem. The numbers of convoluted roadblocks the authorities dreamed up for any possibility of universal learning were overwhelming. Legislators did this to control the ballot box. But Lila did not give up. She said that if the Lord was willing, she would even find a way for her children to go to Talladega College, which was just over the county line. The Lord was apparently not willing, so the children did all they could as long as they could with one teacher at Mt. Zion.

Jerry, Lila's third child, wasn't much bothered by not going to school anyway. He loved trains and not much else from the time he was small. It was quite natural that he would leave home in his early teens and find his way to the North & South Railroad to get a job. That railroad took him far away from home.

When he did come home, he and his father walked together along the steep ridges of Blount Mountain discussing the world the way it was. They stopped sometimes to look across the valley at the last ridge of hills where his great grandmother Lella's house once stood.

"Jerry, nobody lives there anymore. Your mother grieves over it because your ancestors are still there."

"Papa, it's still a fine place. It's a refuge for climbing vines and nesting birds. I think they would like that."

"You see it in a good way."

"Maybe I will build a house of my own on it one day."

Bradford shook his head. "Mr. DeBardeleben wants to dig another mine on that land."

"I heard."

Bradford put his hands in his pockets and looked down at the valley below. "You are gone now, Son, and it won't be long before the rest of my children follow. I don't think it's good for you to be here, anyway. The mine owners are grabbing every man they can and sending them down into the mines. There will never be enough men for their mines, and I don't want you to be a miner."

Although the Coosa and Cahaba coal fields produced plenty of ore, chasing ore deposits become a pursuit secondary to building and running blast furnaces like those in Cedar Creek. Operators replaced slaves now with anybody they could round up, mostly men who had never even been inside a mine. In slave times, at least three miners a day lost their lives, and that had not changed.

Long before Jerry's visit, Bradford had come home to find a letter waiting for him. Bradford could think of no reason anybody might have to write him. Lila had read the return address to him first. "DeBardeleben and Underwood, Inc."

Then she stripped the envelope open with her fingernails and read.

> *Sent to inform you that Mr. Charles F. DeBardeleben will be in your area on the nineteenth hence. He is prepared to discuss the use of minerals upon your land, the rights to which he already owns.*

> *This in no way indicates any desire upon his part to own your land, which he understands is rightfully yours, but the gentleman mentioned will discuss this in detail upon his arrival. He plans to take the 10:15 out of Birmingham and arrive around noon at your home. We trust this will be convenient for you, but if it is not please respond to us at the address above. He will be there at the appointed time if we do not hear from you.*

> *Regards,*

> *W. T. Underwood.*

4. Onward and Upward

William's first child, Will, was a little over a year old when baby Frederick came into the world. Malvinia died giving him life. The family in Waukegan buried her on February 20, 1862 in Oak Wood Cemetery in Waukegan.

That same day, while snow lay on the battlefield, William, who knew nothing of his young wife's fate, rode his horse from Chicago to Fort Douglas, to muster in for the second time.[16] Company D was about to be absorbed by Company K. By the time word of his wife's death reached him, William was hundreds of miles away.

Weeks later, the sergeant told him about the death of his wife as gently as he could, but William took it hard. He could not sleep, and he did not hear reveille. All he heard was his own voice telling him he was 24 years old and had two baby boys to feed and love, and he could not even go on leave to console them. He was alone and shed his tears in silence.

He mustered out in 1865 after the fighting ended. He rode his tired horse the whole way to Waukegan without stopping so he might scoop up his boys and make them the same promise his father had made him. He swore he would never send them away but, perhaps because of battle or perhaps he was only wiser, in his heart he knew life would separate him from those he loved.

Engineers spent their lives almost everywhere but home. William worked for Massillon Bridge Company by now, which sent him traveling from Iowa to Missouri to Alabama building bridges for the railroads. Sometimes it took as many as fifty days to go from one job to another, and he was exhausted. He swore to his parents that he believed a new mine or railroad started up every day. He was close to right. Johnstone and Elizabeth would have to be both mother and father to his boys, at least for now.

In between these trips, he urged his horse back to Waukegan where he took his children walking along Lake Michigan, or to Chicago to see the horse shows. The boys loved watching hired hands ride bucking horses and lasso bulls. Will and Freddie took turns riding on his shoulders, wrapping their arms about his neck and pulling his moustache. William found their laughter almost more than he could bear. His visits were too short.

In 1868, William met a Mr. Henry Everhard from Newcomerstown, Ohio who needed a man to survey some land for its potential. William left Waukegan for Newcomerstown with no more directions than to look for a house with the name *Everhard* written on the gate. As he trotted down the main road toward town, and well on the outskirts of town, he thought he saw it. A carriage stood in front of the only stone house on the street, and on the gate was written "Eberhart." William was confused but pulled the bell cord and waited.

A man in riding cap and jodhpurs appeared from the back side of the house and quick-stepped his way toward William, followed by a pair of hunting dogs. William took in the man's old dress boots, of a style long out of fashion, but he took off his hat and offered his hand to this Mr. Eberhart.

"You noticed the spelling on the gate, did you? That's the old spelling. My grandfather changed it to 'Everhard.' Are you ready to walk the property? But I forget my manners. Would you like a drink of water?"

"A walk would be just the thing, Sir. I'm very grateful." William was tired but saw no need for delay. The two set out toward the boundaries of the property.

After a half hour, Everhard suggested they rest. They sat with their backs propped against an elm tree. This time when Henry offered William a drink from the well, he accepted. The two rose to go to the well, and Henry's hunting dogs, who had trotted close by his side, took this as a signal to wander. William watched until the dogs took off running. They were after something.

In the far corner of the field, a young woman sat in a cane chair in front of an easel, sketching on a large canvas. She did not look up, so absorbed she was in the work she was doing. The dogs ran up to her and stood by her side, wagging their tails and quieting down. When she saw the two men walking toward her, she put her brush down and stood to greet them.

"Emma, this is William Stafford." Everhard introduced him. Then he turned to her, "and William, this is my ward and niece, Emma Melsheimer."

"I am so glad to meet you. What brings you to Newcomerstown?"

The older russet hound stood close to her and let her stroke his brow between his ears. Everhard excused himself to go tend the well house.

"You have a fine friend there," said William, indicating the dog.

"Thank you. He is my favorite subject!"

"I did not mean to interrupt you. Your uncle hired me to see what minerals he might have on his land, so I will be wandering around a few days. I hope you will not mind me."

"Not at all. As a matter of fact, I will only be here a few days myself. I am still in school—art school that is. It is just a matter of days before I have to head back to Cincinnati."

"Oh? I attend lectures in Cincinnati when I can. When do you think you will be going?"

"That depends upon my friend, Ida Saxon. It is her father who will take us. From what Ida tells me, he won't be coming before one day next week." The two stood awkwardly, saying nothing. Emma broke the silence.

"Toddy poses for me," she laughed, indicating the pointer. "I have to take advantage of him while he is willing." She seated herself in front of the easel again.

Henry returned, but William only half heard what he was saying. He watched Emma paint. He saw her chestnut curls brush across the back of her blouse every time she turned her head, and he noticed how tiny her hands were when her free hand dropped absent-mindedly on the older dog's mane. He heard her gentle command to the hunting dog she was painting as the dog began to loll about. The dog obeyed, pointing into the wind.

The scene stuck in William's mind forever: the mottled setter facing into the wind, eyes alert, back straight, tail parallel to the ground—a brown and white brush stroke against a red-orange sky in an otherwise cold landscape. William could hardly believe the dog's discipline or the ease with which Emma brought him to life on the canvas. She had turned the rudiments of an admirable cur into an all-but-finished hunting dog.

Emma herself could not have been much more than four feet ten inches tall. Her plain taffeta dress was some mysterious color that shone like pure gold in the sun. In the depths of the folds, in the waning light, the dress was only a simple brown, the color of her eyes. But in the sunlight, the material took on a brilliance of color he could not describe.

He found a boarding house for himself nearby in Massillon. As he dragged the assay on, William learned how Emma came to live with Henry Everhard.

In 1849 when Emma was four, her staunchly Lutheran parents, the Rev. Edwin Melsheimer and his wife Rachel—died of yellow fever. The little girl went to live with her Melsheimer grandparents in Canton, Ohio.

Grandfather Melsheimer, who was also a Lutheran minister, was of the old school and still spoke German at home, even though his family had been in the United States since before the Revolution. The Rev. Melsheimer spent his days sitting at his huge desk, writing treatises in German for other theologians, most of which made their way back to the scholars in Jena, the great School of Theology in Thuringia, Germany.[17]

He taught Emma the classics, Latin and French, and gave her music lessons on a rosewood square grand piano with claw feet. He bought the piano for her from an artisan named Everett. It was only the seventh one the man had ever built. Her grandfather certainly never intended for her to play show tunes on it, but she could not resist.

Instead of buying sweets the way the other children did, she saved her money to buy the music for "The Flying Trapeze." This was a mistake, she learned. She had not asked his permission, and was banished to her room without supper. Later, her grandfather came in and sat by her bed, his eyes twinkling even as he administered her reprimand. She loved him dearly. It broke her heart to think that she had displeased him

In 1858, when Emma was thirteen, her Melsheimer grandparents both died and left her an orphan once more. That was how she came to live with Uncle Henry and Aunt Mary Everhard.

William heard her out, and when she finished thought it a perfect time to ask Emma to take a walk with him. She accepted. She pulled on her wool bonnet, stuffed her hands into her muff, and the two set out for a nearby hill. By noon they had climbed almost to the top and stopped to rest.

He told her he intended to come see her at her school in Pennsylvania. She looked concerned, then.

"The school will not let me see you alone!" She teased him. "I could never see you alone, but I might be able to visit with you a while in the school's parlor—if somebody else is there watching us."

"That shouldn't be so hard for you to arrange. What about your friend Ida? She will be at school, too, you know."

"I will ask! I know her—she would sit over in the corner so we could talk. She is very frail and quiet, you know, but you will like her." Emma looked out over the horizon, her mind elsewhere..

"My Grandfather Melsheimer took me up here once. I shall never forget it: He waved his hands along the horizon like this." She demonstrated. "Then said 'Everything you see in any direction will one day be yours.'"

"I almost wish you hadn't told me that."

"Why not?"

"Because. . ." William turned away, then blurted out. He had two children back in Waukegan. He was not a rich man. He did not own a mountain.

"I know."

"How did you know?"

"Well, actually, I suppose it was more of a guess. I saw their little letters to you. I wondered."

Two letters were forwarded to the Everhard house, scribbled in a child's hand. William did not know what to say.

"Those letters are from my boys, Will and Freddie. Their mother died when Freddie was born. Will is seven and Freddie is five. They are good boys."

Emma was relieved. She had been hesitant to go walking with him. Now that they had cleared that up, she chattered on about Uncle Henry.

"Uncle Henry is generous. I am *so* grateful for all he has done for me, but he rarely speaks to me. He and Aunt Mary leave me to myself, and I confess that in all these years I have never felt quite at home."

William thought a long minute. "I have only known you a short time, and I am not settled enough to have a real home for my boys—much less for a bride, but . . ."

This did startle her. Not so much that he had brought up such a subject but more that she now knew William was anything but shy. He, on the other hand, knew in an instant he should never have spoken so frankly.

"Forgive me," was all he could think to say.

They sat together on a large flat stone for a while and warmed themselves in the sun, close enough to touch, but they did not. Emma pulled her boots off and rubbed her feet on the soft rock moss. They sat quietly for a while surrounded by falling leaves. Emma found herself laughing to herself. She could not help it. William, she told people later, looked for all the world like Wild Bill Hickok. He wore a silk vest, and his moustache drooped like Wild Bill's but nothing about Wild Bill could in any way apply to the sweet man in front of her.

Stone houses lined the streets in the valley below as the afternoon sun covered them in shadow, the tiny steeple of the old church still light. A string of horses and carriages moved along the darkening streets like ants. About then she felt the warmth of a gentle hand helping her rise to make the journey back home. When that arm encircled her waist, she leaned ever so slightly into his strong body. She was so much in love that she would have married him then and there, no matter what.

"I will speak with my uncle," Emma said. It was her turn to be bold. For William, walking beside her was harder than anything he had ever done. They held hands, and he walked her home in silence.

The next morning, Emma greeted him at the door. He heard frustration in her voice.

"Uncle Henry will not stand in our way, but. . ." Her voice trailed off and she looked down at her feet.

William encouraged her to go on. "Tell me. Whatever it is, you can tell me." He wanted her to look at him, but she would not.

"Uncle Henry says there is nothing left. I have no dowry, no money, no land, nothing."

William was relieved, but could not tell her that. He had been so afraid she would tell him he was too old. He was a good ten years her senior. "Do you think I care about that? I love you whether you have a dowry or not."

"Do you know what else he said?" She drew herself up indignantly and began to imitate her guardian. "'My dear child, I sold that land for you. I gave you clothes, I gave you an education, I let you travel, so there is no money and no land. Do you understand?' I understood quite well, but all I could say was 'You have been very generous, Uncle.'"

William then made another foolish promise. "If you will have me, I will make you rich." It even sounded foolish, but he believed he could accomplish it for her. Nothing so far compared to Emma the lovely, Emma the fascinating, Emma the artist, Emma the worldly, Emma the kind. She was everything an engineer could never be and he would not give her up. "Now may I go talk to Uncle Henry?"

She nodded her head thoughtfully. "But I am the one who must decide."

That evening William joined the Everhards for dinner. It was his last night in town. Emma played the piano.

"Isn't that a beautiful sound?" She turned on the bench. "My grandfather bought it for me, and even with its big ugly paw feet it has comforted me my whole life."

"Then we will take it with us."

Everhard heard the music and came in from the library to join them. The men talked frankly. Soon Henry gave his permission if Emma first finished school. William would wait. He wanted to tell his sons anyway, and a trip to Waukegan would take two long dusty weeks on horseback.

He refused to take the train on those trips because his boys expected him to ride up on his horse. Besides, he loved this magnificent country, its huge oaks and sycamores, its wild life and open spaces. He hurried, though, cantering along the dirt roads and highways, navigating around cows and deer. Closer to Waukegan his horse was an anomaly among carriages and trains and city dwellers. The animal slowed to a trot, happily kicking up mud all the way to the corner of Gennessee Street and Tenth.

Both boys were waiting for him near the street, swinging on the gate. He rode close, and while his horse did its slow dance, he scooped Will and Fred up into the saddle. They screamed and laughed and grabbed him about the neck.

"Take us for a ride," they said.

"And where would you like to go?"

"We want to see the horses," they chimed together.

"Well then, just let me go say hello to your grandmother and wash my face, and we will be off." He lowered them to the grass and dismounted.

The boys ran ahead while he tied his horse. Inside, Elizabeth was busy in the kitchen, scooping up large pats of butter and cheese to go with the corn sticks she was making. William couldn't help but lift the lid of the stove pot for a look. In it was fresh lamb stew. Elizabeth wiped her hands on her apron and wrapped her arms around William as though he were a child, and he was happier than he thought possible.

"Why didn't you bring Emma with you?"

"I wanted to see all of you first," he looked down at his two boys. "But most of all, I wanted time to tell Will and Freddie that they are about to have a new mother."

"We're going to have a new mother?" Freddie asked, glowering. William could not tell if his son was upset or just curious. Just curious, he decided.

"Indeed, you are." He went on to describe her, what she liked to do, what she liked to eat, that she liked dogs and that she liked children. Finally, he got around to the most important thing at that moment. "Now let's go see the horses!"

Emma opened her first letter from him while she was at school. She read some of it to Ida. By the time the next letter came, she was back in Newcomerstown. William thought he had a home for them. He told her it was perfect. She could bring her piano, and it was big enough for his boys.

They married in Newcomerstown on Ascension Day, May 21 in 1868. Uncle Henry gave her away and kept his promise to let her take her beloved square grand. William went ahead to Iowa.

Before summer came in earnest, Emma and her piano were packed and ready to go. Uncle Henry and his friends loaded the Everett on a wagon and hitched it to the coach. Uncle Henry kissed her goodbye on top of her head, handed her the heavy valise, let her embrace her aunt one last time, and sent her on her way to the train station. Emma promised she would visit.

What she had no way of knowing was that when William reached Iowa, nothing was as he expected. Gold mines in Iowa, some of the richest in the rush, were petering out. The mine owners wanted William to find new seams, but there were none. The owners spent all their money trying to find more gold, but William could not help them. The mines began to close, and the miners drifted farther west. William made other plans: Missouri, he thought, or perhaps Alabama, where operators were already tapping the State's four great coal fields. The South was now a blip on his horizon.

Emma fostered misgivings about them all: Iowa, Missouri or Alabama, but she would not let him know. The misgivings grew as she set off on her journey. She had never anticipated the horrible bumpy rides or the coughing and choking from clouds of dust that smudged her face and dug into her clothes. Alarms went off in her head when the very first coach, the one that took her to the train station, lost one wheel after another in the city's rain-filled ditches.

The train track finally ended in Iowa, but she had to endure several long coach rides before she even crossed the Missouri state line. The final leg of the journey was by covered wagon. It took three men to load her crated piano into a cart that looked far too small for it. The driver assured her it would be all right. The coach passed through towns populated with swaggering men and Indians. She felt small around such men and was afraid of Indians. How dingy she felt now on the road to Missouri.

Worst of all she felt shame when she had to stand outside the coach and raise her petticoats to relieve herself. She knew the coachman watched. But when the coach stopped at a clean inn along the way, or when a passing stranger gave her a sweet, or when she rested with her sketchbook in her hands, the romance of it returned. She felt tall and adventurous.

Until, that is, she became the only passenger. The coachman picked up speed that day—so much so that she had to hold tight to the sides of coach. When she opened her curtain to see why they were speeding so, she saw a band of Indians. They were running from Indians. The wagon slowed when the band surrounded it.

One of the Indians signaled the coach to stop, then motioned for her to get out, but she would not. He motioned once more. When she refused, he opened the door and took her elbow to help her out. Knees shaking uncontrollably, she obeyed, too frightened for tears. The wind caught her cap, and she reached for it out of habit, but the man kept his grip on her elbow. He was not so much rough, she thought, as he was determined. She waited for the driver to defend her, but he did not. She looked wildly for an escape route, but there was none. To her amazement, her captor released her and retrieved her rolling hat. He spoke English.

"What is that? What do you have in there, Ma'am?" He pointed at the lumpy cargo.

She was astonished. He called her "Ma'am."

"It is my piano," she said. "Here, let me show you."

He looked puzzled. He helped her as she struggled to climb up onto the wagon. The coachman took the nails out of the crate, and together they lifted the lid. She was afraid what she might see underneath. Then she made a quick decision. She reached over the crate and opened the piano to display the keyboard. With her hat between her knees, she played on the keys with one finger. It still played. She made a little tune then.

The rest of the curious band, one by one, urged their horses to step closer to the wagon. A few dismounted and actually climbed into the wagon with her and gingerly touched the piano keys. They put two or three notes together to make their own tunes. Time passed. The music they made together was unforgettable. Catbird songs. Point and counterpoint. The Indians laughed and joked until finally the wagoner ordered them off. They remounted and rode off in high spirits.

Emma made her way back to her seat, the coachman cracked his leather whip, and off they went. Emma felt different somehow. She had met fear with a kind of practical bravery, but she knew it might not always turn out so well.

She reached her last stop in Missouri, and William was there to meet her. All her brave intentions, all her stoic resolves, everything in her gave way as she dropped her suitcase in the dust and held her husband close. She let her tears flow, let him comfort her, let him take off her misshapen hat and stroke her matted hair. He brushed her tears from her cheeks and smoothed the tangle away from her brows.

Only then did she look down and see two pairs of eyes looking quizzically up at her. The two boys hung behind, Freddie clinging tightly to William's coattail. William stepped back.

"Freddie, this is your new mother. Emma, this is Will. He is seven, and Freddie here just turned five." Will came forward and bowed.

"How lovely! Thank you for that nice bow, Will." She let go of her husband and bent down until she almost sat on her heels. Her skirts billowed around her in the dust.

She looked Freddie in the eye and asked if he would like to hold her hand, but Freddie scowled and fell back. Once they were in the coach, Emma let the boys talk about things important to little boys. Not knowing what else to do, she told them she knew a song they might like, because she had sung it to children before. It was the song she sang to runaway children, runaway slaves who made their way to her grandfather's church in Canton. It was the only children's song she knew. The language didn't matter.

"I will sing you a song in German and in English," she said. And she began:

"Ich bin klein, mein herz ist rein, / Soli diemand drinn wohner aber Jesu allein."

Then she sang in English.

"I am small, my heart is clean, / No one will live there but Jesus."

Will smiled, but Freddie held his hands over his ears.

5. The Concordia Beneficial Society

The Concordia Beneficial Society built a new clubhouse back in 1901,[18] thirty years after Birmingham was born. Those of German descent built it for themselves.

People from all over the world, seduced by the promise of riches, came to Birmingham. They were from everywhere: Russia, Italy, Germany, Greece and of course from states like Ohio and Pennsylvania. Even Charles Linn, perhaps Birmingham's most civilizing influence, came from Finland, where his family owned ironworks.[19] Linn understood how important it was to transform raw iron into pig iron, then ultimately to steel. He also understood that Birmingham had to attract the best engineers, masons and ironmongers in the world.

They came and built the mining towns that looked just like the villages they left behind. They used the same designs, the same stones and mortar, and the same metal and woodwork they had used in their old countries. Birmingham came into being with exquisite spires and domes, stone churches, craftsman-style houses, stone masonry walls, wrought iron gates and homes with intricate wood carvings. Entrepreneurs and artisans alike organized their clubs the same way they organized their houses—just like those they left behind.

German immigrants and others who studied in Germany at the School of Mines in Freiberg or Saxony or Teubingen or Goettingen, joined the Concordia Beneficial Society. Its members held their meetings in German and wrote their minutes in German; and there were a lot of members. The Concordia Beneficial Society became the place where decisions were made—its members changed the future of the city.

Charles DeBardeleben, Henry's son, waited restlessly outside after one of these meetings. He was waiting for a lackey to bring him his father's horse. He had to meet his father at the L&N Railroad Station, and they planned to ride home together. While he waited he wanted somebody to talk to. He cornered the first likely fellow leaving the meeting.

"Philips! What did you think of *that* speaker?" The club's guest that day was a Mr. Heflin, a legislator from Randolph County.[20]

"I doubt we will forget him!" Phillips struck an orator's pose and mimicked Heflin's preacher voice. "'This is our country by virtue of inheritance. It is right that we should rule it. We will rule it!'" Philips always astounded Charles with his recall.

"Great line," said Charles. "I might add: 'Damn the unions and the Catholics!'"

They laughed and Philips quipped "Shall I give you another quote from Wilhelm II? I believe he was speaking to all of us Germans when he said we must 'bear up like the Huns of Attila.'"[21]

The lackey arrived with two rider-less horses, one for Charles and one for Henry. Phillips shook Charles's hand, and the two men parted feeling very good about themselves.

Charles mounted his horse and trotted over to the station with his father's horse trotting along behind, tied to his saddle. When he approached the platform, he tethered both horses, ascended the stairs and waited. The steaming carcass of the train came to rest next to the platform, and Henry disembarked. Father and son descended the stairs to Morris Avenue together. Henry had begun to stoop, to show his age. He had mellowed, too, Charles thought. Henry touched Charles on his shoulder as a thank-you and tipped the red caps. They mounted their horses and trotted off down Morris Avenue.

On the way, Henry rattled off his entire inventory, all the different mines and associated enterprises he owned. This recitation lasted most of the journey because Henry owned substantially everything that had anything to do with mining, including more than 150,000 acres of land. Charles knew how the conversation was going to end.

"Things are good, but there are still more seams out there. Who knows which land will yield good ore! Get busy. Go buy those lands. Start your own farm, so to speak."

"You have something in mind? Something in particular?" Charles already knew.

"Well, yes, I do. There is still land in St. Clair County. Nothing much there yet. Rails in place. Old mines not operating. Some of those properties could be very profitable, you know, but there's those who will put up a fight when you try to buy them."

"Who said buy 'em? The old chief's daughter is dead, and the granddaughter married that Negro, and you know Negroes can't own property in Alabama."

Henry was pleased. Later that day Charles and Henry met with Mr. W. T. Underwood, their attorney and Henry's partner from twenty years before. The two men formed *DeBardeleben and Underwood* in the 1880s. Henry counted on his partner to keep him out of trouble, but Underwood was growing older, too.

"I think you're right there about the mineral rights." Underwood looked up at them from over his spectacles. "You don't have to buy anything. Save your money. Owning the mineral rights may be better than owning the land. If you own the mineral rights you do not have much liability. Just get hold of the mineral rights." He was fond of repeating himself.

"See, Father, what did I tell you? I mean, there are other ways to skin a cat."

"You need a deed," Underwood continued. "Then you'll have the right to put buildings and equipment on the land, you'll have the right to install pumps and wells, you'll have the right to open a commissary, you'll have the right to provide housing for the miners, you'll have the right to storage."

The DeBardelebens stopped listening, so Underwood put both fists on the table, leaned forward and continued. "It needs to be legal. You cannot just go in higgledy piggledy. You have got to justify improvements as necessary to the project."

"I say that's too much work. I'm inclined to give that one up," said Henry.

"But I'm not," said his son. "I'll tackle St. Clair. Watch me." It was exactly what Henry F. wanted to hear. Charles was just like him.

In 1905, Charles DeBardeleben and his Alabama Fuel and Iron Company opened a mine in St. Clair County. By 1908, he had named it *Margaret*, for his wife. The Company's other operations nearby included mines at Acmar, Acton, and Overton. The Company brought workers into St. Clair County by the hundreds. For every worker who died, two more came to take his place. The villages exploded with personnel.

Lila read the letter from Mr. Underwood to Bradford. They could not prevent these men from coming. She didn't know what to do other than to make provisions for the visit. She cooked a skillet full of fried corn, fry bread and fresh tomatoes.

The men came. Lila walked with her husband to the road to greet them. But she never had a chance, not even to offer her visitors something to eat.

Charles DeBardeleben brushed past her. "You know why I'm here, don't you?" he said to Bradford.

"I expect I do, but we are not interested in selling. Not at all." Bradford stood with his legs apart and his arms folded over his chest.

"Do you think I want to *buy* your land?"

Bradford hesitated. "You tell me."

"Now don't get me wrong," said Charles DeBardeleben. "I don't want to buy your land—you can keep it. I do not want to take it from you." Charles stared at Bradford until he made Bradford uneasy, but Bradford never flinched. Charles continued. "Mineral rights, sir. That's all we want."

"Mineral rights?" Bradford wanted the whole story.

"Means we can mine underground."

"And what else does that mean?"

Charles skimmed over this part, mentioning they might have to build a road or two. He forgot to specify camps, houses, commissaries, imported workers, wells, storage, pump houses or much of anything else.

"If I own the mineral rights under your farm, you still own your land." He repeated himself seven times during the conversation. Bradford counted them.

"I will pay you of course. I will just need your signature so I can break ground. When you do, I can guarantee you and your neighbors many jobs." Charles ticked them off: brick mason, blacksmith, cook, hauler, pump operator, rail attendant, and so on. Then he stepped close to Bradford.

"You know, I can take the land even if you don't sign."

"Give me some time to think about it," Bradford said. He would consult the others, Lila and his neighbors. It might help them understand better if he drank the bitter drink with them. Truth and wisdom prevailed when men drank the bitter drink. How much benefit would they receive, or would such an agreement prove fatal for them all?

"I can guarantee your town will grow," said Charles.

"Two days is all I ask," Bradford said. "I will meet you here again in two days."

"Wednesday afternoon at two o'clock, then?"

Bradford never held that council because his son Jerry knew a man who knew a man who was an attorney who worked for a Mr. Sloss in Birmingham. Bradford and Jerry found the man and went to see him. The lawyer saw the potential in Bradford's land and advised him that he had nothing to lose. So when Wednesday came, Bradford signed the agreement.

Charles DeBardeleben announced the progress in Margaret to his Board this way: "I was the eagle, and I wanted to eat all the crawfish I could— swallowing up the little fellows. I did it!"[22]

Deep holes appeared like pox all over Bradford's corner of what once was his farm. The sound of drilling woke babies and disgruntled the old people. Accessory buildings popped up like boils. Miners and cooks and mule drivers and suppliers and chain gangs crowded into Margaret. They stored dynamite and dangerous compounds and tools in Bradford's shed. The Company built a trunk line on the land so workers could load coal directly onto a coal car. Employers only showed up on payday.

Children clung to their mothers' skirts, afraid of the strange new men. Grown-ups distrusted the Company's supervisors. Bradford's crops were trampled and turned under. They could no longer live on what they could grow.

The day came when Bradford could take it no longer. He cranked up his truck and left for Birmingham to see Mr. DeBardeleben. It took him half the day to get there, but he found the right office before quitting time. He knocked politely on the door, his hat in his hand.

"Excuse me, Missus, but is Mr. DeBardeleben in?"

"Which one?"

"Mr. Charles, Ma'am."

"You just wait right out there and I'll go see." The secretary disappeared. Bradford sat for a good hour or so. It turned dark before the secretary finally returned and informed him that Mr. DeBardeleben was busy. Bradford left and made the long trip back to Margaret in the dark.

He came back the next day and the next, until finally the secretary said Mr. DeBardeleben's general manager would see him. Bradford tried to sound business-like, but it was hard. He told the general manager that all the dynamite and destruction were not what he bargained for and he was asking for help.

"He's paying you rent ain't he?"

Bradford allowed as how he was.

"Well, ain't nothing I can do about that. He's got every right. But he's not a man don't care about you, you know. He says you can come work for us."

Such a proposition never entered Bradford's mind before. Its ramifications were mind-boggling.

"It's good pay. You won't need to farm no more. You'll be hauling for us—hauling timber for the railroad. You'll be a hauler."

"What will happen to my crops?"

The general manager looked at Bradford as though the conversation were over. "Make up your mind. You can't have it both ways," he said.

The payment he received for his mineral rights wasn't much, Bradford admitted to himself. It failed to cover their needs. If he had just known. He had already mortgaged what little yield he had on his crops to make ends meet. Now he owed the company store money for seed, too. He was still strong, though. He believed he could haul timber for the railroad and continue to farm, so he agreed to take the job.

Early on he received good pay, but later the company claimed bad times and paid him less. Finally, after World War I broke out, even though he kept on working, kept on hauling and farming, there was no pay at all.

6. Freddie

For a time—for much longer than they expected—Emma and William stayed with the children in Johnstone's house on Gennessee Street. When Emma and William went for a walk, Will went along, but Freddie hung back. No amount of sweets would entice him.

Freddie was older now. He sullenly refused to say good morning or slammed the door on his way out. William came down hard on Freddie, but Emma understood him. She had wanted to slam doors when she lived with Uncle Henry, and she tried to tell William how it had been, but William saw himself as a stern father.

"They are afraid they will lose you, my love. That's all. Be patient," she told him.

"And I am afraid I will lose my temper," was what he said. He never lost his temper, but he sometimes made Freddie march out to the garden to cut his own switch. William was the mildest of despots and wielded the lightest of switches, but any switching brought tears to Emma's eyes and to a lesser degree to the defiant Freddie. Emma's mind sensed that, with convoluted little-boy reasoning, Freddie took some small pleasure in tears.

"Freddie will come around. He doesn't mean anything by it, it's just that he doesn't know what else to do."

William did not stay in Waukegan long enough to develop the necessary patience. Engineers were in demand. Every state and every river needed bridges; every railroad in Missouri, Iowa, Illinois, and Ohio needed bridges. William had to go wherever his company sent him. The couple moved from place to place at a clip they never anticipated and never wanted. Will and Freddie stayed with Johnstone and Elizabeth, but when it came time to go, Freddie clung to his father as though his heart would break, and Emma's already wounded heart almost broke in two. She tried to reassure the boys that their father would soon come back to fetch them.

Emma would not leave her husband. She endured nasty weather, horrific river crossings and dust storms, heat and cold, lack of companionship, bad food and water and birthing her first child, Edwin. Her fine shantung dresses soaked up mud she could never wash out. After Missouri she had no need for finery, even though she missed it. In the end, she tore her nicest dresses up for rags. They did not make very good rags.

After Edwin was born, she refused to take another stagecoach. She traveled thenceforth by rail, which had some advantages—speed being one. The food was a little better, too, but the train had its own dangers.

In about 1874, she made a train trip to Iowa with two babies, Edwin and Alice, and she was pregnant again besides. When the train went around a curve, the nausea grew worse. She held tightly to her children, and the three of them jerked and swayed. Finally, the train rolled down from the hills and chugged lazily across the wide plains. Grateful for the respite, Emma called the porter to make her berth and settled in with her children for a long night's sleep.

At around midnight, Edwin stirred and began to cry. The train had picked up speed and was tossing them side to side again. She felt the change before she was fully awake and dreamt they were outrunning a band of Indians until she realized Edwin was not just crying, he was gasping for breath, colicky. She woke then and picked Edwin up, trying to ease his pain and stop the crying. Only then did she see the strange light flickering through the opening in the curtains. She thought at first it was morning, but it was only midnight.

Then she saw smoke. Her compartment was full of it. The train was in a forest, and the whole forest was afire.

She covered her children's noses with wet handkerchiefs and prepared for the worst. Flames licked at the sides of the wooden car until she could no longer see anything out of the window beyond the wall of fire. The train sped through that awful night while she prayed her babies would not die. She made a thousand promises to God that night. Then just before daybreak, about the time Emma had all but given up, the train broke through.

None of them died. The engineer had pushed his train to an ungodly speed, almost beyond the engine's capacity. Had he recorded his time, she said later, she was sure he would have broken all previous records, but nobody recorded it. She never saw anything about the fire in the press. The railroad never mentioned it, either.

In 1878 the papers were full of stories about the infinite pleasures of travel on the Eerie Canal. Articles glorified the boats' elegant and comfortable quarters and described the wonders a passenger would experience meandering through the great glacial chasms along the Mohawk Valley. She remembered taking such trips as a child, waiting for water to fill the locks and thrilling as the boat rose to the top. She heard the lugubrious sound of horns, and she longed for the ease and leisure of traveling with her grandparents.

After that hideous train journey, she fell again into her husband's arms. She counted on his goodness and could not survive without it, especially when her babes came so close to death.

Her third child was born in Iowa and the last one in Cincinnati. She had too little time in between to become accustomed to any one place.[23]

With every move, she and William begged Will and Freddie to join them, but the boys never did. There was always a reason. Johnstone and Elizabeth always answered, saying how important it was not to unsettle Will and Freddie any more than necessary. Waukegan was no longer a little frontier town but quite a metropolis with doctors, schools and churches, plays and music, a good sheriff and new academy. The boys needed to finish their education.

The boys became Johnstone and Elizabeth's reason for being. So Emma and William moved closer. William built Emma a lovely house up on a hill in Cincinnati, and this is where Edwin and Cyrus, George and Alice grew up. Will visited them, too, on all the holidays. On one of these visits, Will told them he had met the love of his life and planned to marry her.

The implications of that announcement did not seem to sink in with Freddie. The news shook Johnstone and Elizabeth to the core.

"What will become of Freddie without you?" Johnstone asked Will. "You boys have never separated for more than a day!"

Will could not answer that. He asked his father William to come back to Waukegan, to talk to Freddie. William took the next train to Waukegan.

His sisters Caroline and Matilda Elizabeth met him at the station without their husbands. A strong wind howled off Lake Michigan, and William almost didn't recognize them underneath all their scarves and mittens.

Caroline's buggy waited outside. The siblings talked happily from the sheer joy of being together. So much had happened after all these years. Only after tea and after Caroline and Matilda left did Johnstone mention the impending wedding.

"We—your mother and I—need your advice. More to the point, your boys need your advice. Will is going to be fine. We are not sure about Freddie."

Elizabeth looked even smaller when she sank into the Chesterfield. She and Johnstone approved of the young lady, whose name was Martha.

"Then I trust your decision on that," said William.

Johnstone touched his fingertips together and moved to the edge of his seat, but said nothing. Elizabeth picked up. "Freddie is taking this far, far too hard. He has hardly spoken to us or to anybody since Will started talking marriage. He needs you, William. Nobody else can get through to him."

"Tomorrow night," said William, "I will talk seriously to them both. For tonight, just let me be here."

Tomorrow night came. Both boys returned before sundown and set off straightaway to wash. When they returned, Will said his hellos before he said his goodbyes and rode off to visit Martha in Cincinnati. William grasped his opportunity.

He and Freddie saddled their horses. Destination: the outskirts of Chicago, not far from the stockyards where William had gone so often to buy leather for Johnstone's shop. Father and son took the back roads until they came to a grassy field with a corral at one end where horses were kept. They stopped here, where they could talk honestly to one another around these beautiful horses.

They had just begun when a group of local cowboys gathered close by. Men often spent their evenings here, turning their horses loose in the fenced pasture to let them run. Sometimes onlookers placed bets on these horses.

This night, dozens of restless horses—too many horses—burst out from the corral into an even smaller pen. From the looks of the frantic prancing, they had been corralled for days. Freddie told his father the horses had indeed been confined to smaller and smaller places over the last few days. This was new to William.

The gate opened just enough to let one horse into the ring. Both Freddie and his father registered horror as the men strapped leather thongs around the horse's groin and cinched them tight. The tighter they pulled, the wilder the horse bucked and snorted, trying to free itself from the painful cinch. Cowboys took turns trying to ride. The more the horses bucked and the more men they threw to the ground and tried to trample, the wilder the crowd grew. The cowboys cast lots again and again until a man succeeded in riding the horse to the finish. The winner dismounted and wrestled the tormented animal to the ground.

Freddie shook his head and turned to his father. "Those bastards should pay. If I were the horse, I would kick the shit out of them until I broke free, and I would never come back."

"Is that what you want to do, Freddie? Kick somebody and never come back? Is there a reason?"

"How would you like to have that band squeezed so tight around your private parts? You'd buck and whinny, too, to get the damn thing off."

"But you are not a horse. You are not being tormented, no matter what you think."

55

"What can I do? I don't know how to do anything but be a shoemaker. Where can I go when Will leaves?" This was Freddie's torment. Freddie anticipated what his father was going to say. "And I don't need your help."

"What would you rather do than be a shoemaker?"

"Maybe I will join the rodeo." He didn't sound serious.

"Maybe after you grow up." William teased him.

Tension in the ring grew. A heavy-set fellow with spurs on his boots strode into the ring and roped one of the struggling creatures. Bystanders and those placing bets chanted encouragement, but the whinny the horse made sounded more like a gurgle.

"That poor horse will be dead by tomorrow," said Freddie. He looked at his father sharply. "You don't know what it's like to be a horse, and you are not being tormented either."

The winner yanked the rope in such a way that the noose broke the horse's neck. Then the cowboy pushed his hands over his head in victory, waiting for applause.

"I'll kill him, Father."

William pulled him back.

"You'll get yourself killed." It took a long while for Fred to stop pacing and punching at imaginary devils in the air.

On the way home, William had an idea. If only Brother Frederick would take him. Frederick "practiced agriculture" in Butler, Illinois, not too far from Waukegan. Would Freddie consider farming with his Uncle Frederick?

"Just for a while," William said to Freddie. "Long enough to know if you want to raise horses. Your Uncle Frederick has plenty of room for you on his spread, and I know you would be welcome. And Uncle Frederick has horses. If you intend to defend them, I would suggest you get to know them more intimately."

7. Brothers

In 1905, Joseph Caswell lived with his wife and five kids in a large enough house on Shades Mountain near the Cahaba River in Alabama. He kept his family clean and fed and sometimes took them to the lake just outside Irondale for a picnic. He never walked out the door without putting on his belt and shining his shoes until that final day when he left for good. This is the story of how he met Alma.

Alma grew up on Shades Mountain near the town of Irondale. She spent her summers walking barefoot along old Muskogee trails, mostly to the river bank where she stopped and cooled her feet and watched fish congregate in pools of swirling river water. One June, when she was fourteen, she picked all the sweet blackberries she could gather as soon as they ripened. After she ate her fill, she stuffed the rest, still oozing their sweet juices, into the pockets of her dress.

Like life itself, in some seasons the berries were seedy and tough, sometimes bitter, sometimes overripe, and sometimes wormy. But picked at the right time, they were luscious and smooth.

Her mother washed her clothes without complaint, but even with all the washings her clothes took on a certain shade of gray-blue that could never be washed out. Other times after she gorged herself on the berries, she submerged herself—dresses, stockings and all, in the Cahaba until its cold waters took her breath away. She told herself this would wash the stains out, but of course it did not. Her mother let her get away with it with only a mild scolding.

Another time, she ate a mouthful of sumac berries by mistake, and her mouth and toes and arms swelled up with angry welts. Shades Mountain was a beautiful place, but it had more dangers than just bears and panthers.

Diphtheria had already claimed two of her cousins—brothers. When Alma found out how sick they were, she ran to their house to see them, but their parents would not let her or anyone else into their room. She could only stand in the doorway trying to comfort them as they lay pale and weak, choking to death. She would never forget how wild their eyes looked before they died.

Two more of her friends died of polio. Her neighbors, afraid that quarry water carried the disease, would not let their children swim in the deep cloudy quarry water, but conceded that perhaps swift-moving icy river water was safe. Alma and her sisters swam in the rivers and never came down with anything more than the usual measles and mumps and chickenpox, diseases that sent them to bed for just a few days. They knew measles might leave you blind and scarlet fever might make you bald and leave you with a tipsy heart, but they escaped the worst, hand-wringing, terrifying ailments.

Hardly anybody Alma's age got smallpox anymore because of the vaccine, but she knew a few older people who had lived through it, at a great price. They bore deep, ugly, discolored pits on their faces and necks. Alma escaped that just by being born later. Her face was smooth and her legs were long.

She helped her father sell fresh vegetables. Some days she left school early to tend the store. She was there when Joseph stopped in, swinging a clipboard in his left hand. He acted as though being left-handed didn't matter to him a bit. He tipped his hat when Alma opened the screen door and stepped inside. There, he took off his hat and held it against his chest before he mustered courage enough to speak to her. He said he was a hungry man and had seen the sign outside about the pickles. Might she have some fresh pickles in the barrel?

She did. She wrapped them in butcher paper for him. Joseph ate his pickles and watched Alma as she busied herself arranging plums on the display case.

When Alma first laid eyes on Joseph, she became aware that she was barefoot and her faded pinafore was an ugly, dusty gray-blue from a whole summer's worth of blackberry picking. Her reflection in the window showed her hair hanging down straight and yellow. She was a mess, but knew it did not matter, really, because he had her in his sights. In spite of her careless looking clothes and her straight hair, she was what they called a *looker*. She was lean and tan and had a bright smile, or so she had been told. It was as unnecessary for her to flirt as it was for Joseph to pay her compliments.

Alma brushed her hair back anyway and never went barefoot or wore stained pinafores again. Still, she was surprised when Joseph came back. It was almost a year later, and this time he came on business and not for pickles.

"Miss Alma," he said. "I'm come to speak to your father. We're having a town meeting tomorrow night. I have come to ask him to join us."

Alma looked quizzical, like she thought he didn't know what he was talking about. "Well, we ain't a town. Really—not a real town. Just a county far as I know."

"It qualifies as a town in my mind." He smiled

She could see that he was tidy, that he had carefully polished his shoes before he came. He stood before her straight and tall, his fine blue shirt tucked into his brown trousers without suspenders. He looked shiny all over in spite of all the coal dust in the air.

"Miss Alma, I understand your pa knows all the men that work in the mines around here. Would you be kind enough to tell him I would like to talk to him?"

Joseph found Alma level headed. They talked a while until her father came in—about things happening in the city, the cost of flour and cotton, and about the future. They talked about what was bad in the world, but also what was good. He was sure there would be a future because the South was in a new century. Joseph Caswell represented the miners union, and that was a position of great responsibility.

Even though Joseph's own family made it through the depression in 1893 by growing beans and making their own clothes and not getting too upset, they kept on and survived the bad times. They didn't have much choice, but nobody stood in their way, either, which was why Joseph did what he did. He had seen men fall apart, not just because they did not have the will to overcome, but because other men stood in their way.

Men and women everywhere wanted to talk, and Joseph indulged them. He was willing, even glad, to listen. Furthermore he believed most men had something to say. He also thought most men knew in their hearts what was right even if they didn't do it.

Alma listened when he talked about hitting brick walls. She heard him say he sometimes feared his quest for fair wages was a search for pie in the sky. He also told her how many times, when union men did ask for a raise, they were met with punishment like having their wages cut, sometimes twenty or thirty percent. Some companies do that even when they know it is wrong, he said, because they belong to a powerful organization in Chicago that has their backs, called the General Managers Association.[24]

In Birmingham, life was excellent. An Englishman named Bowron figured out that if he reduced the silicon and sulfur content in pig iron, he could make steel, by far the strongest possible construction material of the time. Overnight, big companies turned pig iron into refined pig iron, fit to be converted into open-hearth steel. Operators had been doing this ever since June 22, 1895, when Henry F. DeBardeleben cast the first steel in his own Alice furnace. Ever since that first run, runs of molten steel lit the skies of Birmingham a brilliant orange at night and caused Birmingham citizens to whoop and holler as loud as they could. The crimson glow on the horizon looked to them like the pot of gold, and they placed their hopes on it.

Times were worse than people knew, though. Mining and steel industries were about to go belly up.

Mr. DeBardeleben left for New York to try to find backers to save his company and the steel industry itself. That was when New York saved the South. Mr. Carnegie and his Illinois Steel Company bought and paid for every bit of that first steel.[25] Alabama and Mr. DeBardeleben stayed rich after all, and this was the event that deserved a true celebration.

Birmingham celebrated its first Labor Day.[26] After the joys of the day, that very evening, Alma agreed to marry Joseph. They planned their wedding for a day in October when the leaves around Irondale would be bronze and gold and purple. They would marry in a chapel near the Cahaba.

Alma's aunt made her a satin dress with bits of Alencon lace on the cuffs of the sleeves. The lace came from a display, unbought for a long time, in her father's store.

The day of the wedding arrived. The little church filled to overflowing with Greek and Italian, white and Negro miners, old men and young. She knew Joseph tried hard to learn their languages, and she knew he would invite them all to supper if he could. The Depression was over and the mood was jovial all around.

On the grounds in front of the church, Joseph stood in his stiff shirt, shaking each man's hand and tipping his hat to each man's wife. Wedding guests crowded around him, talking about their troubles, a sickness in the family or a child working long hours in the mines. He listened patiently, sometimes giving the speaker a smile, sometimes an encouraging pat on the back. Later, when they were alone, she asked him who all these people were and was astonished when he named every one and told her who they were.

"Good people," he said. "Working for a dream, you see. They want to build something good here. The South is their world!"

"Mine, too," she answered. He was her world, and he waited for her with his arms outstretched.

The honeymoon was shorter than anyone could have guessed. Before the next day even dawned, one of the miners knocked on their door.

"Hey, Joe. Wake up. You gotta do something."

"What is it?"

"We just caught them convicts . . . them that ran last week. We been looking for 'em and now we got 'em, but we got a problem. The sheriff didn't take 'em back to the mines. He just put 'em in chains and took 'em down to the jail. Says it's for safe keeping, but we know better. A lot of men talking, telling everybody to be afraid, telling them they're in danger with convicts around. Can you talk some sense in them men? They're assembling down the east end of Main Street, and they're armed."

Joseph told the miner "You go talk to them—hold them off. A shooting like this will set us back, way back. It will hurt our brotherhood."

Joseph needed to think. He tried to figure out what Samuel Gompers, head of the Alabama State Federation of Labor, would do. Gompers demanded that his union men be "models of fair behavior."[27] Killing prisoners would not set well with him. He was trying to stop the leasing of convicts altogether.

"How much time do you think we have?" asked Joseph.

"They probably ain't going to go about it in broad daylight. Maybe after dark."

"Then hold them off 'til dark. I think I know somebody they will listen to, and I think I know where to find him." The miner left.

It just happened then that Samuel Gompers was in Selma looking for a place to hold a conference.[28] On his agenda was convict leasing in Alabama's mines, which brought Alabama's State Treasury and the mine owners magnificent benefits, but too often the price for the convicts included phony extensions of sentences and more time in the mines. Because the most likely thing to come out of a mine was a man's dead body, a convict had a powerful incentive to escape.

The mine in Tracy City alone worked 400 convicts. The situation had reached critical proportions. Sheriffs and deputies arrested young men indiscriminately, especially Negroes, on charges that were either nonexistent or exaggerated. Almost as soon as they were thrown into prison, these men were sent to the mines.

Joseph reached Selma in time to see Gompers, who arrived from New York, coming out of the mayor's office. A strong fellow with piercing blue eyes, Gompers sported an elegant white beard and a goatee. Gompers recognized Joseph instantly and shook his hand. He had one fine handshake.

"How did your meeting go in there?" Joseph began.

"Not well, I'm afraid. We're being put off again." Gompers shook his head. "They won't let us use the hall because we have Negroes coming to the meeting."

"Well, Sir, that won't happen in Birmingham. Come on, we'll arrange for the auditorium in Birmingham." Joseph gave him an encouraging pat on the back.

"You think Birmingham is different?"

"I do. I most definitely do. I know the men in Birmingham."

"That is not why you came. Is something else wrong?" Gompers' sharp blue eyes zeroed in on Joseph.

"Sir, we're in a bad situation back home involving escaped convicts. They've been caught and are in our jail. Word is they will probably be killed tonight. We need a real persuasive voice, and you've got the most persuasive voice I know. Do you have time to ride with me to St. Clair County and help me out?"

Gompers agreed, and Joseph gave him a brief version of the whole story while they saddled up. Gompers could not guarantee a good outcome, but he would try—as long as it didn't interfere with his reason for coming, which was to hold his conference. Still, he conceded, stopping a killing came first.

"Now you know I don't have control over the convict situation," he cautioned Joseph.

"No, but you do have control over how union men behave. So I think we are about to put you to the test." They both grinned.

The two rode into town before dark and approached the men and women milling about the jail. Most of them were there out of curiosity, but others were the kind who were proud of the notches in their guns. The latter had either dodged coming to grief over something or had demonstrated their power over others in a lethal way. In either case, these men's guns stayed cocked and ready.

"Gentlemen," Joseph began. "Mr. Samuel Gompers here is my guest tonight. I want you all to meet him. He wants to speak to you." Neither man descended from his horse.

The crowd, mostly on foot, gathered around respectfully, as Joseph knew they would. The gun-toters lowered their guns. Gompers was a man of his word. He spoke with authority.

"Fellow citizens, we have a situation here. It is hard to decide what to do. I don't know what these men have done and you may not know what they've done, but these men in your jail deserve a trial. In this they are no different from you." He looked down at each set of eyes looking up at him.

"What you decide tonight will make a difference in how you will be treated in the future. You are the backbone of this place and this union. How you behave tonight will be seen by eyes around the world, so take plenty of time before you act." He dismounted. Then he began again.

"Time is the most valuable thing on earth: time to think, time to act, time to extend our fraternal relations, time to become better men, time to become better women, time to become better and more independent citizens."[29]

He strode through the crowd and spoke to each man. Not a one disagreed. The trouble was over.

An October cold front chilled the auditorium in Birmingham. Someone tried to turn up the heat, but for some reason it would not work. Men removed their hats and seated themselves in the cavernous room as the program began. Representatives from every union in Alabama were there. They were part of the Alabama State Industrial Union Council.

Joseph sat in the center of the first row, his dark hair combed fashionably straight and parted down the middle. He wore a dark brown, double-breasted gabardine jacket. He handed Alma his broad-brimmed hat and made his way to the stage, shaking hands as he went. The audience quieted down as he stepped up to the podium.

"Brothers, welcome to this warm hall." Some laughter. "I have a few announcements. Then I will turn the meeting over to our president, Mr. Samuel Gompers."

8. Posted to Birmingham

For a while, letters from Freddie were newsy. Uncle Frederick sent him to work for a neighboring farmer, Mr. Williamson Smith. By 1888, Freddie wrote he wished he were back at his Uncle Frederick's. He had some rough things to say about Smith. Maybe farming was not for him, he said, and maybe he should join his half-brother Edwin in Birmingham.

Edwin was married now. His letters were full of children's incoming teeth and the Episcopalian mission church he attended in Woodlawn, the Calvary Mission Church.[30]

William and Emma loved Cincinnati, but William never missed an article about Birmingham. The *Cincinnati Enquirer* was full of Birmingham, and the more letters Edwin wrote about his city, the more William thought about slowing down. Not stopping, of course.

"Holy Mackerel! Look how much land they're using down there—just for mines! Just for digging ore!" William did a quick mental calculation. "Do you know what this means? Alabama's seams dwarf those in England. They make Germany's mines look paltry by comparison. What do you think, Emma? You always said Germany's mines were its golden egg!" He handed the *Enquirer* to Emma. She was not quite prepared for what came next.

"Emma, you need to know I have been writing some letters. I wrote to a Mr. Linn in Birmingham who is looking for engineers, and to a Mr. John Turner Milner. He helped build the South and North Railroad. From what I hear, Milner is another Ormsby Mitchell. He started out as assistant engineer just like Ormsby, only on the old Muskogee Railroad! That's now the Columbus and

Macon, you know.[31] I am inquiring about positions there, my dear. I know you won't mind—especially since Edwin is there."

When Freddie's letter came, saying he might consider going to Birmingham, too, that was the tipping point. William had been in Birmingham before, while Massillon Bridge built its first bridge in Gadsden, just north of Birmingham.[32] Before much longer, William and Emma were packing up Cyrus and George and Alice and boarding a train for Birmingham, where they hoped they would soon see Freddie.

The train roared through the tunnel. The brief darkness stopped their conversation, but when they reached daylight, they began talking again. Emma tended to her sewing, Cyrus and George stood up to stretch, and Alice perused the paper for teaching positions.

"Birmingham schools are looking for Latin teachers!" Alice was genuinely surprised, because she was a Latin teacher, and she had her doubts.

"Latin? Looks like they need everything but," said Cyrus. "Jefferson County has hit bottom as far as teaching those children to read."

"Too much time in the factories, too little time in school," Alice added.

"You have to remember, Dear, sometimes that's all the income a family has—whatever a child can earn." Emma did not want to discourage Alice.

Other states had the same problem, William said. West Virginia, for instance. "Looks like West Virginia is planning some kind of *Conferences for Education in the South!*[33] He turned to Emma. "Have you ever heard of a place called *Capon Springs?*"

Emma had not.

"Excuse me." The man sitting across from Alice spoke up. "I couldn't help but hear. I know Capon Springs; I am just coming back from that Conference. We are trying to spur on industrial training for Negroes." He turned to Emma. "Your son is right. No Latin I'm afraid."

The man introduced himself as Mr. Baldwin. Emma introduced her family, then commented how good it was to hear that whites and Negroes could work together in the South. But their fellow passenger said it wasn't quite like that yet. No Negroes were invited to the conference, only some moderates and some educational reformers—and a few white southern businessmen.

"Did they invite any missionaries?" The Lutheran in Emma made her ask. Lutherans she knew came south to teach miners and Negro children. But no, said Baldwin, no missionaries either.[34]

Alice noted she had never heard of any such conferences on education going on in Alabama.[35]

William looked at his daughter's serious face and broke in. "Now, Alice. Alabama no longer has slaves. They will most certainly have such things sooner or later."

Mr. Baldwin nodded.

"The benefits of a Negro population properly educated is infinite and incalculable. An educated black work force is the key to a strong Southern economy and a force to prevent unions from organizing."[36]

"Are you a Southerner?" William asked Mr. Baldwin. William didn't know many Southerners yet but hung on to the hope that all citizens, even miners and Negroes, were better off in Birmingham than in other places he had been in this country. Emma deserved something better.

"No, Sir, I hail from Boston. But I love it here, and you are riding on my train! Great service, don't you think?

"Oh, it certainly is," said Emma, taken aback..

"Fried chicken is our specialty. We have Negro cooks on these lines now." He changed the subject. "And, Mrs. Stafford, with Christmas coming, what are your plans?"

"We—at least I—am going to invite all my new German neighbors to join us for Christmas carols. There are a lot of us Germans in Birmingham, you know, and Germans love Christmas—especially Lutherans."

Mr. Baldwin began "Ein, zwei, drei, vier, funf. . ."

"Oh, so you speak German?"

"No, no, no. Just cardinal numbers."

"And the minute that's over we start making plans for May Day!" Emma finished.

The little group fell silent as the rhythm of the train wheels slowed. A steam blast signaled the stop. The couple exchanged pleasantries with Mr. Baldwin and invited him to come visit. They had an extra bedroom they kept for Freddie, whom they had not heard from in a while.

Mr. Baldwin picked up his luggage and made his way along the platform to a waiting Rambler. William could not take his eyes off the car.

When the Rambler pulled away and they were all settled into Edwin's buggy, William asked Edwin: "Did you see that extra tire? Did you see the steering wheel? It has a steering wheel and not just a tiller. . . ." And he went on rambling. At Edwin's, they received news that took the joy away. Elizabeth had died. The family grieved for Johnstone.

Later they learned that Mr. Baldwin was vice-president of a whole line of railroads. The train they had been on was the Southern, which was controlled by *the* J.P. Morgan, and it was Mr. Morgan who sent Baldwin to look after his investments.

By 1889, the family was settled into a house in Woodlawn big enough for the five of them plus a bedroom for Freddie. Emma set about looking for a Lutheran Church or a Women's Christian Temperance Union or even a band or a quartet, but found no such things, and William discovered Alabama had more engineering challenges than he ever dreamed. It was not blessed with soil of any uniform consistency. Its ore ran for ludicrously great distances in unstable seams among layers of impossibly sticky clay in between sandstone layers that wore away in the presence of water. Unlike land in Iowa and Missouri where the banks of rivers were relatively stable, central Alabama included mountains and valleys with fragile caves and unmapped underground rivers

But William loved this kind of challenge. He was home. He set about working on bridges and designing a recreational lake in Lakeview that would be home to football games and entertainers.

Best of all, he found another Englishman who became his friend. Karl Daly also lived in Woodlawn. Whenever they could, William and Karl took the trolley from Woodlawn Junction at 14th Street and 1st Avenue North out to Shades Mountain to hike in the hills. One time, they found an old abandoned cabin among the blackberry brambles on a piece of land that had a most beautiful view. The owners were dead, and the cabin had been left to perish on its own. The two men bought the property—Karl took the parcels to the north and William took those to the South—and brought it back to life.

Alice declared that it be named *Farview*, and it was. The family went there to escape the city's coal dust and smoke. Emma set up her easel there and painted the hillside below.

About then they received a long letter from Freddie. He had left the Smith farm and found a job with a bond company in Tennessee. At the end of the letter, Freddie told them how much he wanted to come to Birmingham.

William had tears in his eyes when he read it. He handed the letter over to Emma. Freddie planned to come as soon as he finished delivering some bonds to a company in Ohio. Emma danced for joy and embraced her husband. Together, they wrote him saying how happy he made them and that his room was ready, as it always had been.

They waited for weeks for a letter, but none came. Freddie had not given them a phone number or the name of his company. Emma kept sending letters because she knew that whenever Freddie came would be the happiest day of William's life. She had prayed for that day for years.

William was not so patient and wrote Will, asking if he knew Freddie's whereabouts. Will did not. He had heard nothing, but he would contact everybody who might.

When another letter arrived from Freddie, it had a strange postmark. It had been written months before. The news was so old it confused them all. Freddie was on his way from Tennessee to Will's house, but Freddie never arrived at Will's house.

The last person who saw Freddie was the postmaster in the little town in Ohio where the letter was postmarked. All anybody ever knew was that Freddie was last seen walking across Ohio carrying a brief case of non-negotiable bonds.

"Nobody would want those bonds," William seemed confused. "Those were non-negotiable bonds."

"No, no. He may be all right. He may have gone somewhere else, done something foolish," said Emma.

"Like joining a rodeo." William held on to that hope, any hope. He spent the rest of his life contacting every sheriff in every county between Ohio and Alabama, knocking on doors, writing letters to hospitals, talking to strangers.

As each year passed, William's spirit broke a little more. Emma never stopped grieving for Freddie or for the life-giving visit that never happened.

PART II

MISFORTUNE

1. The Tram Cars

By January 1905, Birmingham's industrialists were flying, and its mountains glowed with runs from the furnaces. William had more than enough to do. He bought a fine new horse named Floy and a National Electric car.

This cold but sunny day, William whistled as he dressed. He put on his heaviest English wool three-piece suit, a woolen scarf that Emma had made him, and a bowler hat to cover his gray hair. He kissed Emma goodbye, then went out into the cold to saddle Floy. The mines were far too remote and the roads too rough for the National.

The mine out in St. Clair County had not been open long, but it already had a poor safety record as many mines did. But the Company did not hire William to address safety issues. They hired him to find out just how profitable that mine might be. If the mine owners determined this mine was worth the further investment, then they would most certainly take precautions to make it safe. Their engineer would make that call, and William was their engineer.

Only the palest of light topped the eastern horizon as William and Floy trotted through the open gate that led to the pit. He hitched Floy to a post and waved at a squat, heavy-set man, presumably a supervisor. The man's coat collar was turned up high, bat-like, to cover his ears against the cold. His shoulders were broad, and he had on thick woolen gloves that made him look like a boxer—or an ape. The man crossed the yard, walking right up almost to William's face.

"Morning. How do you do?" said William. He held out his hand, but the man refused it.

"Not from around here, I take it." It was not a question but more an indictment. The man looked William up and down, then scowled.

"Well, no. Not originally." William realized his bowler hat must indeed make him look strange.

"State your business, then."

"Today? Well, today I'm simply making a report. I won't be long, though. Perhaps an hour?"

"You ain't going to find nothing," the man said, hitting his gloved fists together. "Take my advice. Make it quick and watch your head."

The man was obviously short-tempered. William found himself encountering a lot of this lately. He could not seem to shake off the image of this particular man's grim face, so stroked Floy's nose for a bit, not sure whether he was reassuring himself or the horse. Then he headed for the cage.

Going down as the only passenger on the lift was not something he enjoyed doing. It meant abandoning the pale warmth of the rising sun to the dank cold of the dark mine shaft below. When the cage came to rest at the bottom of the shaft, he saw only two other men in the room near the drift, one white and one Negro.

The Negro, in miner's cap and boots, stood quietly resting on his shovel. The white man also wore a miner's cap, but his other clothes didn't mesh with those of the miner's: He wore wool trousers and well-polished, ankle-high boots. The man in the shiny boots came over and offered his hand to William.

"Joseph Caswell, Sir, with the United Mine Workers." Caswell paused. "Just so you'll know, I'm not their favorite visitor these days! And you?"

William gladly took his hand. "William Stafford, Sir, independent civil engineer. I expect I'll be down here at least an hour." As they parted, the man gave him his card: "Joseph Caswell, Representative. United Mine Workers, Anniston, Alabama."[37]

William moved on. He sat below the first outcropping and took out his notepad and a slide rule. He measured the pillar and began to calculate load-bearing capacity. Then he concentrated on listing the various aggregates he could see in the room: coal, potash, stony rubble. He estimated the quantities, then began his calculations.

The pit seemed extraordinarily quiet for a weekday morning. Where was the boss? The silence made him uneasy, but perhaps the men had been there all night and were taking a break or maybe they were waiting for some kind of equipment. The air hung heavy, but it always did in the mines.

In the next room, a few miners and their mules lolled about, their work not laid out for them yet. It was still early for the day shift, William figured. Whatever rest these men could manage would serve them well. The day would be another back breaker for them.

William worked his way slowly along the drift, where two or three more miners stood with pickaxes. Convicts by the looks of it. They seemed friendly and interested enough in what he was doing to come up to him, curious. William spoke to them, but these convicts were not being supervised. The mining company's foremen were nowhere to be seen. Even if the company foremen had been there, William knew they had no authority whatsoever over the convicts. Alabama law stated that convicts could only be supervised by state supervisors, who were noticeably absent that day.[38] Convicts, supervised or not, had a reputation of deadly fights, rampages unchecked for no apparent reason.

Killings happened too often in the mines. Strangely enough, violence under this system worked in the operators' favor. Not only could operators not be blamed for it, but they could bring complaints against any violent man, which often resulted in an extended sentence for the convict and more profit to the owner. The State of Alabama alone benefited from the system by at least a half million dollars each year.[39]

The question remained: How did a company protect its men? Nobody was around that day to ask.

As William made his way back toward the bottom of the shaft, he spotted a boy of about six years of age still in short pants, riding down in the cage alone. William looked around to see who might be accompanying him but saw no one. Young immigrant boys often worked in the mines—black and white, but this boy was no immigrant. He wore glasses and a pair of home-made suspenders holding up his trousers.

The decibel level rose as work began farther down the tunnel. Heavy metal struck rock as men broke it up with pickaxes to feed it into waiting cars. Chains ground away as the pulleys brought loaded cars to the tipple. William tried to call the boy.

"Son, what are you doing down here?" He called loud enough to be heard all the way up the glory hole, but the boy didn't answer. William let it go and began making his way toward the shaft, with the Negro man walking a little ahead of him with his mules. When the miner turned back to check on his mules, he took his hat off and wiped the sweat off his brow with one hand, which left a whitish streak across his forehead.

Above him, William saw the shadows of two men moving about at the tipple: one tall stooped figure and one squat and heavy with apish arms. William stared for just a minute, a brief attempt at identifying the shadows, but turned to watch where his feet were going.

The lights from the miners' caps behind him now lit the ragged sides of the tunnel like fireflies. The miners were waiting near the down shaft for a string of empty scoop cars to fill. William stood at the bottom of the return shaft now, waiting for the cage. Somebody near the tipple barked an order, its words muted by the sounds of wheels rumbling and blasts from distant dynamite. William did not see the trip of loaded cars begin to move.

Four scoop cars flew unmanned and out of control down the slope at lightning speed, far too fast for anyone to get out of the way. The string hit the Negro man and his mules, crushing them, killing them instantly. The burdened cars rammed on unimpeded, then pinned William to the rock wall.

Everything after that William remembered in slow motion, without sound. He smelled blood, just as he had in battle, and he vaguely remembered looking around for the boy before he slipped into unconsciousness.

They hauled William up and carried him to the sanitation building. The man named Caswell was inside. By afternoon, someone had sense enough to say somebody had to ride to town and tell the family. The coal boss ordered one of the miners to ride William's horse to the dying man's house. He sent the Negro miner they called Bradford and told him to return straight away.

Emma opened the door to a stranger that cold January morning. The man only had on a pair of rough work pants and a ragged brown cotton shirt. She asked him his name and if he needed to come warm himself in the kitchen. Bradford told her the mine boss sent him. He was not that cold, thank you, because he rode Mr. Stafford's horse hard.

"Mrs. Stafford, Ma'am. You might oughta come on down to the mine. A accident. It's your husband, Ma'am. He's still alive, but you need to come on."

"No. Oh, no." She shook her head, sure it was not, could not be William. "It was just routine. It's not William. He promised he would never take any more risks. He promised."

"Yes'm. I mean no, Ma'am, it is him and he's hurt pretty bad." Bradford remembered his hat and whisked it off. "He was down in the shaft, Missus, and some cars got loose."

The significance of the words escaped Emma. "Was it an explosion?"

"No, ma'am, it weren't no explosion."

"A cave-in?"

"No, ma'am, it weren't no cave-in."

"Cars, you said?" She could not seem to move her arms or her legs. She was frozen, trying to understand. "Where is he?"

"Ma'am, he's there where they brought him up. They got him on a litter in the sanitation shed."

"Then we're going to get him." Emma's eyes clouded over with tears as she threw on her coat and grabbed bandages and blankets out of the cupboard. Bradford helped her hitch Floy to the buggy and drove her back to the site.

When they arrived at the entrance to the mine, Emma jumped out of the buggy without waiting for Bradford and ran to the fence. A squat man with heavy gloves on blocked her way. She was not allowed in, he said, but Emma could see the commotion around the shed and the sign over it that read "Sanitation."

The man's belligerence meant to intimidate her, but it made her angry instead. She became a woman afire. She shook the gate and shouted at its guardian. "I am a friend of the President of the United States, and if you don't let me in right now, I will have you fired and hauled off to jail."

She didn't think twice about her half-truth: She did know the president, but that president had just been killed, and there was a new one in his place. Her friend Ida had married William McKinley, the president who had been shot. Roosevelt had taken his place. Emma didn't think either Ida or President Roosevelt would mind.

The ape man let her in, mumbling "He didn't have no business being down my shaft."

She ran toward the sanitation shed where men bent over her husband trying to give him water. When they parted to let her through, she saw her husband's blood dripping on the bare earth and staining one side of his face. Emma took his hand. He lay deathly still on the litter. She looked up at the men standing around her. "Why haven't any of you taken him to an infirmary? Why is he just lying here?"

The men stood silent, all except one, a skinny clean-shaven young man who seemed to be in charge. "Ma'am, we got him out as fast as we could but had to go slow you know. Didn't want to move him because it could be his back and all. Nobody knew who he was until now."

Joseph emerged from the sanitation building. "Excuse me, Sir, but I think I can help this lady."

Emma leaned close and kissed her husband's cheek. "We're going to get you out of here, Darling. Right now. You are going to be fine." She kissed him again and again, then added "You were always at risk, you know. What do you expect when you go under a bridge or into a mine? No more of that, my darling."

Joseph supervised as miners loaded William into the carriage, then Joseph took the reins from Bradford and drove Emma and William over the rutted country roads to Birmingham, to Dr. Robinson's Infirmary. It took more than two hours.

While Dr. Robinson examined William, Emma and Joseph waited outside the room. Emma begged Joseph to tell her what he knew.

Joseph said as gently as he could that best he could tell the train had careened down the track, knocked down some mules, then pinned William to the wall. He could not bring himself to tell her that not only had all the mules been killed, but the mule driver, too, and it was a bloody mess down there. He did tell her that his own son was down in the mine when it happened, and he was sure the boy saw it all. He promised to ask the lad what he had seen.

On many nights after that, Joseph sat with Emma and the family at Dr. Robinson's Clinic, as though he somehow felt responsible for them. In a few weeks, Emma was so sure William was growing stronger that she begged Dr. Robinson to let her take him home, and he let her. Emma cheered William on, telling him not to give up. Mostly she assured him of her love over and over, "I would have married you no matter what."

When he seemed ashamed for her to see his mangled nakedness, she laughed and tried to reassure him. "I have seen it all," and "I will take care of you no matter what."

He believed her. He believed she could do anything, but he never answered her questions about the accident. It was Edwin who extracted as much information out of his father as he could, which was not much. William confided in Edwin that he did not believe Emma could handle the truth. Clearly his father was the target, and Edwin could not refrain from commenting to his father.

"That bastard, whoever he was. He did it deliberately. Tell me who it was? Just tell me."

Emma shushed her son because it upset William. She asked why anybody would want to kill a white-haired Englishman? An engineer?

After Emma left the room, William tried to raise his head off the pillow to speak to his son.

"Let it lie, Edwin," William told him. "Even I don't know the whole story, but I know part of it. They were after the union man, and they got me. When they figure out they got the wrong fellow, they will go after the one that got away. It's best just to let it lie."

Emma sensed William knew more than he was telling. It made her so angry when he refused to discuss it that she took herself upstairs and beat on the walls and let tears of outrage come. Not being able to right a wrong done to her husband hurt her as much as watching him suffer.

She scoured the papers looking for something, anything that might help explain what happened, but William was not yet a fatality. The death of the mule driver was noted, though, but with so little detail that everybody figured his death was an accident. The papers said the dead man was "a good worker." The State of Alabama counted the man's death as one of many such fatalities in 1905.

William had lived through the Civil War; Emma had foiled death from childbirth several times over; both had escaped Indian attacks. Wars and attacking Indians and childbirth were dangers people understood, even anticipated. But the violent streak in the South was a danger tucked away, never discussed, and neither prevented nor punished.

"We live in a hornet's nest," William told her once, laughing.

"I think you are telling me they are big hornets!" she added, and they laughed out loud together. Now, as he lay in his sickbed, he reminded her of it.

"They are indeed big hornets," he said quietly. Then he looked into her brown eyes: "And you are my angel."

Dr. Robinson knocked on the door. Emma welcomed him in and invited him for a breakfast of kippers from England and newly preserved figs. The figs came from a giant fig tree by the back door that bore enough golf-ball-sized figs to feed not only their own hungry children but all the birds and squirrels on the south side of Birmingham.

Weeks passed. William lost weight, and his eyes began to sink deep in his forehead with pain. Dr. Robinson spoke about the hard things.

"William may fool us yet, but if he makes it, he will most likely be terribly crippled," he told them. Then he turned to Emma. "Emma, it is time now. You may give him all the laudanum you wish. Don't hesitate to call me any time. The clinic is right across the street, and I can be here in minutes."

After Dr. Robinson left, Emma dragged the little round oak table next to William's cot and helped him sit up. Like the piano, the table had traveled with them in the beautiful and in the sad times. It wobbled on three unsteady legs, which no amount of glue or nails seemed to steady. She set the table for him with flowers from the garden and prepared a coddled egg. He ate a tiny bite just to please her. He died later that day.

Emma changed that same day into the mourning clothes she would wear for the rest of her life: a black dress with mutton sleeves sewn as much like Queen Victoria's as Emma could make it. When the Queen's beloved Prince Albert died, she too had gone into mourning for the rest of her life. Emma admired her greatly and did the same.

Johnstone died in 1909. Emma called it not right that a father should outlive his own son. Life went on in Birmingham without Emma for a while. Indeed, it picked up speed and left her behind. The entire South turned to industry even as it pointed to the Comer family's Avondale Mills as evidence that cotton was king once more. But Birmingham had little else to claim it was in any way a city of the Deep South. Birmingham rightfully claimed to be the Magic City with all of its growth and in all of its glory and manifestations, including hungry coal-mining families, immigrants, and small children working in factories.

Emma and Alice saw that poverty daily, and they watched the numbers of orphans grow. The teacher in Alice said, "Those children need to be in school," and the wanderer in Emma added, "and out of doors."

They agreed that alcohol caused the downfall of many a family and rejoiced when a branch of the Women's Christian Temperance Union came to town. It was the WCTU that took on the care and feeding of orphans, and it was Alice who took on teaching them.

Emma had a new reason for being then: She sewed clothes for the orphans and read to them. Her vitality began to return. She took the family to Chautauqua festivals in Talladega so they might hear great music and attend great lectures, she took them on vacations to a place called Monteagle in the mountains of Tennessee, and she took them on long walks among the lovely hills that William and Karl Daly had walked before them.

Her children were grown now. Alice was teaching Latin at Woodlawn High School, Edwin and Aileen were raising a houseful of children, and Cyrus was off to Cincinnati to become a lawyer for the L&N Railroad. The last unfinished child was George Timothy, the dreamer who clerked some at night but would rather dabble in designing houses or furniture. It was their old family friend, Karl Daly, who decided to turn that story around, and the best way to do it, he decided, was to find George Timothy a suitable bride.

"George Timothy," he said to William's youngest. "You know my old friend Lyman Berry? The fellow who owns Mercantile Supply over there on Second Avenue North and 22nd Street?"

"Yes Sir, I certainly do. We go there often."

"Well, he has a daughter I would like you to meet. Her name is Margot, and she's just your age."

"Thank you, Sir. That is mighty thoughtful of you."

Later that week, Karl called Emma and announced his plan. He executed that plan with almost no delicacy at all.

"So it is done," he said. "I have invited Margot to dinner next week, and I expect George Timothy and all of you—parents included—to join me. Her family will be here, too."

In his complete dismay, George Timothy tried to get out of it. "I'm clerking that night, Sir. I won't be able to make it."

"Son, I took care of that. You have that night off."

The Daly house was brand new and beautiful. It faced the distant hills across the valley. The night they came to dinner, stars shone. Margot made her entrance on her father's arm, charming them all. When she spoke, she spoke with that peculiar Southern accent that comes only from Mobile. When she smiled, she brushed her long blonde curls back to show the sweep of her neck.

George Timothy was intimidated and said almost nothing. Later, though, he made the fatal mistake of confiding to his older brothers that he could not stop looking at Margot's beautiful brown eyes. His siblings took his timidity into consideration and decided to take matters into their own hands. In this case there was too much at stake.

From then on, the brothers included Margot in all their plans. Sometimes Margot came by herself to visit Alice and left her calling card in the tray by the front door. Wherever George Timothy went—on rides or picnics or parties—Margot went, too. Finally the brothers were worn out with it and decided what they had done was enough. They had done their part. It was time for their younger brother to do his.

"George T.," said Cyrus. "In different times and different places you might need more time to get to know Margot better, but there is no time like the present. Anything can happen. It's time you did your own courting. We're done."

Karl would not let up either. His insistence pushed George T. right across the threshold.

"I introduced you to a lovely girl from a fine family who has been raised properly. I expect you to do the rest."

The couple became engaged, but at least one member of the family had doubts. Alice gently suggested to Margot that they consider postponing the wedding, just for a little while so the family could get over some of the sadness and financial hardship.

"We will soon be back on our feet, you know. It's just I think it's too soon. Mother is in mourning, and there are accounts in Ohio and Illinois that have to be settled. I expect my brother will have to go up north for a while to deal with them. I hope you understand, dear."

Margot sulked. "Leave it to the Yankees to spoil my wedding."

Apparently she never noticed the surprise on the Staffords' faces when she spoke about Northerners as though they were criminals and she their personal victim. She poured her angst onto the backs of Yankees, and as far as she was concerned no Yankees were among her acquaintances. *Yankees* could be blamed for all the world's wrongdoings and mistakes.

Emma realized she might have trouble convincing Margot that those she loved, like her beloved Grandfather Melsheimer, the Yankee Lutheran minister who was universally loved, deserved more than categorical condemnation. But this young woman would soon be her daughter, and for her son's sake she kept quiet, which was a hard enough task for her under any circumstance.

In the end, the wedding took place. George Timothy reassured the family he was quite capable of handling this new phase of his life, including the care and feeding of a mother, a sister and a wife. The honeymoon began.

Champagne was in abundance in the ballroom of the paddle wheeler. George Timothy and Margot danced to music from the steam-powered calliope and wandered the decks on starry evenings. They had a glorious time, except occasionally during discussions of their future when George T. found himself talking to the wind. Once, he asked her whether they should live with Emma for a little while—or would it be better for her to come to live with them?

He held her hand and looked deep into her eyes. She answered yes, by which she meant "Whatever you say, Dear."

The honeymoon came to an end. They docked near New Orleans with mahogany sideboards and tables, Bavarian china, chairs and fine new materials to make into dresses. George T. had a time tracking down enough drivers and carts to bear the load of all their purchases. After visiting all of Margot's cousins in Mobile and Orrville, it took another week to make it home.

"Can you find a boy to help us with our luggage?" asked Margot.

"I declare, Margot!" said George T. "Don't you know I'm the boy who helps with the luggage?" He couldn't help but laugh. She looked so serious.

The couple did not live with Emma, nor did Emma live with them. They rented a cottage on 10th Avenue South between 11th and 12th Streets, then they moved in with Grandmother Berry at 1610 Cullom Street. It was all temporary.

The day finally came when Emma could no longer be silent about the Yankee thing. She swore to find a way to bring it up without offending Margot. Margot had a strange way of sometimes finding evil in what was good and making excuses for what was bad. Perhaps that kind of confusion came from an unbending upbringing or perhaps Margot just succumbed to the misfortune of being a girl sheltered by the times. Either way, Margot harbored an eternal child inside that dared not but live up to all the expectations laid upon her.

Margot called upon Emma twice a week, always asking beforehand if it was convenient, which gave Emma time to prepare for tea. Margot always arrived on time. For many months after the wedding, Emma and Margot met in the living room and sat on the large divan together drinking tea like two strangers. Margot limited their conversations to the weather and the goings-on at church.

But Emma soon tired of this. As far as she could see, Margot was her daughter, just like Alice. She looked forward to the day when they could have a really good talk, one in which Margot bared her soul and she could, too. This way they would grow to love one another. She finally told Margot that the next time she came, she would like to see what her childhood had been like and suggested they tell stories to each other.

They took their tea to the little round table in the kitchen. This was Emma's lucky table. When the two ladies poured their tea, Emma began.

"Do you have stories for me, Margot? I would love to hear them."

Margot demurred. "Only if you begin," she said.

Emma thought it best to begin by saying that she spent her young life in Massillon, Ohio, and because she was raised by a Lutheran minister, she was expected to participate in the many activities related to his church. She paused, waiting for Margot to ask what activities, but Margot did not. Emma believed it best to say what she had to say now rather than later.

"People came to our church from faraway places. Grandfather Melsheimer expected me to behave like a good Lutheran adult and welcome these visitors whenever they came, day or night." Then, Emma took her deep breath.

"Most of the strangers who came were Negroes. We let them wash or rest a little, then took them on to Spring Hill." She paused again. "Spring Hill was a charming white frame farmhouse nearby, but it was also part of the Underground Railroad. It was there that our guests received food and blankets and got a start on a new life."

Margot let Emma's words roll over her head and out into the ether. She smiled a smile designed to let Emma know she was not really listening.

Emma had gone this far, so she went on. She told Margot how these people came tired and dirty, children and old people, scratched and bruised and covered with mud. She described the wash shed out back, and how she sometimes read to the children when the older ones fell exhausted on the pews. Emma never used the word "abolitionist" because she had never heard it. Only many years later did Uncle Henry tell her she was one.

Margot politely and patiently waited her turn to tell her story, which was a proud story.

"My father owned slaves. When he joined the Confederate army, he knew that many of the plantation owners sent slaves to fight for them so they could stay home, but he never did that. He went to battle himself. He fought at Chickamauga, and the Yankees took him prisoner."

Emma was aghast. "Your father fought at Chickamauga? William fought at Chickamauga, too!"

"Well I declare." Margot said. "My father called it the 'War of Yankee Aggression.'"

Emma bit her tongue and refrained from mentioning that the South fired the first shot.

Margot continued. "Now my mother's grandfather, Judge Chapman, who was too old to fight, learned that the Yankees were coming and instructed his servants to bury the family silver in the back yard, which they did. He then hustled his family out of the city and as far out into the countryside as he could go. The Yankees came, of course, and soon dug up the silver.

"After the war, the Yankees took over our government. Some of our friends were so afraid of what might happen that they took their own lives. Even my family waited for years before they finally went home. When they did, they found an empty hole where the silver had been."

"Oh, I am so sorry," said Emma.

"Well, that was not the end of the story. One of those Yankee legislators invited my uncle Reuben to dinner. That was not so long ago, of course. It was about the time they were writing our new constitution.

"That Yankee used fine bone china and some monogrammed silver that looked just like our lost silver. Reuben waited until after dessert, then he spoke to his host. The Yankee heard the story and returned the silver. Isn't that a coincidence?"

"Perhaps all Union soldiers are not devils after all," Emma said.

"I have a piece or two I can show you." Margot fished in her bag for the few pieces she had and held them up to the light.

Emma conceded this was indeed a telling story, but Margot just smiled and made no concessions. Emma then commented that she did not think much of this new constitution. As far as she could tell, all it did was divide people into two categories—desirables and undesirables—with all the privileges going to the desirables.

Margot ignored her and brought another treasure out of her bag: a tiny silver snuff box.

"Lafayette gave this to my grandmother," she said.

Margot's family were fine people, though. Not only were they polite, well dressed, well spoken, prematurely gray and charming, but the men were kind and put women on a pedestal. For this, the family won Emma's approval.

87

Margot rambled on then about how she and her new husband were planning a trip to Mobile, where they would attend Mardis Gras and mingle with their cousins. Margot would take her creamy silk dress and the silver belt made of old Spanish coins. She had shown that to Emma, hadn't she? Then, after Mobile, they planned to visit the Pettuses in Selma. Emma did remember that Senator Pettus had taken in all of her grandmother's children and raised them as his own after their own parents died of Yellow Fever? That was the kind of thing you did—take care of widows and orphans—if you were the Grand Dragon of the Ku Klux Klan.

The round table talk came to an end. Margot went on her way.

The South had not been particularly good to Emma, but she loved it anyway. She loved the way farmers let their mules and sheep and goats roam the hillsides, the camaraderie, and the excitement of something new on the horizon almost every day. She loved the dogwood that grew wild in the valleys, the great water oaks towering above her on her walks, the smell of honeysuckle permeating the summer woods, the thousands of migrating goldfinches that turned broad meadows into carpets of sunshine when they landed in open fields. She loved looking for the foxes that darted out of their dens in the abandoned mines on Red Mountain, and she loved sitting for hours on outcroppings of flat stone on Shades Mountain to paint or just carry on living.

So she would love Margot. But when Margot made comments about slaves and the colored, she knew it made George T. uneasy. It made Emma indignant, but she held her tongue.

Emma made herself a new life as best she could. The Dalys visited often and kept her abreast of who was who and what was what. She was grateful to them. But she had another visitor whose visits she looked forward to even more.

Her most welcome visitor was Joseph Caswell, the man who was there when they brought her injured husband up from the shaft. Joseph looked in on William almost every day during his last days and still did what he could to help Emma. He tried time and time again to claim that William had joined the union so that Emma might be entitled to benefits, but of course he never had. Emma told Joseph he was a kind man for trying. But after all was said and done, William was an independent civil engineer, and civil engineers did not join unions.

Joseph represented to her at least a small part of the world outside. He knew whenever some major thing happened at city hall or at the capital in Montgomery. He was certainly privy to some of the darker secrets of Birmingham. And, she thought, he probably knew who killed her husband, but he would not say. Joseph talked freely and in confidence to Emma about everything except what happened that fateful day.

Joseph still held on to the ideals of the very young. He celebrated when a union man made a small victory and grieved when one was struck down. He worried because furnace operators were the most powerful men in Alabama, perhaps even in the nation, and that they fought their battles with money, which he considered unfair.

He advised her when Birmingham's streetcar workers were about to strike, and because he knew the Birmingham Trades Council would strike back even harder, when it would end. He also told her something else: After recent discussions between furnace workers and management, that Council convinced furnace operators to lock out 300 workers before the strike even began.

"Those are the workers who suffer most. Furnace men dare not complain, or they will lose their jobs and be evicted from their homes, just like these men."

"How can that be?" She was baffled.

"Because there are plenty of men around to take their places. Railway Power and Light just discharged 200 more men for no good reason. When the newspapers interviewed those men before this happened, they had dared say nothing more than that they might *consider* joining a union."[40]

"But not all companies are like that. Not the L&N Railroad. My son Cyrus is an attorney for the L&N in Chicago."

"I'm sorry to say—them too. L&N discharged employees too.[41]"

Emma was stunned. Cyrus was part of this. She defended the operators. "I know some of these men you describe. They are talented. Some even studied in Germany. They are well thought of here in Jefferson County!"

"I understand," Joseph brooded. "But remember, they belong to clubs with hundreds of members and one thing in mind: Kill the unions."

"But not all of them, surely. There's Mr. Hillhouse."

James Hillhouse ran the Tutwiler Company,[42] and William thought highly of him. She chided Joseph saying Hillhouse attended union meetings and listened to the men.

"Well, yes," Joseph ventured. "He is a good man. He does come, and he doesn't seem to make much distinction between black and white. Maybe I have painted too bleak a picture."

"Blacks and whites in the same hall?" Even Emma caught the implications.

"Sure enough," he added. "Women, too, although they just formed their own union."[43]

When Joseph came on his next visit, Emma showed him a column she had cut out of the *Birmingham Age-Herald*. Columnist Frank Evans loved to call Negro citizens ignorant, but this time he actually suggested lynching Negro union members for letting black and white women meet together.[44]

"Such things make me think you are not safe," she said.

"He's just a rabble rouser," said Joseph. "Don't pay any attention to it."

Emma wasn't so sure. "Still, it is my duty to make you aware of these things."

"Changing them will just take time," he said. "Change will come through the ballot box."

Emma and William saw change for sure, but not the ballot box kind. When they came to Birmingham, huge companies were consolidating and steel was replacing iron. They watched the mining industry turn topsy-turvy and marveled at how one man from New York, J. P. Morgan, could swallow up Andrew Carnegie's TCI and tuck it into a small corner of his own U.S. Steel.

"But if, for instance, Birmingham has this dark side you talk about, and it's these men in power who run this dark side, aren't you afraid of what might happen to you?"

"I don't have an answer," said Joseph. He hoped Emma might have been somewhere, heard something that might help him find that answer.

Emma had not and could not. Joseph was a kind man who had done more than his duty. Even if he was not aware of it, he was her tie to the outside world. All Emma knew to do for him was to share her beloved books with Alma and the children.

They came away from those visits happy—she with a glimpse into the world beyond newspapers and he with an armload of books. As he rose to say his good-byes, he held his hat in his hands and backed out the door. Only after he turned to go did he put his hat back on his head. She watched him walk the long block to the trolley.

That last week she did not insist he stay. She had been busy with George Timothy's wedding at St. Mary's Episcopal and with the couple's wedding trip up the Mississippi to St. Louis and Ohio.

When it was over, she spent a long day tidying up around the house. Life seemed to be returning to normal. She retrieved the evening paper from the front porch and was startled to see two papers lying there instead of one. She had missed an issue! She opened them in order. Yesterday's headlines sent her reeling.

"Union Organizer Kidnapped and Deported."[45]

It was Joseph! To Emma, this was like another death in the family. She feared she might never see her friend again, and she did not.

2. A House Divided

George Timothy Jr. came along some time later. They called him *Georgie*, which he grew to hate. They all lived with Grandmother Berry, which had its advantages: Georgie had six or eight parents rather than two, all living within shouting distance of each other.

Grandfather Berry's hair turned stark white during his stint with the Confederate Army, and the family suggested it might have been the result of having to eat mule meat. Whatever caused it, his white hair afforded him a great deal of respect. He built his own store downtown, became treasurer for Howard College, and served as the perfect grandfather. When it snowed, which was about once a year, Grandfather Berry rolled Georgie over and over in the snow until he turned into a human snowball. Margot fretted that the soaking would surely kill her child, but of course it did not.

When Georgie was older, the family moved in with Emma. By the time Marjorie came along, Margot could stand it no longer. She insisted they have their own house.

George Timothy had planned for this day. He had already designed their house, which he would build next to Emma's on Eleventh Avenue South. The house plans showed a garage that would shelter both the National Electric and old Floy, who up until now had shared quarters. The only problem he faced was that Emma's house sat right in the middle of two lots, and George T. had to figure out how to free a lot for himself.

He consulted the Berry men. With their combined engineering skills and by begging or borrowing bits of equipment, they managed to maneuver Emma's house over enough to make room for another. George T. started work, and finished his house just in time for World War I.

German-Americans constituted 26 percent of the entire population of the United States then, and all 26 percent were worried. Germany boasted it had the best ground forces in the world, but its maritime forces fell short. When Germany declared it would soon have the largest Navy in the world—even larger than Britain's, German-Americans silently applauded, but when these same Americans watched the Kaiser invade first France then Prussia, and tensions grow between Britain and Germany, they were horrified.

Emma took it hard; her family was proud of its Prussian roots. She pored over the news, but her eyesight failed her. She reluctantly asked Margot to read the news to her—only when it was convenient, of course. She was a little surprised when Margot agreed.

Emma sat by her window until the news boy flung his paper on Margot's porch, then she waited until Margot brought the newspaper in. After what she considered a decent interval, Emma made up a basket of cakes or fresh figs and walked next door. Once inside, she picked up the daily and called to her daughter-in-law.

"Margot, I can read this headline, but what else does it say?"

"Hmmm," said Margot. She put down the piece of embroidery she was working on and took the paper from Emma. "Today is the tenth anniversary of the passing of the Alabama Constitution. It says here that Mr. McMillan of Wilcox County is pleased to say that Alabama's Constitution is definitely keeping the Negro from voting."[46]

Emma could not contain herself. "Do you know what a travesty that is? I don't have any use for all that nonsense."

Margot went on as though nothing had been said. "Mr. McMillan says he will continue to keep the Negro out of politics, too. And out of our schools. He says he'll keep foreigners out, too." She looked at Emma.

"Humph. My family came here before the Revolution and so did yours. God knows where everybody else came from. We are all foreigners."

Margot laid the paper down. That was all she would read that day, she said. But Emma was not finished. She brought the paper up close to her failing eyes and read laboriously from the editorial page.

"There's a letter reprinted here from a Mr. William H. T. Holtzclaw, a Negro gentleman, I believe. A response to Mr. Wilcox. It says 'I sincerely believe that if you lay down a law which will operate in favor of the white man because of his ancestry, and operate against the Negro because of previous conditions over which he did not and could not have any control, it will be a great step backwards.'"[47]

"Well, I declare. That word 'gentleman' should not be used when speaking about the colored," Margot said to Emma.

"That," replied Emma, "was a beautifully written letter, and he is as much a gentleman as you are a lady." Emma tried mightily, but she could not keep quiet in the face of Margot's opinions, in spite of herself. The two always ended up arguing.

The children heard such politeness and were confused by it, until they reached school age and were no longer home to listen. Being old enough to go to school meant they were old enough to attend the church down the street. Emma agreed that the church down the street, which happened to be St. Andrews Episcopal, might be a reasonable substitute for a Lutheran Church. However, other than holidays and events, which she loved, Emma did not attend.

Georgie's parents signed him up to sing in the boys' choir. The choir director said he had the voice of an angel, but something about that church terrified Georgie.

An iron grate hung on the wall between him and the altar. Behind the iron grate he could see nothing but a dark cavern. Between hymns, Georgie heard air rush into that darkness and noises that came from deep within the bowels of the church. The stone walls crackled and the metal frame popped. Surely it was the Holy Ghost.

He kept it to himself and would tell nobody he was afraid, but every Sunday he begged to stay next door with Emma. The choir director put up with only so much of this before he threatened to kick Georgie out of the choir. Emma taught him the music when he missed practice, but it happened so often, she took him by the hand and the two of them went to church together.

She took him and his cousin Cy on other adventures, too. When he and his sister Marjorie were eight and ten, and Cy was spending the summer with them, Emma took the three of them by streetcar to Woodlawn Station on First Avenue, and from there by train through parts of Shades Valley to the end of the line near Irondale. The train stopped to blow off steam and let the little family disembark.

Emma gathered all the food and supplies and gave each child a share of the load. They walked the last mile to Farview singing "I've Been Working on the Railroad."

Farview by now had a new straight up-and-down house that Uncle Ed Berry had built. As soon as the house came in sight, Emma sent the children off to the hills, then set up her easel and began to paint. They would spend the night there.

They had a merry afternoon. After a supper of cheese and bread, they read by candle light until bed time.

Late in the night, the children woke to heavy footsteps on the roof. Whatever it was paced back and forth overhead until the children climbed out of bed, terrified, looking for Emma.

Emma stood beside the door with her husband's Civil War rifle in her hands. Whatever it was continued walking from one edge of the roof across the hip of the roof to the other side. Finally, after what seemed like hours, the creature made up its mind to depart and leapt off the roof onto a low-hanging tree branch and disappeared, but not until it let out a horrible cat scream. The children knew in an instant that a panther had visited them that night.

Not much sleep took place after that, although Georgie said he was not afraid. He had seen his grandmother wield that shotgun on a Saturday night not long before, the night after all the children helped her de-feather and dress a chicken for Sunday dinner.

That Saturday night, the chicken went into an icebox that sat on the back porch. The icebox had been robbed before, so this night Emma planned to stay up and defend her chicken.

The thief came. She got him in her sights and pulled the trigger to scare him off. It worked. The thief ran through the back fence, leaving a gaping hole and most of his coat. The family thought the whole thing very funny. If Emma would do that to protect a chicken, she would do even more to protect her grandchildren.

The windows of the house at Farview were open all during that night. Nothing had stood between them and the panther. Now, Georgie ventured toward the window. He knew without being told that his had to be the first move, so he peeked gingerly over the sill. The only sound was an occasional bleat from a lamb or a goat.

A green-gray fog greeted them. The morning mist was just beginning to burn off. The family stood in a tight knot around Emma, imagining screams in the woods. Cy joined Georgie now, and the two poked their heads out, looking for whatever was making the noise. They didn't have to scan far. The bleating came from under the house.

Georgie nudged his cousin. "Cy! It's a little goat! Its nose is sticking out from under the stoop!"

"It's hiding. It's scared." Cy pushed Georgie over so he could get a better look.

Marjorie finally let her blanket drop and crossed the floor barefoot to join her brother. "How pretty! It's a little kid. He's trembling. Is he hurt?"

"I don't think so," said Cy.

Emma went out first and approached the animal quietly so as not to frighten it. "I think it is just as Cyrus said. The kid is scared, and probably hungry, too. Here. Give it some oats."

Emma parceled out handfuls of oats to feed the tiny creature, and the children made their way outside, the panther forgotten. The kid nuzzled in their hands. The children played with it for hours, entranced, until the mist lifted off the hillside and they spotted a farmer walking up the trail.

The farmer meandered up the old Indian trail behind his herd. He wore his trousers loose with a sturdy rope belt and a wide-brimmed felt hat to keep the sun off his face, a hat that likely served double duty as his Sunday best. The goats moved along, bell-less, in slow silent waves, grazing nonchalantly. The kid, happily fed, ran off to join its family.

The children sadly watched it go. Georgie vowed that one day he would own a goat—not necessarily that goat, but a small goat of quality.

When Georgie turned twelve, he kept his vow. He rode the Irondale car by himself, walked along the trail to the cottage, and bought himself a goat. He named it "Goat."

3. Margaret

Gertrude turned ten on the twelfth of January, 1922, the day of the big snow storm. She and her father and mother, Bradford and Lila, gathered around the cook stove where an iron pot full of venison stew boiled, for which they bowed their heads and were grateful. Snowstorms were blessed few in northeast Alabama, especially in the valleys. Blessed because for Bradford, snow meant no timber to haul, but few meant no income.

Gertrude pulled her blanket close around her while her three sisters huddled together, giggling. They clutched a package wrapped in a scrap of flowered cotton, tied with string and decorated with a perfectly round pine cone. Gertrude guessed it was for her, which it was, and broke into a grin, which was thanks enough for the whole family. She let her blanket slip away long enough to untie and unwrap her gift.

Inside she saw the first half of a quilt made just for her out of scraps of material from almost every dress the sisters had worn. She let her sisters hold it out between them so the last rays of the setting sun could let them all admire it. Gertrude smiled again then, and ran her hands over the stitches. She thanked them and told them she would add patches to it herself, and that one day, when she decided to marry, she would call them to help back the quilt. Then it would be finished.

"How did you do it? How come I didn't see you all sewing?" Gertrude asked.

The sisters just giggled. Bradford and Lila looked into each other's eyes and were happy.

When the snow finally melted, the children planted cuttings from the remaining turnips in the last patch of ground the mines had left them. They added the few odd carrot and cabbage seeds they had saved from summer and worked them into the soil. It was too early for anything else. They fed their few laying hens, the ones the foxes missed, which they kept in a pen.

Bradford took his axe and left for work. The forest was drying and men were hauling whatever timber they could still find for the railroad down the old Creek trail. When they reached Mudtown on the Cahaba they floated the timber to Oldtown on the Warrior. From there it would go on to Montgomery.[48]

During the Civil War, everybody had plenty of work. The war needed every able-bodied slave not only to work the mines but to use their skills as blacksmiths and workmen for the foundries, which were still plentiful in and around Leeds and St. Clair County. The men learned their skills long before the war, which made them the principal munitions workers supplying the Confederacy. They built and repaired roads and drove supply wagons into enemy territory.

When the Union Army burned everything down after that war, work stopped. Beehive ovens shut down and coke production ceased.[49] For a long time there was no work for either white or colored. But when the first World War came, things began to change. Then after that war was over, post-war entrepreneurs resurrected the old St. Clair and nearby Coosa and Cahaba coal fields, salvaging whatever they could find—tools, dynamite and any other equipment—to store in barrels and hastily built sheds like the ones on Bradford's farm.

In town, Alabama owners traded assets, vying for position. Henry F. DeBardeleben had made his fortune and sold his vast holdings to Andrew Carnegie's Tennessee Coal and Iron before he died.[50]

Henry F.'s son, Charles F. DeBardeleben, watched his father's holdings fall into another man's hands and determined to build his own kingdom. By this time, his Alabama Fuel and Iron Company owned just about every inch of St. Clair County worth mining. Charles carefully assessed and built mines at Acton,

Acmar, and Overton. He opened another mine in the county that he named Margaret, for his wife, in 1905. He named another Alice for his mother, and another Overton for a friend.

Bradford's land, once called Negro Hill, fell within the bounds of the new town of Margaret. Bradford was pleased, because his half Indian children no longer had to pretend they didn't hear the jokes the miners made about the niggers on Negro Hill. They could say they lived in Margaret. Then Lila died, and it broke Bradford's heart. He told his children that they must look down the road and not give up, because one day the mines would be gone and a better day would come. But that day took its time coming.

Jerry decided he was old enough to go along with Bradford to haul timber and lay track. Besides, he loved his father and thought he might cheer his father up. He had watched workers build railroad tracks before, all his young life, some on their own land, almost up to their front door. Jerry wondered why that had been necessary. That tiny slip of track was no more than a pinhead in the hundreds of thousands of miles of track that crisscrossed north Alabama, but it loomed large in their front yard.

Bradford gladly took Jerry along. He took the deed to Lella's land, too, because it went wherever Bradford went. He knew the law had always said women couldn't own land and now it said Negroes could not own land, but the land was rightfully theirs and he would not let go of the deed unless something changed or a title was given or somebody signed a new deed.

Mr. Charles DeBardeleben made it clear to Bradford that he only owned the top layer of his land, if at all. This meant that Bradford could continue to plant on the top layer but had no control over the bottom layer. The Company owned the mineral rights, and there was nothing Bradford could do about it.

Company men built sheds alongside Bradford's garden. Strange boots trampled their corn. Heavy equipment ripped blackberry vines and fig trees apart. Dirt roads turned to rutted mud, and livestock starved from lack of pasture. Even the grass died. Any green shoot that dared dig its way up was instantly trampled down. The land was a shambles, and Bradford had six children to feed.

The Company once offered Bradford a job as a miner, but there was more than enough railroad work then, and he declined. In 1928, the year Lila died,[51] Margaret mine produced 326,450 tons of coal in 238 days, and 173 men were injured. Margaret had been lucky. Three men died in the nearby Bragg seam at Overton. Bradford could not risk it.

The railroads were nearing completion, though, and as railroad work became scarcer, Bradford took more odd jobs with the Company. Because he was a Mason, the Company called him as worker of choice. He built roads, put up temporary housing for supervisors, dug wells, and built pump houses and storage sheds and wooden covers for cesspools. He had no time to farm. Like his neighbors, he fretted more and more as he came to depend on the commissary. They all realized early on that their pay would never be enough to avoid the staggering debt they would soon owe the commissary.

Jerry listened to his father's worries as they made their way past a shed that held God only knew what: Tools and dynamite—rusty tools and leaky dynamite at that. Company men crawled around in the boxes and threw useless and broken items out on the ground. The children in Margaret had to be careful where they stepped.

Dynamite was a great blessing for miners—far superior to TNT. Even a single stick, if laid in a hole precisely in line with other sticks, could collapse an entire mountainside or cut a ditch deep enough to hold a river. But old dynamite was unstable, vulnerable to friction and a great curse when it fell into the wrong hands.

Explosions became more frequent after the incident in Ensley back in 1894. Ensley union men asked for a pay raise, but management refused to negotiate. That was when it began: Somebody set off dynamite and killed a Negro miner. Some blamed management and some blamed the union. Sheriff George Morrow investigated, but no one was ever held responsible, and the dynamiting went on.[52]

Without Jerry at home, Gertrude was left in charge of the house. She cleaned and cooked and took care of four-year-old Charlie. But she didn't mind. She had turned fifteen, still a girl really. Charlie wanted her to play, and she loved it. He pulled at her skirt, asking for an unending game of chase, demanding attention, laughing and running from her. She eventually caught him and swung him breathless in the air.

Charlie enjoyed that game best of all. She did too, obliging him by playing the chase-and-scoop-up game until both of them laughed uncontrollably. When Gertrude laughed, everybody laughed, and Charlie was no exception. His laugh made her heart light. If he wandered too far, she swung him up into the air then put him down close by her. This was the game they played that morning, and it went on for a while until Charlie began to tire of it. Finally, he settled down, seemingly content to watch a large beetle climb a wild pokeweed.

Gertrude went around the cabin to check on the heavy cookpot filled with boiling lye soap that Geneva left for her to watch that morning. She let the fire go out, then stirred the liquid until it cooled. She tested the liquid, then left the laundry soaking in the pot, then went back to the front of the house.

Pale new leaves appeared on the sweet gum trees, turning the canopy to green lace as the sun played through. The breezes were soft and the sun warm. Every living creature was outside. Even if the weather had looked alarming—which it did not—she would have taken Charlie outside that day, but they would not have wandered so far. They would have stayed in sight of their cabin, played only in their own clean-swept yard. This day, when almost no adult was home and it was such a beautiful spring morning, most of the older children had already abandoned their homes and run far down the hill and down the road toward the outskirts of Margaret, all by themselves with nobody to stop them, probably headed for the creek that ran through the valley. They were nowhere to be seen.

Charlie ran in circles now, running his hands through the air and making vr-o-o-o-m noises, pretending he was an airplane. He watched her as he ran, looking at her out from under his dark curls and stopping about every third round to pull at her skirt. He begged her with big dark eyes to play.

"Charlie Boy, I still got a few things to do, but I'll come play with you in a few minutes. You just got to be patient, now." The miners reported to work before sunrise and were long gone from the hillside. Her work was almost done.

Gertrude finally took his little hand in hers, feeling him tug her forward, and she let him pull her along. The morning warmed her and she found herself walking with her little brother along the crest of the hill toward all the activity. She loved watching the men work in the distance, listening to them shout to one another. Sometimes they spoofed one another, bantering the way men do when they work, and sometimes they shouted orders or disapproval. Intriguing echoes from invisible men. It didn't matter; she loved those living human sounds, grown up sounds that seemed so far away.

When they reached a place on the hill where she could see the mine in the distance, she told Charlie he could go play but not to go far. She sat down in the long soft grass to dream about how beautiful she would be when she grew up, and how she would be rich—rich enough to take care of them all.

She picked white clover blossoms and plaited their stems together to make a tiny posy. Just to the left of the clover patch, she watched a line of ants stretch as far south as she could see. She looked hard to see where they came from, guessing they lived somewhere in the forest beyond and were out foraging for who knew what. Straight down the hill and to the west, she saw men scurrying around very much like the ants, coming and going out of holes in the earth. Far down that hill was the road from Birmingham that came to Margaret. She could see bits of railroad, too.

The men shouted louder now, and their shouts changed. They seemed nearer, and something told her they were trying to attract her attention, so she turned toward them, looking for Charlie at the same time. Charlie was not there watching the beetle. He was gone.

"Git away from there, nigger!" The men were shouting at Charlie, who was half way down now, between her and them. She saw him then, running at top speed away from her, his little legs carrying him toward the men.

She jumped to her feet and ran toward her youngest brother who was by now almost in the field with the men. Gertrude ran after him, calling his name. He stopped at the sound of her voice and turned to look back at her, but instead of starting back up the hill, he squatted down and began to dig around in the dirt. The men kept on shouting.

Gertrude ran until she was almost at him. Charlie stood up now, showing her what he found. He paused just a minute, then began to run toward her with his treasure in his hand. She didn't remember much else after that except that Charlie was holding a stick of dynamite, running, bringing it to her, showing it to her. She knew instantly that it was an old one, one of the old leaky ones stored in the shed, and she remembered the warnings that went along with such dynamite. Her father told them all many times: "Don't *ever* touch them. They leak and they will explode—even if you just jog 'em. Stay away, do you hear?" He meant it.

She reached her little brother just in time to grab it away from him, yanking it out of his tiny fist and knocking him down in the process. In that instant she knew she would have to throw it as far away as she could. She remembered standing between Charlie and the dynamite before she let it fly.

It came at her like a gunshot, and she felt it with her whole body. She didn't see it because her head was turned away, her eyes on her baby brother. A jolt to her body, a sharp hammer blow to her right hand was all she felt. When the haze lifted a little from her mind, she wiped her hand on her apron and saw blood where her fingers had been, nothing but blood. The blood would not stop gushing. She tried to wrap her hand into the folds of her apron, but the hand was not right. Under the blood and burnt flesh she saw most of her fingers dangling limp, barely attached to the rest of her hand by shreds of burnt skin. She went into a kind of shock.

The miners reached them, and one of them took Charlie's hand, gently leading him away from his wounded sister. One of the men ran to the closest cabin to look for another woman, because it was women who knew about healing, not men. Medicine men knew diseases and herbs, but women knew what to do in an emergency.

The women close by heard the blast and were already running toward them. They saw Gertrude looking dazed at Charlie, her right arm hooked under her waist, blood everywhere. One of the women took the baby and hid his eyes from the blood. Another pulled Gertrude's arm gently away from her apron and examined what was left. The two women put her between them and half carried her back up the hill, where they dipped a rag in the lye soap to wash the wound. Gertrude sat on her own steps rocking her body back and forth silently, overcome, letting them do what they would. She did not yet feel the pain.

"Can we tie them back on?" The teacher was the first to arrive.

"Can't see... Don't know." An old woman fingered the wound and tried to separate the mess into five different bundles. "That's where the bone goes. Get me some binding."

"Lay her down, I'll go fetch my scissors."

The old woman placed the girl's hand on a block and sawed the mangled fingers off cleanly, trimming the shreds of skin as best she could, trying to fashion a smooth edge that would take a needle. She intended to sew a flap to close the spot where three of the fingers had been. She wanted to make a few stitches at the base of the remaining thumb, which had only lost its tip. She would try to save as much as she could.

When the preliminary work was done, the woman stretched the remaining skin tight across the top of the now bare bones and sewed it to the palm of her hand with big black stitches, which she knotted tightly. She steadied the remaining two fingers with sticks wrapped around with the same black thread. Her handiwork was good. Gertrude would just have to make do with what she had left of that hand for the rest of her life.

105

They laid her down right there on the wooden slats of her porch. Gertrude saw crowds of neighbors standing around, but she was confused. Somebody folded a towel and put it under her head, and she remembered no more.

For once, even the miners were quiet. They came up the hill when the ruckus began and now stood quietly at a distance in Gertrude's yard, watching helplessly, most of them with their hands folded in front of them. They looked at one another, wondering if they dared try to call the union doctor out there to treat a colored, but they figured it was probably too late for that anyway. There weren't any doctors that treated the colored for at least fifty miles. The closest one was in Gadsden—much farther than that.

The teacher took the baby home with her to relieve Gertrude of her duties. Then the other women worked by splashing cold water on her face and body to bring her out of her stupor so they could help her into bed.

Gertrude lay in bed by herself that night, feeling the pain come on strong, but grateful the child was not there. When Gertrude's older sister Geneva came home late that night, she tried not to let Gertrude see her cry.

"Oh, Honey," she told her. "I am so sorry. I am so sorry I was not here." She said it over and over.

Bradford and Jerry arrived several days later, about the time the fever broke. Geneva told them what had happened and that she thought Gertrude was going to be all right. The skin was still hot to the touch.

In a few months the skin began to heal over the wound, but the disfigurement took Gertrude down. That stump of a hand had to be made useful. She worked with what was left of her thumb and her little finger until she could do almost anything. Her crowning achievement came the day she threaded a needle with only two fingers. That day the women came over to visit and watched Gertrude thread that needle time and time again. They had no idea how many thousands of tries had gone before, but they knew she had reached a milestone, and they considered it a miracle, which in a way it was. They oohed and aahed over her and brought her cornbread and shelled butterbeans already cooked so nobody had to cook that night. They sat together, relief spreading like sunshine through the community.

1930. Bradford was downgraded to a day laborer for the Norfolk and Southern Railroad at half the pay, which was when he learned that no amount of hard work and no amount of talking to white men made much difference, if any. Then the rail work and carpentry jobs finally came to a halt. His life seemed to be slipping out of his grasp, which made Bradford swear he would spend every minute of the rest of his life trying to promise a better one for his children. This effort in itself kept some of the despondency away, but it did not bring in any income.

For a while after Lila died, he had become inconsolable. He sat rocking on the porch for hours, well into the night, blaming himself for the harm that had come to his family.

The other older sisters married and left home or took live-in jobs in Talladega or Birmingham. Geneva, Gertrude's favorite older sister, married before she was seventeen, and she and her new husband left Margaret for Chicago. It was both a sad and a happy day for Gertrude. The couple assured her she could come visit.

Gertrude felt the need to work stronger than ever. Besides, she longed for someone she could talk to. White women usually looked at her hand and told her they didn't really need anybody right then but they would call her if they needed somebody to help out. Mr. McGinnis, the foreman of the mines, felt some sympathy for any family who had come on hard times and looked for work for her. The best he could find was temporary work, but he kept his promise..

4. John Jones Comes Calling

When Gertrude turned eighteen, she took her last job in Margaret as a maid's helper. It was a temporary position to help Mrs. Rich, whose husband worked for the Company, entertain some of his boss's important visitors from Germany. It was only for a few weeks, but during those weeks she learned how to make pastries and heavy cream puddings without lumps in them, and how to grind meat for sausages. The lady of the house was pleased with her, she thought, but when the Germans left, Gertrude was no longer needed.

In 1932, Charles DeBardeleben once again offered Bradford a job in the mines, and this time he accepted.

These were glory days for St. Clair mines. The Company brought in new equipment almost every week, and the commissaries were filled with miners and miners' wives who had nowhere else to go to buy food and clothes. These latter day mining ventures were perhaps even more dangerous for these families than the earlier ones, because the convict leasing system ended back in 1928. Family men replaced convicts under conditions no better than those of their predecessors. Now the Company's annual report listed six fatalities and 57 accidents at Overton.[53] By 1934, the Company was pleased with its record: Only one man died in Margaret mines that year.[54]

Alabama Fuel and Iron Company, like all companies, fought unions with everything in its power, and violence was within its power. The boss gave his men only one option: They could not assemble, but they could join company-approved, company run black or white "Welfare Societies." They told every workman in St. Clair County that if he even looked at the Steel Workers

Organizing Committee he would lose his job. Governor Perry assured the workers this would not happen, but the threat was real enough to keep unions at bay, at least for a while. Unions were like carrots, always just beyond a man's reach. They were a workman's vessel of hope and despair, misunderstood, a topic of speculation.

One night, when the Lodge brothers met at the Bradford house, Jerry—who was twenty now—read the *St. Clair Aegis* to the men.

"Damn." Jerry's voice rang out over their heads as though he were talking to the trees. "Look at this ad! Our bosses made a $104,370 profit off us at the Commissary."[55]

"Let me see that paper," said one of the men.

Another responded "What for? You can't read!" which brought howls from the other men.

The men began to talk all at once.

"That ain't all of it—we owe 'em lots more than that. Mebbe twice more. We're fools to keep on buying." The young fellow speaking had just announced the birth of his fourth child.

Jerry added, "And when we die they don't even print our names."

"Don't pay up bereavement either," Bradford said.

"So what can we do?" asked Jerry.

"Think we can go talk to the Boss?" asked the new father.

"Again? Don't know. We could try, but from what has happened so far, I'm afraid it would just make it worse." Jerry signaled them to be quiet and went on reading the Company's ad:

"The employees are well satisfied. They have nice gardens."[56]

After the laughter subsided came the reality that the Company refused to listen to an outfit even as respectable as their Black Masons. So, they wondered, what could sway the company? Somebody suggested the workers put their own ad in the paper.

A long silence followed before a balding, middle-aged man in checked shirt and overalls added: "Brother, they wouldn't even allow it to be printed. They would just call us communists."

"Communists?" some indeterminate person asked. The room began to buzz again.

The man they called Elmer, the one in the green shirt with suspenders, stood up and shouted, "Hitler don't like communists."

"Who says?" the bald man asked. All eyes turned on Elmer.

"He said it," answered Elmer. "Mr. DeBardeleben said it. He said the Germans just arrested a thousand communist priests."[57]

"We ain't communists." The man in the plaid shirt was standing now, shaking his fists in the air.

"No. But they ain't going to listen to us," said the balding man.

"So who will listen?" Jerry wanted answers.

"The Steel Workers mebbe?" Elmer suggested, but the bald man gave him a look.

"You dumb? If we talk to them we'll lose our jobs for sure."

Jerry spoke again, telling them a second time: "Governor Perry says it ain't true. He says we won't lose our jobs if we join the union."

"Well, ain't none of us done joined, Jerry, and they cut our pay anyway. Maybe the governor don't know what he's talking about."

"You're wrong, Brother. Some of us do belong already. Mr. Ramey already done organized a local down at Overton."[58]

The men sat in stunned silence, listening to a man who had kept silent until that minute. This was the first they had heard of that. Even Jerry had nothing to add at first. Then Jerry found his voice.

"So, like we said," Jerry took advantage of the silence. "Let's go talk to them. The men down at Overton. Who wants to go?"

"Hey, we already tried that." Old Man Jones was speaking. His curly black hair had turned a silver gray, and they respected him.

He rose slowly from where he had been hunkered over and began his tale. "Three of us Margaret men walked over to Brown's Station just last month, just in July."[59] Some of the men nodded. "To talk to a union organizer there. All we wanted to do was talk—we thought we should at least go see him, but we never got inside. Before we could see the meeting hall, we heard shooting. But we kept going. When we got close, we saw the sheriff's deputies. Sure enough those deputies were firing right into the meeting hall. When one of them saw us coming they stopped and pointed their flashlights right in our faces. They told us if we went one more step they would shoot us."

"That's right," said one of the other men. "And we turned around and went home."

"Well, this ain't no union organizer meeting," said Jerry, his voice calm. "We just want to talk to the Overton men, see what the union does for them, and while we're at it find out what they do for the union. We don't know nothing but what we hear."

They agreed they didn't know. Some were for going and some were for staying, but Jerry kept on persuading. It shouldn't amount to much, really. Mr. Ramey's men were down at Overton but Mr. Ramey was not. Many of the men agreed to go one morning early, between shifts.

Later, after the meeting was over, Bradford told his son he was proud of him. He hardly ever gave anybody credit, much less his own children, but this was different.

When word got out that Margaret's men were going, the men at Acmar wanted to go, too. Some of those laid off at Acton sent word they would meet them half way.

It was on a Thursday, early in the evening of August 1, 1934, before the miners were due home, that John Jones came calling. He lived just a few houses down Margaret Road, just past Gertrude's house, so it was quite natural that he would stop on his way. Bradford was the town councilor, and his house was where any man needing to talk could go. But on nights when the Company sent Bradford to the West Blocton mines, Gertrude let the men wait there for her father. When he was this late, Gertrude fed the younger children and put them to bed. When John came calling, he knew she could listen just as good as her father.

This stop was a habit now, a rest after his eight-mile walk up from Overton. John Jones was in no hurry to be home because there was nobody there anyway—just an empty chair or two and a couple of beds in the one room where he and his brothers had grown up. All of his brothers had houses down at Overton now, near where their mother lived.

He tossed his coat on the porch beside the rocker as he always did, then took a seat on the top step and called to her inviting her to join him. He sometimes talked to her like a father—sort of like Bradford, then sometimes he talked to her like a brother, but whichever way he talked to her she listened. She was taught to respect her elders and almost everybody else.

Gertrude came out with a bowl of peas still in their shells, drying her hands on an apron that bore traces of turnip juice and pokeweed. He waited for her to settle down, looking out over the peaceful valley, waiting for her to put the peas down, too, before he took the grass out from between his teeth and began.

"That your mama's apron?" She only said Yessir nothing more.

"Sure is too big for you." Then he turned away, looking into the distance. "You know I ain't never condemned the Catholic people, although I sometimes condemn what they do." He paused a minute, then stipulated, "But Mr. DeBardeleben don't like Catholics one bit."

Gertrude pulled the bowl of peas close to her and started shelling.

"And I ain't never condemned the Protestants, neither," he added. "Mr. DeBardeleben says he's a good Protestant."

"You don't have to believe the same things he does."

"But I ain't either one." He looked over her head. "He just made me president of his Colored Welfare Society. That's as high as a colored man can get."

"So what has that got to do with what you believe?"

"Just that I ain't neither, but I'm still duty bound to stand for what's truth. See? I know God will appreciate me if I be honest and sincere." He was struggling something awful.

"Go on," she sensed a revelation coming on.

"They've got a union at Overton." It took him a while to gather his thoughts. "Seems the men of Margaret are planning to go talk to the men at Overton about getting a union for themselves. Your pa, too."

This got her attention.

"The Boss says we don't need no union in Margaret; he says we have black and white welfare societies, and we should be grateful for what we got. What he means is, *he* don't want no union in Margaret, and he says *I* have to stop 'em, not let 'em get through to the men at Overton. He's give me orders." His voice began to shake. "Them's my brothers, Gal. He wants me to dynamite the road my brothers are going to be on. He done told me to dynamite that road when I see men coming. Your pa is one of them who's coming."

She froze unbelieving, terrified of what might happen to her father.

"Mr. Charles DeBardeleben . . .he done moved here personally hisself to keep John L. Lewis and them mine workers out,[60] and I'm the one he wants to do it for him."

Gertrude had heard that Charles DeBardeleben called himself the greatest believer in white supremacy, the mightiest of the white supremacists.[61] She wanted to put her hand on John's head to console him, but she didn't.

"It ain't right. It ain't right." John was shaking now, his head in his hands.

Gertrude trembled too, then. John made her promise not to tell her father but to keep him at home, which she was not sure she could do. She promised. Then after he left, she went back inside and locked the door behind her, waiting for her menfolk to come home.

The next day dawned and the family rose from sleep. When Bradford went to open the windows for some morning sun, Gertrude walked right behind him and closed them again.

"What you doing Baby? It's going to be a hot day. Give us some air!"

"No, Papa. I can't." He tried again, but Gertrude resisted. "I'm telling you, I can't." She would not look at him.

"Well, then, I need to know why not."

"Might be something awful out there." She tried to warn him with her eyes, but he would not be shushed.

"What on earth you talking about? I ain't going to stop what I'm doing just because something *might* happen. If it *might* happen down to Overton then there ain't nothing to worry about."

"It's something you don't know."

"What? There's something I don't know, huh? Well, I don't know nothing except it's my day off and Jerry's not going down to Overton by hisself."

"You ain't neither of you going nowhere if I can help it!" Gertrude was choked up by now, her dark eyes trying to hold back tears. "And I can't tell you nothing, so don't ask."

Jerry came in and walked over to the wash basin to wash his face. He was just splashing the last of the soap off when he realized his father and sister were on the verge of shouting at each other. He looked up, water dripping unnoticed down his chest. He took a towel to it then walked over to the table and sat down.

"You two don't never fight." Jerry just made the observation offhand-like.

"We ain't fighting. I just don't want my family going down to Overton Mine."

Outside, the road seemed strangely quiet for that time of day. No hullos, no footsteps running, no hammers banging in the distance, no wives running after their husbands with sacks of food.

"Just look out there—ain't nobody going down that road." Jerry sounded puzzled and said under his breath that maybe nobody was going after all.

"Ain't no hurry anyway. I made pancakes. I want to see by the expression on your face that you are enjoying them." Gertrude stalled.

After a second round of breakfast, Jerry announced he was heading out pretty soon, regardless. He had to meet some men down by the crossroads.

"Oh, no! No, sir. No you don't. Ain't none of you going down Overton Road." She was wild-eyed. "Not on my time you ain't."

She looked out at the sun, which was well over the horizon, and calculated John was most likely safe by now, had most likely done what had to be done, and she couldn't hold back any more. She told them both. She told them she knew that somebody was going to dynamite that road when they saw men walking toward Overton.

Bradford looked at his daughter sternly. "How do you know that?"

She shook her head "I can't tell you, Papa."

"You know I love you, Chile, but now I got to go. I'm one of 'em."

"You can't do that. I done told you so you wouldn't go. I broke my promise."

"Tell me now, then. Who told you?"

"Don't make me tell. If I tell you and you go there and they catch you, you'll go to jail. And the man who told me will get hurt. I can't."

She had never held anything back from her father before, but this time she did. She paced back and forth, wringing her hands. Her father pressed her and pressed her.

"Papa," she finally stopped. "He didn't have no choice. None. He's president of the Colored Welfare Society and he ain't got no choice. It ain't his fault; he's got to do it, and if I let you go down there he will know I told you. "

"So, that's how somebody gets to be President of the Colored Welfare Society," said Jerry. Bradford stood up as though he had been hit by lightning. He knew.

"My God in Heaven. His pa is my friend. I can't let nothing happen to him."

He and John Jones's pa went back, way back. The elder Jones owned a pair of serviceable mules. On sunny days, the dirt on the main road through town—a dirt road that crossed a creek that mostly was a trickle—was always packed

115

hard from wagons and horses. But in times of deep rain, the creek flooded something awful and churned up a heap of mud.

When the two men were young, they waited for dark clouds to appear overhead, then as soon as it started raining, the two of them would head out for the branch to rescue travelers. When the creek overflowed they were ready. They could pull out just about anybody and make a little money on the side. Since Bradford started working for the Company, Jones hitched up those mules by himself when it rained.[62]

"No," she said again. Gertrude stepped in front of him this time. "I will follow you, and I will bring Charlie." This was the first time she dared threaten her father. Charlie was just waking up, his feet dangling over the edge of the bed, sleep in his eyes.

The longest day in their memory ended sometime after lunch, although nobody ate any lunch. A lone miner came dragging up the hill at about two o'clock. Bradford and Jerry ran down to meet the man. Gertrude sat down, exhausted. She watched the three men talking then start together down toward the road to Overton. She heard their agitated voices.

The teacher from next door came up on her porch. A small crowd of women gathered, but for a long time no more men came up the hill. Then finally they saw them coming. Bradford was in front.

"Our Margaret men never made it to Overton," he told them when he reached the porch.

One of the other miners spoke up. "We was just walking along on down the road just as pretty as you please, not minding nothing, when, well. . . somebody—and I ain't saying who—sets off some dynamite."[63]

"Men ran every which way," Jerry told them. "Don't think anybody got killed, but they took a couple of them to Gadsden to the hospital there. That's where most of the men are now."

"But before they took the injured off, they just let them lie there in the dirt. The deputy sheriff came up and walked right up to John Jones like they knew he done it. I don't know what made them think John did it, but they took John and that broke us all up. He's down at the jail. He's another convict."

Gertrude worried John would be sent to the mines, even though the laws said the government couldn't do that anymore. Convicts ended up there anyway. Not with chains around their ankles but as trustees, of no particular value to anybody. Gertrude didn't forget but she had no power to help him.

Charles DeBardeleben shut down Overton Mine the day after the dynamiting.[64] In only two days, he had evicted all the miners and their families, even the innocent ones. John's two brothers, who had nothing to do with it, lost their house and were banished from the mines forever.

If the mines at Overton had to be closed, Alabama Fuel and Iron determined that the men of Margaret would work twice as hard and produce twice as much as they had before. Toward that end, the company conscripted 300 more Negroes from South Alabama, Negroes who had never seen a coal mine before.

These new men began to arrive in dribs and drabs at the mines in Margaret, Acmar and New Acton.[65] Margaret families, already struggling to stay alive, tried to house the new men, sometimes two or three new families to one house. Margaret families grumbled as much as they dared.

Since the company installed electricity in company housing, Margaret families paid the bill.[66] The new men were no help paying light bills for sure. Then there was the pay cut they had already taken. The Company had already reduced wages by 30 percent and cut their hours by 60 percent. Even then, the Company told its stockholders that their employees were highly appreciative and very happy and contented.[67]

Gertrude learned later that the men of Margaret tried to make their case to the Company several times. They even went to talk to Mr. DeBardeleben in person, but he only asked why anybody would go to Overton on a Saturday. Some fool upped and said that the only reason they went to Overton at all was to talk to the miners, nothing more.

It was then that Mr. DeBardeleben said that if they even thought about joining the Steel Workers, if they even spoke to the union's Organizing Committee, they too would lose their jobs and their houses. And if they dared join in a strike . . . well, he said, we keep men armed with machine guns around the Company to shoot pickets.[68],[69]

The men wrote Governor Perry again. A letter came back assuring them once more that what they were hearing was not true: No one was going to shoot the pickets.

The time came when there was nothing left for Gertrude in Margaret, and she knew she would have to go. Her cousin in Birmingham, who was married to a fine baker, called her one day and asked her to come help out. Gertrude's reputation for baking had gotten around. As Gertrude was about to leave for Birmingham, her father took her aside and told her it was best if she not come back. He didn't explain. He just decreed it.

In October, she left her father, her cousins, her friends, and the neighbors who helped her in bad times. She went to live with the cousin and her husband in Homewood, just outside of the city of Birmingham. Together they made pastries for the finest restaurants in town. She wrote her teacher neighbor some, but she was losing touch.

Then Eddie Carter came to see her. Eddie was John's best friend; they had all grown up in Margaret together. He brought news about those who survived the Overton disaster, that the mine closed without so much as a final paycheck and that some of the miners found work in West Blocton but most of them left. John was alive the last he heard. That was not much to go on, but it was something.

Eddie had the strong broad shoulders of his Creek ancestors and moved the way muscular men do, swaying slightly from side to side. But he was surprisingly light on his feet. He was a good man. He kept his hair cut tight on his head and had ditched his overalls. His shirt was straight off a shelf. She noticed, but she was annoyed, too. He came right on in without so much as a nod and helped himself to whatever he wanted, cutting himself a slice of pie or cake. When he put a friendly arm around her waist, she couldn't decide if she liked it or not.

"Go on now. Get outta here. I ain't studying you." But she said it in a laughing way, and Eddie put his hands down because he was a good man. Soon as he'd finished eating he would be off again, quickly enough that Gertrude missed him.

She kept Eddie's visits pretty much to herself because she really didn't want any gossip. Eddie always brought news and sometimes a bit of lard or some flour as a gift. He watched her work away, ironing clothes with her stump of a hand. Sometimes she caught him staring at her hand, but when she did, he looked away and tried to make up for it.

"You sure do look pretty today."

She answered "You're just saying that!" or "Go on" meaning go away, but her words had the opposite effect and encouraged him to keep on talking.

"Seems like the Company can't find enough workers from around here for their mines." He scratched his head in puzzlement. "Seems like they bring in new men all the time and more men on top of them, and everywhere you look we have men walking around without jobs. Can't understand it." He drifted off a minute. "But them new Negro men work for less than the whites or us."

"Uh huh," Gertrude watched out the window for her cousin.

"They cut our pay thirty cents for every dollar and still hire new men from around Mobile. I guess they out-cheap us."

"Where are they going to sleep?" She was concerned for what her father must be facing. The iron flew over the apron she had spread out on the ironing board.

"Well, you know, we jus' don't know now, do we?" He laughed out loud. "Could be just about anywhere." He loved goading her.

"Stop kidding me, Eddie."

"Lots more of them coloreds are on their way, and there just ain't time to build houses. I guess we'll just have to move over!" He wasn't quite as cheerful when he said that. "It just don't make sense."

"No. It sure don't." Gertrude heard every word, but she didn't look up. "What are they going to eat?"

"That's a good question, too. A real good one."

5. Doric Lodge No. 58

During his railroad construction years, Bradford became a Free and Accepted Master Mason. Like Masons everywhere, these men banded together to help each other in times of need. As the Lodge grew in numbers, it began its long uphill battle to become chartered.

The night the charter for Doric Lodge No. 58 was approved,[70] the brothers set out whooping and hollering, foraging wide in the mountains for a wild hog to roast. The animals, naturally skittish anyway, made themselves very scarce, but the brothers were determined to bring home as many of those grunting pieces of four-legged pork as they could find. They ran through the forest chasing the sounds they knew so well until, eventually, the grunts and shufflings under the brush turned to squeals. The men whooped and hollered even more, which is quite natural in times of victory.

The wild hog round-up turned into a jubilee. Half a dozen fires lit up to cook what they trapped, and that night the whole town ate lard-covered, spit-cooked, coal-fired pork for supper. They never forgot that night or that fine feast. It made them think they would have many more days to be brothers and many fine years for their children to grow up in Margaret.

That night, as dishes were being cleared and everybody quieted down, the discussion turned again to John Jones. No one knew where he was. Jerry said John was still one of them in spite of what he did. He spoke of how the men of Margaret were being used wrongly and every man there said *amen*. Adrenalin flowed, and they all agreed that it was time to go down to the courthouse and find out what had become of John.

In days before, immediately following the dynamite at Overton, some of the leaders gathered their courage and went down to the Ashville courthouse to tell the judge that John was not to blame, but they were told the judge just was not there. When they told the secretary they would wait, she explained that the judge was so busy he would not have time to see them for weeks and besides, he was holding court in Pell City. After weeks passed, the same men went down to the Pell City courthouse for the same reason. St. Clair County has two county seats, Pell City and Ashville, which makes it handy for an official who does not want to be found.

"Weren't nobody in town in Pell City," said Bradford after the second visit. "They were all down to Ashville. The whole town was down there looking at the new Stanley Bridge."[71]

But the miners were not ready to quit. In the end, after several trips back and forth between the courthouses in Pell City and Ashville, they managed to catch the judge in his chambers.

The judge was also a politician and knew how to avoid an issue. "What do you boys think happened to that old bridge? Now I know you all know something." He was practiced at this. If he could not avoid seeing them, he knew how to turn the tables.

"We came here to talk about John Jones, Sir." They were not so easily diverted.

"Well, I don't want to talk about this John Jones. We're talking about the damage you fellows did to the old bridge."

"You mean the old Auberg Bridge, Mr. Judge?" They looked surprised, all of them.

"You know what I mean. That's the one. Somebody broke that steel bridge apart and stole it in the middle of the night, piece by piece. You wouldn't know anybody who done that, now would you?"

These were familiar words. It was not the first time they had been accused of causing the incident, but if they knew, they weren't talking. It didn't matter if they did it or a white man did it. They would lose out whichever way if they talked. So they didn't talk. That was the code.

"No, Sir, Mr. Judge. Not that bridge. We don't know nothing about that bridge. 'Scuse us, Sir, but we heard you were dedicating the Stanley Bridge today, so that's why we come here. We been here before, Sir, a couple of times."

They took that brief, single minute afforded them by the judge to make their case.

"We came to talk to you about the dynamite that went off on Overton Road back in August and about your prisoner, John Jones," said Jerry.

Elmer broke in. "It weren't Jones's idea, Mr. Judge, Sir. The Company done told Jones to set off that dynamite. He was just doing what he was told. Just ask Mr. DeBardeleben, Mr. Judge, Sir, and I believe he'll tell you."

The judge said he tended to believe them, but he couldn't just let Jones go. Jones, after all, was just an ignorant colored man like they were and could not have planned the whole thing by himself. No, he was pretty sure of that.

"Yes, Sir, Mr. Judge. I think you are right. You are a fine judge, Sir. Somebody else had a hand in that dynamite. We just want to see if we can't get Jones out of jail."

To nobody's surprise, nothing good came of all their efforts. The last Bradford heard, John being the President of the Colored Welfare Society didn't do him any good at all. The citizens never found out where he was being held.

6. The Annual Meeting

The directors of Alabama Fuel and Iron Company were saved from having their names smeared across the front pages of the paper by an Act of God. The Perseid meteor shower made the front page in the *Birmingham News* instead. Meteors blazed across the clear night skies all through September of 1934 for days after the dynamiting, so the incident was buried somewhere amid the ads.[72] It never was covered much anyway because Margaret, Overton and Acmar Mines were insignificant compared to Alabama's other mines, nothing at all compared to those now belonging to U. S. Steel.

The Company's Board of Directors called its annual meeting for March 1935 in downtown Birmingham. Board members climbed the marble steps of the First National Bank Building to the meeting room on the second floor, arriving in time to have a smoke and a chat beforehand.

When the call to order was announced, those assembled pulled their chairs across the Aubusson rug and up under the polished oak library table. Tendrils of smoke from a half dozen Lucky Strikes crept up the sides of the mahogany panels and hung at ceiling level like thunderclouds. Because it was cold outside, nobody opened the windows and the smoke grew thicker. But when the president pounded the gavel, some of the directors tamped out their cigars, and those who had racked their chairs back leaned forward to set themselves square.

"Let's get started. Are we all here? Affirmative nods went around the table.

"I believe you have the minutes before you. Are there any corrections?'" Negative nods around the table and a few *No*s. "Then they are accepted."

"Looking back at 1933 and 1934, looks like all the mines made a gain."

"So why did we have to close Overton so fast?"

"We'll get to that in a bit," said Charles DeBardeleben, who was chairing the meeting. "Suffice it to say we've already announced the closure in the papers. So you will all know, we don't need that kind of publicity. Overton is closed indefinitely." He rapped his knuckles firmly on the mahogany table, then looked around the room, engaging each director eyeball-to-eyeball.

"Right now our stockholders are asking questions, and we've got to let them know we're not dead. We can tell them Margaret mines are doing great, what with all the new nigger blood. We need to get that message out. Should have had it out last month and we wouldn't have all these questions."

"Uncle Charlie," the men present chuckled at their own joke, they called Henry's son *Uncle Charlie* now. He was no Henry, but he was no stranger to power and acquisition either. He learned all he needed to know from his father, including how to control a situation. Like most operators, he long ago mastered deflection and rationalization and saw dissatisfaction among miners as nothing more than a public relations challenge. His answer was to present a new public face to the world, a face he described as *benevolent*. He began Black Welfare Societies and White Welfare Societies in the mines and called them benevolent societies. No one contradicted him. It worked then and would work now. It was his legacy.

"Uncle Charlie," one of them went on. "Looking at what you just handed out to us—with the gains at Margaret—we ought to be able to market Margaret coal for many years to come."

"That's about right!" Charles F. agreed. "We have a few liabilities, though."

"Still owe on compassionate claims? Attorneys still working on Overton?"

"Well, balance owed for compassionate claims at Overton as of January is $3,638.27.[73] We don't have all the figures yet. And we've got five more—four in Acmar and one at Margaret."

"Excuse me, Sir, but do we have any names?" the stenographer asked.

"The foreman keeps track of that. We don't."

"So how many accidents did we have?"

"Don't have the numbers on that yet, either. Somewhere around 200." He nodded at the stenographer who was trying her best to keep her skirt over her knees. "Will you check on that, too? I know the numbers at Acmar and Margaret were worse than Overton, though."

"Well, Overton has been closed since September! Sure they're worse."

"I say we have to make a note on that one: Blame the losses on the unions—doesn't matter if the losses are money or men." He turned to the stenographer again: "Take this down: 'If labor hadn't stirred up these troubles,' then go on and say Overton would still be in operation."

"And of course, we have to tell them about the additional Negroes. . ." The Treasurer took notes.

"How many from Mobile already got to Margaret?" asked Judge Alto Lee.

"At this point it's about 300. Another 200 on the way."

"What's the ratio now? Negroes to whites I mean?" asked the Judge.

"We've got it down like we want. Margaret shows about 70 percent Negroes to 30 percent whites. That's about the right ratio to keep up the proper loyalty and cooperative spirit."

"Like we said, we ought to be able to market Margaret coal for many years." They all agreed.

"Uncle Charlie, let's swing some of that extra money into the election. Jim Simpson is up for the Senate, you know."[74] Judge Lee never underestimated the value of politics.

Borden Burr, their attorney, made sure they followed procedure. "Now, Alto, you know that's new business. Just hold it there for a minute. First, let's wrap this report up so we can get our ad in the paper."

"Okay," Charles F. went on, dictating to the stenographer "Write: 'Labor agitators are trying every means to have our men desert the contract they have with us and come under the domination of the United Mine Workers.'"

"Contract? What contract?" Burr questioned Uncle Charlie again.

"Well, you know how it works. We have to be careful. If we are losing money, we sometimes have to do things like cancel their insurance—but they understand. Now you understand, we only cancelled their insurance because we were losing money."

"I thought we were making money," said one of the other directors.

"Well, the books will reflect that Overton wasn't profitable." The directors shuffled their papers in front of them, looking for the figures.

"It says here that after the Overton incident, you evicted the occupants of company housing. Those houses now lie vacant. Is that true?" The Treasurer was working on Assets and Liabilities.

Uncle Charlie just picked up where he left off dictating to the stenographer. "Correction here: Right after 'houses' and before 'lie vacant' say 'houses occupied by undesirables' now lie vacant." Uncle Charlie looked back at Judge Lee. "That should take care of it.'

"Another correction:" Judge Lee spoke this time. "Add: 'Our workers reward us by joining the UMW.' That will be a slap at Mr. Mitch."

"SOB. He deserves it," said one of the directors. "What was that statement Mitch made? You know, when he was talking about who we hired?"

"Which statement in particular? The 'No moral stamina' statement or the 'they wink at rottenness' statement?" They all laughed.

"Enough. Don't put those statements in the minutes." Charles shifted gears back to the Overton catastrophe. "Take this down. 'I saw no reason for our Company to continue this operation and suffer the loss its continuance would incur. Therefore on August 11, 1934, we closed the mine for an indefinite period. The houses being occupied by these undesirables made it most disagreeable. Therefore, I inaugurated eviction proceedings in November, but have met with a great deal of resistance and practically no sympathy from the courts until very recently. We now have only a limited number of these undesirables, and we hope in a short time to be relieved of them.'"[75]

"Next paragraph: 'The three hundred Negroes the Company brought from South Alabama have never seen coal mines before but are now mining at Margaret, Acmar and New Acton.' Then we need to mention that the tonnage is way up in these mines. Way up."

"What's the dividend looking like?" the first director asked Charles.

"Not final, but looks like about $1.50 a share."

"Does that include income from bonds?" the director continued with the questioning.

"Add that in: 'Liberty Loan Bonds at 4.25%.'"

"I move we adjourn. Type up the ad, then get the final figures for the minutes and approve them next month. All in favor say aye."

The ayes were heard clear around the table.

7. Goat

Goat grew up along with the boys, but it did not grow up as well.

"It has no manners," Margot said.

Emma loved her roses, and Goat loved wandering around, eating their leaves and growing heavy. Emma held a soft spot in her heart for Goat, even though it was no longer a kid.

"He just wants to play," she said, excusing him.

Georgie turned twelve not too long after the new house next to the old one was finished. His father and his uncles put him to work with an assortment of tools, then left him alone.

The family settled into the new house before the garage was finished. One crisp autumn day, in spite of his plans with his friend Bernie Evans to do something else, Georgie was conscripted to lay the foundation for the garage. No amount of pleading made any difference. The remainder of that day, Georgie held planks of wood horizontally in place while his father nailed them together. Georgie checked the angles with his T-square and level, then moved on to the next joint. About this time, Marjorie called out to her father.

"Daddy, can I go spend the night at Rosalie's?" She knew the answer, it was always the same. Always *No*.

"Why not?" She waited for the "because I said so" but instead she was told "because you need to take the shovel and work on this concoction in the wheelbarrow." She did as she was told and stirred sand into the wet cement, but she was not a good sport about it. "What's that going to be?" asked a passersby.

"A garage," answered Georgie, thinking the fellow didn't have good eyesight.

"Oh, I see," said the fellow. "Go tell your father he has to pay for a permit to have a driveway. The city will not cut a curb without a permit." The man thought perhaps the boy didn't understand and repeated himself. "Son, without a permit, you cannot have a driveway."

The man walked on. Georgie dutifully reported what the man said to his father, who confirmed with the city that this was indeed true. Georgie told Marjorie that somehow he had let his father down.

That hot summer night, Georgie threw off his one sheet to let the cool air flow over his body. He lay awake until he could stand it no longer. With everyone else in deep sleep, he slipped on his shoes and went quietly outside, where his father's sledgehammer lay next to yesterday's now hardening slab.

Emma woke to loud pounding underneath her window. By the time the family tied on their robes and went outside, Georgie had bashed in six feet of curb over which any automobile could drive. He gave the curb one final blow.

"So, Father, will you call me George from now on?"

"George," his father let it roll over his tongue. "I think so."

They waited, expecting to hear from the city, but they never did. When George turned 18, he bought the shell of a Model T for $5, but he did not have to carry it over the curb.

Marjorie settled herself on the stone bench to watch him. He was tinkering as usual, trying to start the motor. "What *are* you thinking?" Marjorie asked.

"I'm ruminating over my legacy." The motor turned once.

"What the heck are you talking about?" She hollered at him over the clatter.

"I think I've got it, Nut!" he hollered back. "It's for the yearbook." They called each other "Nut" a lot.

"Okay, what?"

"'To take the hill of life without shifting gears.'"

When Emma came outside, he ran it by her, too, and she approved. With cold still in the air, her roses were at their peak. She began to cut them, carefully, so as not to ruin the over-all effect. She saw her garden as a painting and bent over to cut at the base of the plant.

Nobody paid any attention to Goat, who wandered at will. He was behind Emma now and without hesitation butted her soundly. Emma fell; it was quite a knock. Goat backed off looking pleased with himself.

Emma lay still a minute, examining her dress, which was hopelessly tangled in branches and thorns. Marjorie was the first to see her grandmother lying there and the first to realize Goat was making motions to give it another go. She shouted at Goat and ran to her grandmother. When they tried to help her up, Emma propped herself up on one elbow and started laughing.

It was indeed a ridiculous sight. They laughed until the tears came. Emma shook her finger at Goat, who retreated to the wall. Then they heard the screen door slam.

George T. came determinedly toward them. He did not think it funny at all. He grabbed Goat roughly and tied him to a tree.

"Stop that laughing. Help me."

Together, arms under elbows, they helped her rise. Only then did Emma feel the stabbing pain in her hips. Her legs fell limp beneath her. She bit her lip and allowed them to carry her, grateful to be eased down onto the velvet sofa. She could do nothing to make the task easier and asked only to be left alone to determine how much damage there really was.

She stayed in the same position for hours, color draining from her cheeks, until even Margot began to worry. When it came time for bed, George and his father tried to ease her up the stairs, but the pain was too much and they had to lay her down in the parlor for the night. After the others retired for the night, she tried to swing her legs on her own, over her make-shift bed, but could not. She could handle pain, but what if she could no longer walk? She tried to reason with herself that it would turn out well, but she knew better. Only then did she give in to her grief, long overdue.

The next morning, the family once again called in Dr. Robinson. He poked around and gave his prognosis. She had, he thought, broken her hip. They should make her comfortable in her own room because mending would take a while.

The definition of her own room changed then. Emma could no longer live alone next door, so she let her family carry her to their spare room upstairs, little knowing she would live there the rest of her days.

The next morning George and Marjorie brought her breakfast on a lap tray—coddled egg and a rasher of bacon. They stayed with her a while then asked her what they could do for her that would make her happy. She could manage, she said. But as months went by, she became more and more isolated. When Margot sent one of the children up with a tray, she did what grandmothers do in the best of times: She read the papers, talked about the old days, her grandfather, the changes in Germany, and the Lutheran church. She was glad her family was no longer alive to see what was happening.

"Jena was a grand university. Your great grandfather Frederick Valentine Melsheimer would turn over in his grave if he could see what they are teaching there now."

She wept when she talked about it: She called it *Enctjudung*, which meant de-Jewing all the teachings in the Bible.

"And they have the gall to call it German Christianity. Do you understand that?" She looked into both sets of eyes. When she was satisfied that they did, she picked a gentler subject. "I think I will learn Spanish. Do you suppose you two could find me some Spanish books?"

Marjorie hunted until she found just the right book for her grandmother, and Emma began her studies in earnest. It took her mind off Hitler. But other than Christmases and holidays, when the men carried her downstairs to join the rest of the family, Emma lived entirely upstairs, dependent to her horror on Margot for everything. The long imprisonment brought Emma and Margot a kind of truce, albeit a one-sided one. Margot took meals to her and on occasion stayed to talk. Emma had lots of time to read, and the numbers of opinions she formed increased exponentially.

"Socialism," Emma said, "is the only thing that stands between the rest of the world and Hitler."

Margot had no idea what she was talking about and ignored her, having no time, really, for such nonsense. She changed the subject to needlework and menus, but she did not sit passively by. Once, when she brought Emma a bowl of soup, she sat down beside the bed and pronounced, "All Yankees have big feet!"

Emma tried not to bite but could not help herself: She fought back. "I wear a size five. What size do you wear?"

Margot wore a size five-and-a-half. In a huff, she took her soup and headed back down the stairs.

Emma endured the silence and the loneliness as long as she could.

"Margot, I won't argue anymore." She called down the stairs. "I was just talking." Having somebody to talk to was far more important than winning an argument. Then something happened that changed everything.

In January 1934, George Timothy died without warning. Heart attack, they said. The two women tried to comfort each other in their grief, but Margot would not be comforted. It was then that Uncle Cyrus persuaded Emma to come live with him in Chicago.

In early May, George and his cousin Cy carried Emma down the stairs for the last time. They placed her gently in the waiting wheelchair and wheeled her down the driveway. At the Terminal Station, a red cap took Emma's luggage and wheeled her on down the platform to the Pullman cars, where a porter waited.

Emma asked the porter his name, then held her hand out to him. As the family watched, she held tight to the porter's hand, pushed herself up to a standing position and balanced on her liquid legs. With the porter and the conductor holding her on either side, she walked.

"I do not want my family to remember me as a cripple," she announced. She managed the stairs. At the end, as the steam whistle blew and the wheels began to crank, they saw her wave goodbye to them from the window.

She wrote them from Chicago to tell them that the kind porter had begun a porter's union and that she really missed Birmingham. When she died, George brought her body home so she could be buried next to William.

8. The Men of Margaret

1935. Transplants were everywhere in Margaret now. Men displaced, uprooted possibly for the third or fourth time, angry at being forced to leave. They only brought with them the memories of what little comfort they enjoyed in Mobile, when they were not being sent to some mining town far away. There was nothing for them in Margaret except pay and little enough of that. They hung out at the company store and went into careless debt.

More than four hundred new black workers arrived in St. Clair County; hundreds more were on their way. Those who had a roof over their heads looked down on those who did not. They divided themselves from each other, the new from the old, the haves from the have nots. Many of the newcomers camped in the woods out of necessity. The few women who came with them could not make soap fast enough to keep the clothes clean. Many residents on Negro Hill turned them away and complained when the newcomers tried to wash themselves in the town's creek.

The dry August heat mixed with wet August thunderstorms caused fierce storms with searing bolts of lightning that killed at least one of the new workers. The citizens of Margaret felt pity for them but it was pity mixed with fear. The numbers overwhelmed them.

Bradford had no such fear. He saw these men as brothers until they proved otherwise; he helped them as he would a brother. He helped many of them find shelter, and moved his own furnishings around to make room for three of the oldest men, whose gear was soggy and smelled rank from nights in the deep woods. Bradford dragged their disgusting sleeping equipment outside

134

and set fire to it, then enlisted his neighbors to make new bed sacks out of whatever old burlap and pine straw they could find.

Bradford was a practical man, a strong man even, but he knew if he did not stay busy, his thoughts would overwhelm him. He saw his dead wife and his absent daughters in every shadow; he saw them each time he took out a kitchen pot or lit the stove.

Before Lila died, the two slept together in a marriage bed that he built with his own hands out of white oak. Their mattress was pine straw with a soft layer of feathers on top. Their quilt was the one Lila began when she was a very young girl.

Lila was very young when she married, so her quilt was too small for any marriage bed. In the days before the wedding, Lila's mother summoned the other women from the village who came, each bringing a scrap of cloth. Together they cut and sewed dozens more squares to make more rows along the sides of Lila's quilt until it was wide enough for a marriage bed.

After Lila died, Gertrude and her sisters shared that bed and that quilt. With no women in the house, Bradford, Charlie and Jerry took the bed and gave the men floor mats that were only slightly softer than the floor itself. The quilt had gone long ago. One of the older sisters had it.

Gertrude took her own quilt to Birmingham. When she had time, she sewed scraps onto it because it reminded her of her sisters and her mother. Sewing brought memories of stews boiling over the fire in winter and light coming in between the logs.

In Margaret, Bradford set the men to washing up the dishes. When darkness set in, in an extravagant gesture, he turned on the electric light. He had never been so extravagant with his women. He held back his tears, then he could stand it no longer and walked outside to be alone. Eventually, he found himself in front of the teacher's house and knocked on her door. He asked her if he might telephone Gertrude. She let him in and handed him the phone.

When Gertrude answered, he heard himself asking her to come home. He told her that if she did not want to come, he would understood. He explained the house was full of transients—the whole town was full of transients—she would have to stay somewhere else, perhaps at the teacher's house. Maybe just for a day or two.

Gertrude's quilt lay on her lap while they were speaking. She saw Lila's handiwork in even the most misshapen swatches, each of which fit exactly where it belonged. She could never make the pieces fit into her quilt as easily as her mother had. Her child's hands were restless and her stitches too fat. She learned later that she needed patience to tear them out and begin again. Her own damaged hands worked well enough, now. She repaired her own stockings and sewed buttons on. She told herself she could do anything.

Her brothers were the men of Margaret now, all miners. They were no better off than the others, either. Without enough money to live on and with nobody to turn to, they suffered just like those who came later. When Gertrude asked her father how many cuts in pay he had taken, he could not remember.

Bradford on the other hand never saw the impossibility of his situation. He held onto his faith that the Company would listen to him. He told her his relations with all of the Company men were good, from the supervisors up to Mr. DeBardeleben himself. He talked to them often, sometimes several times a day. He told them he did not want his sons to be miners, and he begged for his old construction job back, but there really were no more construction jobs. He took what he could get.

He dreamed of being able to plant fields around his house again and watch his grandchildren play, but that dream was fading. He had a second dream that seemed more likely to come true: that his sons would find something better somewhere else. He wanted them to leave Margaret, too. He would stay and be happy with a patch of piney woods where enough light shone through so he could see to carve blocks of wood. Perhaps he could grow corn on a small piece of land.

He hated the mines. He always hated the mines. What had he done wrong that his family suffered so? He asked Gertrude these things over the telephone.

Gertrude thought maybe God knew, but she said she sure didn't. She tried to cheer him up and told him not to worry, that things would work out. Then she gave in and said she would come.

A month went by before she found the courage to leave Birmingham. When the time came, she took the train to Margaret and arrived late in the evening. The anticipation of seeing her family turned to disgust. If she had bought a return ticket, she might have turned around right then. As the train pulled into the station, she saw a sight she would never forget. Nothing looked familiar. All across the valley what looked like one-room shacks lay like discarded cracker boxes, ugly and misshapen. Unfamiliar men in overalls and a few women wandered the streets nearby, strange human beings in every stage of dishevelment. She turned away, refusing to see. Then, when she forced herself to look, she saw that the old schoolhouse in the Mt Zion Baptist Church still stood where it had been when she attended school there, and she was somehow comforted.

She trudged along up the long path to her father's house not knowing what to expect and knocked on the door. A strange man with a cane opened the door.

"You must be the daughter."

"I am. And you must be his friend? Is he here?"

"No, ma'am. He's gone off walking like he does in the evening. He'll be back when it gets dark."

"Well, I guess I should have told him when I was coming, but I'll be back. Just tell him hello and that I will see him in the morning." She went to her sister Evelyn's house for the night.

The next day she took her nephew, Evelyn's child, with her and went to spend the day at her father's house. Father and daughter breakfasted together amid the chaos of miners hurrying off to work. Bradford rested his forehead in his hands and talked. He went on and on while she listened.

"Baby, I am so sorry I sent you off."

"It's okay Daddy. I'm doing just fine."

"I never would have done it except I thought you were interfering with men things, and now I know you didn't have no choice. You had to do what you had to do."

"We all do, Daddy."

"And now you're back. But now this ain't no place for you."

They walked outside in the pea patch for a while. The child picked pea pods until he could hold no more. Gertrude found a little basket for him.

They walked together again after lunch. Her father could not stop talking. It was as though he had saved up everything he ever had to say his whole life and was letting it all come out. He talked about Lila, about the new men, about the Lodge. He was proud of his boys, of Jerry standing up for himself. But at every pause, he told her how sorry he was he sent her off. The conversation continued until her father left for the night shift in the mine.

It was still the middle of the afternoon, so she and the boy went back to the old cabin for a while so she could tidy up for her father and mend what she could. She needed to talk now, so she talked to the child like he was old enough to understand, which he wasn't.

"Baby," she said. "Your granddaddy blames hisself. He thinks he's let us all down." The child looked up at her and broke out in a big child's grin like he was really part of the conversation.

"'Auntie Trude!" he said. "Auntie Trude!" He laughed and pointed to his aunt. She couldn't help but laugh back at him.

"He swore on his Bible he would protect us. I heard him. Now your Grandmama's gone, and he can't do nothing about it." She felt a tear start down her cheeks and wiped it off quickly. "He's trying, Baby. You know I ain't much use to him now."

She realized the boy's bucket was full of vegetables.

"Now look at you! You got a heap of peas you picked. Thank you kindly!" She let the purple hulls run through her fingers, nodding her head approvingly. She smiled her dimpled smile, so the baby smiled, too. She let him run.

She adjusted her bosoms under her blouse with the stump of her hand and smoothed out her apron. Today was not a good day to ask the other women for help with babies. They were overwhelmed with work.

After a while, she followed where the child had gone. He was an obedient little fellow, so she knew he had not gone far. She caught sight of him digging for fishing worms off near the pea patch. She was busy watching him play and about to turn to go back in the cabin.

For that brief moment when her mind was elsewhere, she was blind to the strange men cutting across their yard, coming and going to the storage shed. Then it dawned on her. "They should be down at the mines," she said out loud to herself. "What do you think they are doing here?"

Just about then, three men stopped dead in front of her, between her and her little nephew. The men were staring at her stump. She hid it under her apron.

"What you got there, woman? Take your hand out your apron, you hear?"

"Yes, Sir." Gertrude hung her head from habit but pulled her hand out from its hiding place and held it close to her bosom.

"Hey Tom! Lookit that! "

"Well, what you expect? Dumb colored gal! She probably got it caught in a meat grinder."

"Now what good's a gal who ain't got but one hand?"

"Especially a colored gal."

"Yea, Tom. What good?" The men edged closer. Gertrude edged back.

"Only one thing I know of . . ." They had her trapped there up next to the house.

"Go on, now. Go on now, you two." She tried to push the closest one away with her good hand.

"Hey, now! That ain't nice."

"Maybe we should just cut that old bad hand off, whatcha say, Tom? It's mighty ugly." They were laughing. Their tools hung in leather belts around their waists. Tom lunged at her like he was playing.

Gertrude held him off with her elbow. Then he grabbed at her good hand.

"You ain't nothing but an old cripple. Now don't you talk back at me! You want me to cut it off for sure?" He had her pinned now, and he drew a knife out of his tool belt, a fishing knife with a three-inch blade. She was too frightened to shake. She froze.

One of the other men spoke up. "Let her go now, you hear?"

The man ignored his buddy and held the blade near her throat, teasing her. "This thing's sharp, you know. Use it to gut fish."

She was glad he had forgotten about her hand and knew in her heart he would not cut her throat. But when she heard a scream, it took her several seconds to recognize it as her own.

"Keep your damn old hand," he said and dropped the knife on the ground.

She didn't remember much more except that there were other people walking on by like nothing was happening. She saw blood on her arm but she could not remember being cut. Automatically she tore a strip from the bottom of her apron and wrapped the wound, although she could hardly see what she was doing through the tears and grime and soot. She tried to pull herself together and go find the baby, but the land around her swam.

As her vision cleared, she saw the corner of the cabin, then her nephew, who was fine and blessedly at a distance. Lastly, she saw an old rooster that belonged to the teacher. That rooster always mistook her house for his own and was pecking away up the hill much too close. He was no more than a few feet from her.

She grabbed the old Red by his gnarly scratchy feet and hung him wattle down—hollering at him, calling him a no-good nasty old rooster not worth cooking. She went on and on that she was going to chop him into little pieces because she was not about to let him go. That old rooster was so bewildered and insulted that he squawked and struggled, up tight and angry, but she did not let him go. Instead, she shut him up forever by slinging him against the cornerstone of the house, which was not a stone at all but some kind of spine-bone from some huge long-dead animal found in the woods years ago. A mastodon bone, somebody said.

Dark was coming just as her men folk came in sight. Gertrude stood with her head thrown back and her arms akimbo beside a fire with flames reaching far too close to the low-hanging limbs. Feathers blew every which way in the wind, sometimes landing in her cook pot, which was sooting and steaming something fierce over the too hot fire. She was holding the head of the dead rooster and plucking remnants of feathers out from around its useless comb with her two-fingered hand. The rest of the old bird boiled away in the kettle, hacked into a million pieces, bones and all.

Her brothers took it all in, in an instant, the horror and the frenzy. They took the rooster's head out of her hands and helped her inside where she began to regain her balance. They were kind people and understood they had to protect her, and themselves, from this new breed of men in Margaret. They talked long into the night, making a plan. They had to send Gertrude back to her cousin's where she would be safe. They spoke of the dangers creeping in around them, not only immediate and threatening dangers from renegades like the Klan, but very real dangers from within their own companies, their own laws, their own unions. They talked about the union organizer who they heard had been taken across the state line to Tennessee.[76]

"He's probably dead," said Charlie. "Would have heard something by now."

"Once they get you across the State line . . . ." There was no need for Jerry to finish that sentence.

For the next few days the boys cared for Gertrude as best they could, bringing her bits of flowers and watching over her as a mother would her child. With all the new worries, they urged her to leave. But she could not. She needed time.

"This is my home, and I want to keep it that way. I ain't give up," she told her father. "I came to see about you and Jerry, and Charlie. I ain't leaving you."

She was determined. Birmingham was out, at least for the moment, but Margaret was no good for any of her family. She would return to the warm ovens of the bakery in Birmingham, but not now.

Time went a long way toward healing Gertrude's wounds. She found solace making pastries, and peace filling a sifter with flour and pinching out the weevils. Most of all she took pleasure in beating handfuls of gelatinous dough into shape and substance under the urgency of her rolling pin. She was happiest throwing dough on a board, slapping it rhythmically into a crust. When that crust finally lay in the pie pan, she pinched the edges and slashed them perfectly round. Those pies were satisfying, something she could control. She was a pastry cook.

"What's going on up there, Jerry?" She pointed down the road as dozens of men milled around in front of the old Mt. Zion Church.

"It isn't what it looks like. It's still a school, but at night it's where some of the new miners bunk."

"You mean it turns back into a school in the daytime?"

"It does—but it stinks from those who stay there."

"Who feeds them?"

"Nobody. They buy from the Commissary . . . if they get to keep any of their pay. Lots of them just wander around." He pointed out little covered stands, temporary shelters where a few of the less fortunate ate and slept.

Gertrude mused that maybe the families living outside were better off. They could escape the stink and the heat, and wash in the creek. Half a dozen women hauled clothes to the water. A few waded in, thigh high, trying to bathe unnoticed. They hung overalls and shirts, and precious little underwear, in tree limbs to dry.

The lucky ones owned trucks and set up camp inside their vehicles, but even they fought to claim a space under a shade tree. The first shift mostly lost that battle and parked wherever they could, with alarming disregard for traffic. Cleanliness and common sense were in desperately short supply.

"The men of Margaret? How is it for them?" She meant those who had been there all along.

"Passable," said Charlie, who was grown up now. "Still no say-so at voting time, though, with all the poll taxes and literacy tests and threats. Some of us like me think unions are our only hope, but that's a dangerous road to go down."

"How come it's dangerous?" asked Gertrude.

"The United Mine Workers and the CIO have reason to be afraid. Too much violence. They do have a local at Acmar now, but haven't done nothing for Margaret. That's what the meeting is about."

After the Overton incident, the men of Acmar had turned to the CIO for help, and the CIO tried to help them. They presented a list of the men's grievances to the Company, but the Company refused to talk to them. Only after that did the Acmar men finally join the union, but the Company made precious few concessions even then. Acmar men were too easy to replace. The Company looked to the men of Margaret to produce more and faster.

Her brothers left to join the other Masons at the church. There were too many of them now to meet in Bradford's house. Gertrude sat on the front porch and waited.

The men trickling out of the door after the meeting were dejected, talking worriedly among themselves. Bradford was among the last to leave, his footsteps as heavy as though he had a load of timber on his back. His Lee jacket was unbuttoned, and his old red railroad scarf was turned around backward.

Jerry explained that when the Company laid off eighty men in '33, they were just beginning. He said that was the real start of the campaign to intimidate the miners. That was when men first lost jobs just for saying the word *union*. The Company paid many of the local women, who needed food themselves, to circulate petitions that said how happy they were, and that they wanted nothing to do with the UMW.[77] The Company also made it clear that if anybody forced them to re-employ any of the fired men, they would just fire them again.

"So we're just fodder." Jerry's discouragement was palpable. "Charlie and I are going to join the Army."

"You're going to abandon your old father?" Bradford only half asked them that. Nothing could get much worse. He simply accepted it and asked if they planned to leave Margaret.

"No, Papa, we're just talking. We're not going to abandon you."

"Papa," Gertrude decided to add her voice, too. "I'm not going to tell you what to do, and I don't want to worry you, but you can't live here and eat nothing but jerk. I'm going to stay right here for a while and cook for my family." She turned to Jerry. "So it's time I went to look for work in Margaret."

Jerry shook his head as though to stop her. "It's no place for you."

"You'll see!" She pointed to a sweet potato pie just out of the oven. "I don't want to hear a word out of you, but I'm going to walk out of here in the morning to see if I can't find work. I'm going to see a lady who hired me once when I was a teenager. She was the one who taught me how to make sausages."

"That was an awful long time ago," said Bradford.

The next day, she kept her word and set out down the Margaret Road. She stopped at a two-story white frame house. On the lawn were a dozen tables draped in white, with bows on them as though a wedding were about to take place. Colored men dressed in black scurried between the lawn and the house.

Gertrude hesitated and turned to leave, but one of the men recognized her and greeted her by name. Her resolve returned. She continued around to the back door and knocked on the screen door, which was hooked from inside.

Peering through the screen into the dimness within, she saw a figure coming down the hall but could not make out who it was, so she cupped her hands above her eyes to keep the light down and squinted as she called out. "Betty? Is that you?" The figure came closer.

"I'm looking for the lady of the house," she said.

To her surprise it was Betty herself, dressed as always in her white uniform, which was freshly starched. Betty unhooked the latch and opened the screen door, then looked down at Gertrude in amazement.

"What happened to you? Where you been all these years? They done throwed a fit when you just didn't show up."

"I figured that. But I hoped . . . ." Gertrude held her breath, knowing she was about to eat a little crow. "I just hoped I might get some kind of job." She let her breath out.

"Well, I'll tell Miz Rich. You ain't going to be welcome here, you know."

Betty stared at Gertrude's hand. "You any better with that?"

"Yes'm. I make pastries for white folks. There's not much I can't do now." Her eyes looked proud and her dimples showed.

"Is that why you came back?" asked Betty.

"Yes." It was partly true.

"Miz Rich isn't home, but I'll tell her you came as soon as she gets here. But she's got a lot on her mind, and I don't think it's going to make much difference. How's your daddy? I hear Mr. Ramey done finally organized all them men up there in St. Clair except Margaret. Is your daddy one of them trying to bring in a union?"

Gertrude froze. "Now I just don't know. I don't know nothing about any of that."

"They're asking around, you hear? All the white families, that is, trying to figure out if the Margaret men are going to march."

Gertrude could not believe what she was hearing. Her father did say something about a demonstration, but he was just talking.

"Well, my daddy doesn't believe in demonstrations. He believes we have to work through the courts, so as far as I know, nobody is planning any demonstration." She let Betty know that, without any details. "What else are you hearing?"

Betty stood at the top of the stoop, kind of not wanting Gertrude to go. She knew a lot.

"Well, I can't help but hear. But you know I can't say nothing." Betty wanted to be begged.

"I ain't no snitch!" said Gertrude.

"Sure, Hon. . . Now nobody told me this outright, but I heard them talking, you know. Seems all the Company men done gone up to the courthouse to get deputized. They have to get deputized to carry guns, you know." She went on, "I think the company wants them to get deputized for something else. They already got guns."

"Who are they going to shoot?"

"Don't matter. They just itching to use them guns. Don't think they ain't. I did hear them say they are going to get Mr. Ramey."

"Who?" For a minute she forgot who Mr. Ramey was.

"Mr. Ramey runs the unions. Now don't get me wrong. I like Mr. Ramey, but he can't do what he wants to do. He thinks the union can help the men when they can't help themselves, but he's going to get himself kilt."

"I'm asking you, how many of them is going to be carrying guns?"

"Well, now, there's about a dozen, I would say. Mr. DeBardeleben of course and the other high-fallutins—the superintendent, Mr. Bell, and the gardener, Mr. Garrison. Then there's some coming out of Acmar, like Mr. Shepherd, then there's . . ." and she went on naming them off.

Gertrude didn't think her legs would hold out much longer, so she backed down the stairs. All she could say to Betty was, "Guess I best be going. No need to tell them I came by. Not much chance I could get my old job back anyhow."

"I guess you best be going, all night. Take care of yourself, Hon." Betty hooked the screen door and watched Gertrude walk away.

Gertrude hurried now. She had heard stories from men other than her father: Coal miners who dared ask for things like their own checkweighmen. Miners were paid little enough for a load of coal as it was, and their pay depended upon how much their load weighed. They believed Company checkweighmen cheated them, used faulty weights and faultier calculations, and even kept part of what was due the miner. Even though these miners knew they risked losing their jobs, they asked anyway. The Company refused them. This was happening all across the country.[78]

146

That night, her father confirmed what Betty said. Workmen, union and nonunion, from all over St. Clair County did plan a march, not just men from Margaret. The marchers planned to head straight to the Company's offices, one mine at a time, beginning with Mr. Charles DeBardeleben at Margaret. They would go as miners only, not as union men, to pay a peaceful visit, with the hope that their numbers might sway the owners.

Jerry believed their only hope was to call on a union, which meant joining the union, but he respected his elders and gave in. Older men tended to avoid trouble, refuse to make noise and give in, but Jerry was tired of waiting. It was he who persuaded his neighbors to make this appeal to the Company this one last time. The miners agreed and voted to go together to the Company. Their women could not stop them.

Early Monday morning, October 28, go together1935, they chose their leader. Virgil Jackson Thomas, veteran of World War I and mechanic for the Company, rode in the first car. In the crisp beauty of autumn, the miners themselves—union and nonunion, black and white—began their treacherous journey down the long road that led to both Margaret and Acmar mines. They walked and rode in silence. As they went along, others joined, until about twenty-five trucks and at least that many men on foot moved slowly down the dirt road, crackling dry leaves as they went. They reached the fork where the two roads parted—one to Acmar and one to Margaret, but they could not go on. Company trucks were parked across the road, blocking their way. Dynamite and machine gun nests lay in wait near the fork at Whites Chapel. Company operators and deputies had their hands on the triggers,[79] expecting enough brutality to stop the nonsense once and for all.

Shots rang. Bullets flew, hitting trees and trucks and men, trapping some in their vehicles and sending others running for their lives. There was no let-up. The Company set off dynamite charges that sent debris into the crowd. Seven Margaret men fell when Company bullets hit their marks.

Nine armed men showed themselves, shooting furiously at miners still within range. The few in the parade who still had control of their vehicles scrambled to turn the convoy around.[80] Virgil Thomas, their hero, lay slumped over his steering wheel, dead, his truck riddled with bullets. The nine did not stop shooting until after the last of their prey disappeared down the road. Then it was over.

Headlines in the *Pell City News* on October 31, 1935 read "War breaks out in St. Clair: One killed, fifteen injured in clash." The story appeared after the fact, gleaned from interviews with Company officials and held back from publication until after the coroner made his report: The first story claimed 200 union miners tried to invade Company property. It also said the coroner confirmed that Virgil took twenty bullets to his head and chest.[81]

Then the reports began to change. The second article, the one that appeared in the *St. Clair Aegis* on November 1, 1935, read "One killed, many hurt." A single paragraph on page 5 called it a "deplorable affair . . . at Acmar and Margaret mines in this county last Monday, when one man was killed and a number were injured." Then the paper went on to say what was about to take place: "Judge Alto Lee called the grand jury to meet at Pell City . . . to investigate the affair . . . . If those killed were trespassing on private property, it is in our opinion, their fault; but if they were on the public highway of the state and county, we feel sure our officials will see that the ones guilty, are punished . . . . No one was surprised, as these mines have been armed camps for some time, and we hope our state and county officials will not stop until these affairs are curbed. We await official investigation before further comment."

Nine Company men went to jail, including the owner, Charles F. DeBardeleben. Birmingham papers did not carry the story.

On November 2, 1935, the Board of Directors of Alabama Fuel and Iron called an emergency meeting.[82] Notably absent was Charles F. DeBardeleben, whose shoes were filled by his brother, H. T. DeBardeleben. Alabama Fuel and Iron Company declared bankruptcy. But because they planned to reorganize, those present set about writing another ad on behalf of the Company.

By November 7, the St. Clair County Grand Jury in Ashville, the first Grand Jury, reported they had examined 21 witnesses in the nine cases.[83] They returned one indictment for second degree murder but at first did not disclose either who had been indicted or the degree of indictment. Judge Lee made no comment on the report, discharging the jurymen immediately after the report was made. In time, the public learned that John Rich was indicted for second degree murder.[84]

Alabama Fuel and Iron Company put up a valiant defense, and their full-page ad appeared in the *St. Clair Aegis* on November 15. The ad assured the public that nobody but the Company could be trusted for the real "facts about the march on Margaret and Acmar mines."[85] An editorial in the same issue postulated that even if both the company and the union used the press to try to persuade the public, the fact was that a murder had been committed. The paper declined to take sides but declared it would await the action of the grand juries, wherever they were seated.

Judge Alto Lee first summoned a grand jury to Pell City on November 18 to investigate the murder of Virgil Thomas.[86] Then Judge Lee reconvened the grand jury in Ashville on November 25. Phone messages from reporters seeking further comment from the Company's executives went unanswered. By November 29, the St. Clair County Grand Jury re-convened in Ashville, after a two day investigation of the slaying. It returned no indictments.

The Alabama Supreme Court refused to stop any appropriate investigation of the disorders in spite of the fact that the Northern Division Grand Jury [Pell City] of St. Clair Circuit Court was sitting in the South Division [Asheville]. The Court could not decide whether such a move was even legal.

By December, the jury handed down fifteen indictments involving 52 men. Nine were charged with murder.[87] In the end, all the charges against the nine men were dropped.

The minutes of that last meeting of the Alabama Fuel and Iron Company contained praise for the company's attorney, Borden Burr, for a job well done.[88] Margaret mines closed. The 500 transplanted miners were left either to return to Mobile or to wander about looking for some other job.

Bradford left Margaret for good; he found work in a mine in New Blocton. Jerry followed his father after he saw Gertrude off to Birmingham. The two men never returned.

PART III

REASON AND PERSUASION

1. Evelyn and George

My mother drew her first breath in 1907 in Birmingham, Alabama. If her grandparents had their way, she would have been born in New York. The Smiths were Yankee financiers, involved somehow with Manufacturers and Traders Bank of New York, which in the late 19th century was one of many banks Henry Fairchild DeBardeleben courted in an attempt to save his fortune and the floundering mining industry in an upstart Birmingham.

Manufacturers and Traders did not save Birmingham. Andrew Carnegie did. Carnegie bought the future of Southern iron and steel, and turned it in to the South's grandest industrial complex of all—Tennessee Coal and Iron, or TCI. Thanks to Carnegie, DeBardeleben saved his fortune and acquired a few lesser stars for recruiting my grandparents to speculate in anything and everything they might find in Birmingham.

In 1883, Ben Coffin left New York to partner with J. D. Kirkpatrick in a sand and cement venture there. He brought his wife and daughters with him, but not his son. His son Harry chose to remain behind, partly because he was in the initial stages of wooing a New Jersey girl, Minnie Smith, daughter of John Edward and Mary Smith of Bayonne.

John Edward made it clear to young Harry that he had serious doubts about the South, and that it would be difficult if not impossible for Harry to marry his daughter and move her below the Mason Dixon line. Unlike his father, Harry was neither serious nor particularly motivated to excel, although in the end, he did both because Father Smith required all of his daughters' suitors to be well established. He set Henry F. DeBardeleben as the example of what a

Southerner could do if he put his mind to it. Harry understood perfectly well, and set about turning himself into Mr. Smith's image of a son-in-law: In between playing whist, boating and bicycling, Harry became a stockbroker.

Then, by a twist of fate, Minnie's mother chose Harry to be her daughter's escort for her own ball, which boosted his confidence. Although he agonized over the wording for some time, Harry sent Minnie an orchid along with a note designed to decide his fate.

> *My Darling Girl,*
>
> *I send you this flower with love. If you come down your stairs with the flower in your hair, I will know you will be mine. But if you should wear it on your dress, I will know my dearest, that you will not have me after all, and my heart will be broken. For always and ever my dearest,*
>
> *Your loving Harry.*

She did wear the flower in her hair. Harry was a happy man until he heard her father's demands, which were phrased as suggestions. John Edward suggested that he build his daughter a house just like the one she grew up in. And, because Birmingham reputedly dealt with cholera and typhoid fever during its summer months, he suggested that Harry allow his wife and any offspring they might have to spend their hot summers away from the unhealthy vapors of the South.

Obstacles at least put on hold if not overcome, the couple married and moved into a house on the upside of 20th Street, overlooking the Town of Highlands. Before too long, Harry built his version of the Smith house on 14th Avenue and Short 18th Street. Then, as June bugs began to fly, the family packed just about everything they owned, rode the train to Gilman's Depot, then went by car to Camp Merriwold in Upstate New York to wait out the summer months..

Even with all those precautions, John Edward Smith lived long enough to watch his youngest granddaughter fight for her life after contracting diphtheria, and see his grandson Harry Jr. lose his life to polio.

Evelyn made it to college, one year at Hollins College in Virginia, before the Depression hit. She returned to Birmingham, to Birmingham-Southern, where she met George Stafford, who had to leave Alabama Polytechnic where he had studied engineering for the same reason. The only magic left in the Magic City during those years was that its young people came home.

Harry must have admired George's honesty because he never placed excessive burdens on his shoulders. George was my father; his honesty came in the form of the two words he used most: *horsefeathers* and *baloney*. My father had no tolerance whatever for sham. My mother and father announced their engagement, which was long. When the wedding finally came and was over, the Sunday April 1, 1934 *Birmingham Age-Herald* read:

> *Society assembled at the Independent Presbyterian Church Saturday afternoon at 4:30 o'clock for the marriage of Miss Evelyn Coffin, daughter of Mr. and Mrs. Harry Welles Coffin, and George Stafford, son of Mrs. George T. Stafford, and the late Mr. Stafford, Dr. Henry M. Edmonds officiating at the ceremony.*

> *Mrs. C. W. Brooks presided at the organ, giving a program of music as the guests were ushered to their places, passing through an aisle of ribbons outlined with white candelabra that alternated with clusters of white snapdragons. Stocks graced the pews. The church was effectively decorated . . . .*

After the honeymoon and for years after that, my father woke my mother every morning singing *Indian Love Call*, which was the sum total of what either of them knew about Indians. He sang:

"When I'm calling you Oo-Oo-Oo, Oo-Oo-Oo," and she responded

"Will you answer too Oo-Oo-Oo, Oo-Oo-Oo-Oo?" Then, in unison:

"Then I will know, our love will come true;

You belong to me, I belong to you," after which my father put on his felt hat and left for work at the Birmingham Gas Company, and my mother sat down at her Underwood typewriter to write short stories for the newspaper.

When, after a respectable year or so, the grandmothers learned I was on the way, they decided that I and any siblings that might follow must begin life in a suitable house in a suitable neighborhood, preferably with a view. Luckily, both of Harry's sisters married architects. Aunt Lottie's husband, Walter Chaffee, was convalescing in Arizona, but Aunt Louie's husband, Harry B. Wheelock, was handily in Birmingham to design their home. They broke ground for the new house on Montevallo Road in 1936.

Any hopes Minnie Coffin might ever have cherished of civilizing my father were dashed during its construction. Her initial error was having her chauffeur drive her to the site every day to watch its progress, because she saw too much.

She watched her son-in-law bring in discarded, misshapen, burnt and cracked bricks from the brickyard's reject pile and asked him to take them back.

"Horsefeathers," he said.

She told him if he deleted the crown molding he would destroy the beautiful architecture.

"Baloney," he said.

Then, to add salt to the wound, he made jokes about his job at the Gas Company. He was welcomed in the best basements in Birmingham, he said.

Minnie also blamed him for not having the house ready when they brought me home from the nursery at South Highland Hospital, the old Robinson Clinic, to the chaos of hammers and nails. Now she was my grandmother, and she almost wept.

Conversely, Minnie adored cousin Cy, who was just as handsome as my father, but in a different way. Equally energetic, equally inventive, he appeared far more serious in attitude and dress, taller and slimmer, quiet and polite, and much beloved.

On his frequent visits, "Uncle" Cy and my father withdrew to the dining room table to invent things: Uncle Cy drawing variations of an engine without pistons, and my father sketching hydraulic assemblies and fifth wheels. When either of them made a break-through, they both shouted "War Eagle," Alabama Polytechnic's victory yell. When Harry Coffin died, which was just after I was born, it was Cy my father consulted. The two men designed a house for my grandmother Minnie right next door to ours, but one made unashamedly of concrete block.

But my grandmother did not live very long after her husband died. I was three by the time my Aunt Florence and her husband Jenks Gillem moved into the concrete block house that shared a driveway with ours. They had one daughter, also named Florence, whom they called "Toots."

My mother began life in a house that was never finished, which prompted her to do everything she knew how to do to counter my father's austerity. She cut flowers for the table and tied neat piles of clean linens with grosgrain ribbon. In those charmed days, she also played tennis, read widely and entertained friends. In a short time, I was blessed with a little brother named after my father whom they called "Tim."

When we grew old enough to understand, Daddy entertained us with poetry, but not so we might learn to appreciate it. His was diabolically garbled poetry, idiot medleys of old chestnuts like *Hiawatha*, the *Yarn of the Nancy Bell* and *The Midnight Ride of Paul Revere*. From him we learned:

> "Listen my children and you shall hear
> Hardly a man is now alive
> Since the midnight ride of Paul Revere,
> When Hiawatha stood and waited . . .
> And found alone on a piece of stone an elderly naval man.
> 'Twas by the shores of Gitchee Gumee
> By the Shining Big Sea Water
> That he upped with his heels and smothered his squeals . . .
> And I on the shores that round our coast,

From Deal to Ramsgate span,

Am the cook and the captain bold and the mate of the Nancy brig . . ."

Then the Japanese bombed Pearl Harbor. Within days Uncle Cy called to tell us he was on his way to enlist in the U.S. Army Air Force. My father hung up the phone, put on his brown felt hat and left for the recruiting office that same day. The recruiting office turned him down. His asthma, they said.

The next time we heard from Uncle Cy, he was already stationed in Europe. Daddy took it hard. He suspected that Uncle Jenks, who was on the Draft Board, had somehow kept him out of the service. So he applied again, because every man in his family answered any call to serve their country. But it made no difference. He was rejected again.

Then the events in our lives took a peculiar turn. He came home one day singing.

"I am quitting the gas company," he said. "I am going to work for the War Production Board and the government of the United States." Then he let out a blood-curdling "War Eagle."

He rented our new home out to strangers, and we left for Mobile. The Marines had landed.

The WPB expected my father to encourage every small manufacturing concern to turn its plant into a war machine, to cease making peacetime goods and begin making accoutrements of war. And he set about turning the country's plowshares into swords. He showed companies that made cereal, toys, silk stockings and automobiles how to make K Rations, ball bearings, parachutes, war planes, tanks and guns for our armed forces. All this manufacturing meant the country had an insatiable desire for more and more trained men and women.

Among those able-bodied men in Mobile who were anxious to work were many of the miners from Margaret and Overton who had recently been made homeless when the Company closed its mines. These men knew nothing about mining when Alabama Fuel and Iron brought them to work in Margaret and even less about making war goods now, but they were eternally hopeful. When Uncle Sam instituted training courses to fill the gaps and keep the war machinery moving, they signed up in droves to learn whatever Uncle Sam wanted to teach them.

Whoever trained got the job. As Mobile's population grew, so did violence. Most of the violence was directed at Negroes as they trained for what some considered white men's jobs. Fights broke out all the time. White workers struck again and again in protest. There came a time when the strikes were perhaps a greater threat to the war effort than the enemy, and the WPB made an urgent appeal to the president, with the result that President Roosevelt declared that unions involved in the war effort could no longer strike. My father was grateful.

The docks experienced an uneasy, enforced peace, but it was not long before a delegation of Negro workers came to see my father in his office. They had one very odd request to make of the WPB:

"Please, Sir, we beg you. Can you do something to help us? We have come to beg you to reduce our pay."

"What on earth!" He was so astonished he could not even form his question.

This, they told him, was the only way they could think of to save their jobs and themselves. They said they faced so much violence every single day that most of them were afraid to go to work. The President's action, necessary as it was, did not address the reason for the strikes. My father obliged, and the men went home with less money in their pockets.

We all lived together during that war—my father, my mother, my brother Tim, my grandmother Margot—by now known as "Bam"—my Uncle Joe, and me. We lived for a time in the old Cochran mansion on Government Street; we were the fortunate ones in all respects but one. My mother confined us pre-schoolers to our own yard because she heard Mobile had sailors, and she had an inordinate fear of drunken sailors. We never went anywhere outside the confines of our own yard except for one thing: Uncle Joe took us on morning walks to the beach on rare occasions. We never saw sailors on those walks, but we saw pirates—or rather evidence of pirates. Uncle Joe told stories about the pirates, who had long ago buried treasure in those sand dunes, and he pointed out exactly where those pirates had been, which sent us scrambling until we found some of the treasure. We always found a coin here and there, and when we did, Uncle Joe reached in his pocket and rewarded us with a stick of Teaberry gum.

Bam always stayed behind. When we returned from these adventures, we found her working crossword puzzles or crocheting, sitting in the same place she had sat all day, which was beside a window in the front parlor of that great cavernous house. She would smile at me when I came in and make sure I did not track sand in.

There were days, though, when I came home after some such outing to find her sitting in a darkened room, her hands folded listlessly in her lap. On those days there was not a single new square in the basket. I carried this picture of her with me. It became my image of sadness, the kind of sadness that torments the old and the useless.

She and I shared a bedroom. We also shared the great mahogany feather bed in it. That bed was so high up off the floor, its turned legs so long, that neither of us could climb in without the aid of a step stool. When we were safely tucked in and the lights went out, we sank into the mattress together and she told me stories.

She painted glorious pictures of formal banquets in houses like the one we were in, elegant balls given before the War and famous visitors like the Marquis de Lafayette. She seemed to grow taller when she told me that Mobile's Mardis Gras was the first one, even before the one in New Orleans. Mobile's balls were more elegant, too, she told me. I never doubted her.

Tim and I never tired of exploring. Behind the great paneled mahogany doors at the far end of the long hall was a grand ballroom. It was a secret room, its doors closed and locked against small children, but we were small and could lie flat on the floor and see everything inside from the gap under the door. Beyond our reach was a vast room, its floors waxed a brilliant red-orange, its walls adorned with portraits of unknown dignitaries, framed in gold.

I saw even beyond that. Elegant dancers, ghosts of ladies in ruffled gowns waltzing, swirling their pastel skirts, offering their gloved hands to handsome men dressed in tails. The man always bowing low to his lady, then leading her away to the next dance. I could not see the musicians, but I could hear dancing music like the Virginia Reel. I saw them plain as day, couples holding hands, flirting and laughing.

When I watched, I waited. I was sure Lafayette would appear any minute, that he would bow at the waist and kiss his lady's hand, which I was certain was my grandmother's hand. I waited for the dance to be over so I might see Lafayette give her the little silver snuff box she had shown me. He never came, but I knew he had been. I had the proof. I had seen the snuff box.

What a blow, years later, to find out that not only did Lafayette give dozens of such trinkets to every young lady imaginable, but my grandmother was not even born when all that took place. I consoled myself with the possibility that it might have been her mother dancing that day. After all, the silver box was real.

The World War seemed both far away and very near. We ate the most beautiful desserts—chocolate cake with chocolate icing, lemon meringue pie, coconut cake, and pistachio ice cream, Uncle Joe's favorite—at a cafeteria called Britlings.

The unspoken edge to this agreeable life came in the form of intrigue. German submarines cruised in Mobile harbor. American sailors drank their way through the streets of Mobile at night. Rumors flew that divers had recovered a German submarine in Mobile Bay that had two dead Germans inside. When the authorities examined their bodies, they found ticket stubs from a local picture show in their pockets. This gave us the shivers.

Meanwhile, the WPB successfully transformed business after business. Men congratulated themselves and each other as Alabama Dry Dock and

Shipbuilding Company went into high gear, launching hundreds of new Liberty Ships every day. Brookley Army Air Field flew at least one new B-2 over our heads every hour. My father reckoned Uncle Cy was flying one. We lived in the midst of perhaps the most productive war endeavor ever. Whatever B-2s and Liberty Ships meant to the war effort, they meant romance and adventure to us children. We felt the tensions of important secrets in the streets. Mobile was not a totally out-of-the-question enemy target.

Bam spent her time instructing us, her captive grandchildren, in proper Southern behavior. As the girl child in custody, I was the recipient of most of the lessons. Tim's quiet smile and big brown eyes protected him from her attentions, even when he was guilty. He was endearing, they said, and endearing went a long way. I, the contrary child, needed a lot of direction.

She taught me every possible embroidery stitch and made me practice on a scrap of cloth every morning before I could go play. At night, she taught me how to walk with a book on my head to improve my posture, and in spite of the intense heat, she insisted I wear pajamas. Then, once I was ready for bed, she brushed my tangled, matted hair a hundred painful strokes. When I protested, she brushed faster. When the tears came, what she said to me made it even worse.

"A woman must suffer in order to be beautiful," she said.

In that case, I did not want to be beautiful. I consoled myself by looking cross-eyed at her, but this also backfired. She gave my hair a yank and informed me that my eyes would stick that way. I would be cross-eyed forever. After that, I was careful not to let her see me do it.

Then came my lessons in the language of the South. These were the lessons we were most carefully taught. We said "yes, ma'am" and "yes, sir" to adults and referred to them as "ladies" and "gentlemen," but if these adults happened to be colored, they mysteriously became "men" and "women" rather than "ladies" and "gentlemen." This made absolutely no sense to me, and as my grandmother had no answer when I asked *why*, I called all people ladies and gentlemen, regardless. This was much easier and fairer for everybody as far as I was concerned.

The only relief from these tortuous sessions came on the nights we had air raids. Bam put the brush down as soon as we heard the loud wailing and hustled me out into the hall and down the stairs. The sounds came at us from every direction. On those nights, once we settled in, Tim and I discussed whether what we were hearing indicated that our bombers were flying away from us toward a battlefield in order to kill Germans or whether they were enemy bombers coming our way with their sights aimed directly at our house.

It didn't matter. My mother treated air raids all alike. She closed the blackout shades tight so no tell-tale flicker of light ever escaped our windows. If we should let that happen, we would endanger our neighbors. Such an act would have been treason. After the last blackout shade was closed and only then, she herded us into a hall closet where she kept a stash of Hershey bars.

Bam sat in the closet with us on those air raid nights, crocheting away by a single light bulb, making crocheted squares. These would become a crocheted bedspread for me when I grew up, she said.

Uncle Joe was our Air Raid warden. As soon as he heard the siren blow, he grabbed his coat and hat and ran out to save us from Nazis, real or imagined. By the time our last blackout shade was closed, he had already made his rounds in the streets.

Then orders came. We moved again—this time to Jackson, Mississippi. Bam did not go with us after we left Mobile. She and Uncle Joe returned to Birmingham, and I missed them. I also missed the house with the gingerbread gables and the wide front porch with its rocking chairs. I missed the empty ballroom and the feather beds and the walks among the sand dunes.

We were just the four of us now—my mother, my father, Tim and me. We took the old Dodge with its sign on the passenger window that asked,

"Is This Trip Really Necessary?"

That sign followed us everywhere, all through the war years. It was all anyone ever needed to know about gas rationing; its words made an impact that lasted my entire life, in the same way the Great Depression affected my father.

As we pulled into Jackson, Mississippi, at least from my vantage point in the back seat, I could not tell where the center of Jackson began or ended. Nothing stood out: no tall buildings and no pretty steeples, just strings of one-storied shops, as bare and regular as a convoy of tanks. The town itself was unwelcoming, discouraging. All its signs gave orders: "Enter Here," "Buy Your Dry Goods Here," "No Coloreds Allowed."

The Dodge slowed down. My father turned into a side street to look for house numbers, but there were none. The task was made even more difficult by the fact that the houses all looked alike. Most of them were row houses with peeling paint and roofs made of some nondescript material that buckled. Each house had three concrete steps in front that led up to a front door, and all the doors had screens. Whenever a screen door slammed, I could tell by the decibels of the slam whether the occupant's mood was good or bad.

Some of the greener yards harbored struggling patches of vegetables we called "Victory Gardens." The bare dirt on the others meant some wartime housing crew had abandoned a new homeowner to a struggle with sticky red clay, on which nothing would grow.

Until that first day in Jackson, my brother had been my sole companion. All at once, I was surrounded by children running in the street, shouting and banging screen doors. Mississippi was on display.

Across the street stood the only house on the block painted Army brown-green instead of white. In that house lived a nervous, skinny kid with wild yellow hair and a high-pitched voice that carried from one end of the street to the other. He wore short brown pants and suspenders, and ran free with two unfriendly dogs that barked and snarled at every passersby. In the evenings the whole neighborhood heard his mother call him.

"George A-a-a-a-albert"! She usually repeated this several times.

When George Albert was at home, his two big mutts sat menacingly on their haunches on the front steps, watching and waiting. They apparently had no names. They answered to "Sic 'em" by dashing into the street to bark and bite at a colored man or to jump on some unsuspecting child. I watched these episodes in horror.

Down the street in full view was the elementary school where I was to start first grade. Nothing I knew could prevent that first day of school when I would have to leave the safety of my own screen porch. When that day came I hung back, waiting for someone from that scary household to feed the dogs so I could sling my first-grade book satchel over my shoulder, take a deep breath and move as quietly as I could down the steps and into the road. Even when the bowls appeared, those evil dogs looked at me and growled. I walked straight ahead and out into the street without turning my head. I usually made it.

One day, though, the barking from behind me came closer until I felt heavy paws push me and smelled horrible dog breath. I went down, a hushed lump of girl human, limp with terror. Then I heard George Albert.

"Hoo boy!" was all he said. All I could see from under that dog was a set of sunburnt bare legs. "Git! Git!" George Albert was not very big, but I guessed he was older than I was. It turned out he was in second grade.

"Hey, boy, I said git." The dog lifted his paws off me.

If this was George Albert's idea of fun, I hated it and I hated George Albert and everybody else in that paint-peeling house. My body shook, but I didn't cry.

About then, George Albert saw the blood seeping out of the scrapes on my knees and running down my legs onto my white socks. Because my mother made sure her children took clean handkerchiefs every day, I pulled one out of my pocket to stem the leak. I could no longer control my sniffling. George Albert came over and snatched the cloth out of my hand.

"Oh, shut up," he said

"If I said 'shut up' my mother would wash my mouth out with soap," I said, and stood up.

For a minute I thought he was going to hit me, but instead he snatched the handkerchief out of my hand and tied it tight around my knee. I had to sniffle on my sleeve. We walked more or less together toward school, he on his side of the road and me on mine, in silence. After that, George Albert kept his dogs off by managing to walk down the street at the exact same time I did every morning. I was not all that happy about it but then again, I probably had no choice.

Coming home was the same story, George Albert walked right through other peoples' yards and stomped on their tiny Victory gardens, picking their peas and digging up their potatoes. He ate them raw and decided I needed to do the same. He crossed the street to my side.

"Raw potatoes are good for you," he said.

"They taste like dirt," I said and refused them.

George Albert also loved fire. His pockets were always full of matches that he loved to strike on the pavement and wave close to my eyes just as they fizzed their brightest. He also flung lighted matches into the bushes along the way home. He was enjoying this particular pastime one day, while we were crossing through a vacant lot, when one of those lighted matches landed in some matted undergrowth and set it ablaze.

George Albert did a dance as the flames took hold, sweeping through the underbrush and climbing up stalks of dead grass, until he had quite a blaze going. A haze of dark smoke began licking at the trees and quickly developed into a black smokestack that reached the sky. He laughed and clapped his hands, jumping up and down, even as we heard sirens.

A fire truck rounded the corner. George Albert grabbed a fallen pine branch that had a tuft of needles on one end as thick as any broom, and began to beat at the edges of the fire. By now the whole field was on fire, with the hottest part in the center, out of control, unreachable. George Albert whacked in earnest.

"Help!" He called out to nobody in particular. It sounded like "Ha-a-a-lp." Then, when the first firemen stepped off the fire truck, he called out "I'm putting it out! I'm putting it out!" He tried to hand me a branch about that time, but my fingers were squeezed into fists right up by my chin by then. I wanted no part of it.

"Now son, you just go on, lest you get hurt. We'll take it from here," was all the fireman said. I had to hand it to George Albert.

Not long after those firemen had the fire under control and we were on the way home, George Albert told me about his club. The club had no name and no reason for being other than to glorify George Albert. He said he already had two boys in his club, and he had decided to let a girl in. But first I had to pass initiation.

I had not come across the word *initiation* yet. *Dare you* I understood. Nobody walked away from a dare. But *initiation?* Apparently that involved a choice. The way George Albert explained it was that when his father wanted to join a certain club, he had to do stuff to prove his loyalty. Once he did what the club told him to do, he was entitled to wear a white robe. That was initiation. I never found out what stuff his father had to do or get any kind of satisfactory answer about anything. But I never turned down a dare and guessed I wouldn't turn down an initiation.

The boys and George Albert and I gathered the next afternoon at one end of the burnt field. The boys were first graders like me, and it soon came to my attention that they had not yet done an initiation either. George Albert chewed on stolen raw peas. I could still escape, but I was curious.

"Dig me up a pie," he told one of the boys.

The kid dug down through the charred underbrush and scooped up a handful of fresh wet dirt and squashed it into a little hamburger.

"Eat it, Rat," he said. The boy took a bite.

George Albert made me eat one tasteless gritty bite before I threw the rest on the ground. He let that pass. We then had to learn the words to *Way Down upon the Sewanee River* and sing it. My initiation ended. I was in.

Then, right in the middle of first grade, before I even had a chance to prove myself as part of the boys' gang, the War ended. My father packed us up and moved us back to Birmingham. My mother wanted to detour to Mobile, just to see it again, but my father pointed to that inescapable sign in the window:

"Is This Trip Really Necessary?"

Mobile was not necessary. We left Jackson for good and headed directly to Birmingham, expecting to move back into our house on Montevallo Road so I could go to Crestline Heights School where I would finish first grade. It did not work out that way, though.

2. The First Vice-President

There was a housing shortage after the War, and the wartime tenants in our house refused to budge. No amount of compromise, no bribes and no humiliating begging stirred them. My father mentioned tear gas, but instead found us lodging in two tiny rooms, three floors up in a derelict brick apartment building on Highland Avenue.

My parents occupied the bedroom. Tim and I slept in the kitchen-living-dining room on folding cots. We shared our room with a stove, a rattling refrigerator and sundry living creatures. We ate together on a table designed for two and served ourselves from casseroles balanced on top of a very old refrigerator. Those dishes shook so from the refrigerator's vibrations that they walked slowly but steadily across the top of the refrigerator and would have crashed to the floor had my father not been quick enough to catch them.

The roaches in our apartment were big enough to catch casserole dishes by themselves. Thus I began to understand my seesaw life. I knew I would always have times of endless desert and times of plenty, sometimes roaches and sometimes ribbons. It would never be the same. We children learned to be grateful.

The squatters finally left, and we went home. My mother cautiously opened each door, and each time she did, another tear ran down her cheek. She found cracks in the windowpanes and water rings on the piano. The house smelled funny, too. She sanitized the bathrooms then shooed Tim and me up to the unfinished attic to set up our Army cots. We spent that first night in the attic with the windows closed against the cold January air, and we slept the sleep of the dead.

The next morning, I crept downstairs to join the rest of the family. We were about to explore the kitchen. My mother led the way.

When we opened the kitchen door, the smell overwhelmed us. Mama went first, meaning to turn on the oven and warm the house, but the minute she opened the oven door, she let out a scream. My father came to the rescue.

In the back of the oven was a nest of squiggly, pink, embryonic mice, very much alive. My father took the rodents outside and gave us children heavy rags, along with instructions to scrub the kitchen with lye soap and rub everything down with alcohol after that. After Tim and I finished, my parents did it all over again

The house cleaned up nicely. Mama resumed tying clean towels with grosgrain ribbon and arranging fresh flowers for the table.

By the time spring rolled around, we were in the habit of spending our evenings gathered around the radio, listening to news of the War. The radio was in a polished oak cabinet that dominated the room. It was as tall as Tim and rounded at the top; it had built-in speakers on both sides of a huge dial that looked like a nose. My mother won it the year before for one of her short stories.

The night of May 2, 1945, the announcer interrupted our program to tell us that the war was over in Europe. Adolf Hitler had committed suicide. Berlin had surrendered. It seemed right that we should go outside, where all our neighbors were doing the same. Standing there in the dark while doors were opening and lights were coming on all around us, it was as though we could actually see all the way to Europe. We were in a world outside of ourselves, and every house in the valley was as awake as we were. The feeling of being awake was palpable.

Aunt Florence came over from next door with her tea biscuits, which she kept hidden in her breadbox for special occasions. Neighbors began to walk through each other's yards, sharing emotional tears and handshakes. We celebrated quietly, still not sure, because our neighbors and Uncle Cy were still away. As the night wore on, we finally gave in and went to bed, and the next day woke to a joyful peace. Our exuberance lasted for several days.

Then came the evening that somebody knocked on our door. Expecting another neighbor, we opened it gladly, only to find two uniformed officers standing uncomfortably on the steps. They handed an envelope to my father and expressed their condolences.

Lieutenant Colonel Cyrus Black Stafford's plane was shot down over France in the early morning of May 3, 1945. The Air Force had recovered his body.

But the war ended on May 2. How could such a thing happen? Routine mission, they said. My father went walking that night, and it was a long time before he came home. He did not sleep that night at all, but between his asthma and his snoring, he didn't sleep much anyway.

In spite of all the cleaning and painting and washing and mowing, my father and I still suffered from asthma. We both struggled for breath. Tim apparently escaped it. Once, when my father was away on business, my mother wrote him a letter. "Dammit," she wrote. "Your daughter has a cold again."

The doctor prescribed a croup kettle, an apparatus that plugged in to the wall and filled the room with nauseous vapors. I lay in bed with smelly steam aimed directly at my head but other than making me feel sick, it did little. It was all I could do to keep my airways open. Falling asleep meant not breathing.

I was my parents' problem. They stood for hours at the foot of my bed, wringing their hands until they could stay awake no longer. When my lights went out and the only sound was my wheezing, my brother padded across the hall. He crawled into bed with me and fell quickly asleep. That was a comfort, but it did not change the reality of my struggling to breathe.

My parents went sleepless for several years before my father finally spoke to Dr. Mason. Dr. Jim was our everything doctor, and he said my tonsils needed to come out.

"How much?" asked my father. This was always the deciding factor.

"Well, the hospital will charge $50 for the room. There will be a small charge for ether and, of course, for me." Dr. Jim never charged much. After all, he told my parents, a tonsillectomy was a common procedure. Most children underwent a tonsillectomy at some point.

My father digested this information for a minute. "You mean Tim might need a tonsillectomy someday, too?"

"Let's say it is always a possibility, but I can't say for sure. Right now we have to try it for your daughter's sake."

"Do you suppose you could do two for one?"

"Really?"

"Really."

So it was decided: Tim and I shared a hospital room, nurses, ether and Dr. Jim. We fought bravely when the nurse smothered us with a mask reeking of ether. We passed out at the same time and woke up nauseous and vomiting at the same time, but we ate our first ice chips free from tonsils. We would survive.

The operation helped me. Tim, however, began to cough for the first time. We came home, one better and one worse.

After the war, my father went to work for Fontaine Truck Equipment Company, but he was always thinking ahead. He kept piles of papers in leather binders and drawers full of inventions and engineering ideas, some of which he gave gratis to J.P.K. Fontaine. He kept a teakettle whistling on the stove and drank cup after cup of instant coffee well into the night. Something about giving his inventions away kept him awake.

The night he turned down the fire under the teakettle and invited my mother to sit down for a cup of coffee, I knew he had come up with a momentous idea. That night he told her he planned to start his own business. All he needed was a little capital, and he had it figured out. As he saw it, he could sell my mother's car, the car she inherited from her mother, our only car, and start his own business.

"No, George." She was aghast. "We need that car. Anyway, it's my car."

"Think about the future," he said. "Think about the cost of school. Think about how much the new baby is going to cost and the doctor bills." She was expecting another, true. But she was not moved.

"George, how can you? How can you even *think* about selling my car? It's all I have."

She argued that he should stay where he was, that he had a real future with Fontaine. He in turn tried to make her understand that a future with Fontaine was not much of a future for him. He had it figured out, and he promised he would make it up to her.

My mother focused on a spot on the tablecloth and her eyes narrowed. In the end he won, of course. The way he chose to make it up to her was by making her first vice-president of his new company. She was not impressed, but said nothing. Instead, she just asked him what he planned to do for a car.

"I can use Brumby's car," he said. Mr. Brumby *wa*s his good friend. He owned a black '38 Chevrolet with a running board. "He suggested it. It was his idea."

"I still think we should wait," she said limply.

"All things come to he who sits and waits provided he worketh like hell while he waiteth."

In April 1946, two years after my brother Harry was born, Birmingham Manufacturing Company—BIRMCO for short—was born. I am not sure my mother ever really forgave him.

My father owned 80 shares in the new company, his friend Harry Ross owned 60, and Arnoldus S. Brumby owned 40—a value reckoned to be equal to rent for a car and an old building on First Avenue South downtown. My father and his first eight men built their first trailer there in one week.

The Company soon outgrew that first shop and moved to a larger facility: a Quonset hut at the airport that Bechtel McCone had used during the War to produce war materials and no longer needed. [89] At the time, BIRMCO manufactured anything anybody would pay for—milk trucks, flatbed railroad cars, floats for Mardi Gras. Birmingham's post-war slump left the government complex all but empty, but the Quonset hut was booming. When a fire destroyed the abandoned building next door, my father sawed off the burnt part and gained 200 more feet.

Southerners never really reconciled to any government. When Alabama voted Democratic, Birmingham turned Republican. The Republican Party was a pretty exclusive outfit at the time. They did obey the law, but in their own way. When the law required them to post public notice of their meetings, Birmingham's Republicans posted them on the back of somebody's tree. They thought it terribly funny.

My father was not a joiner then. He had no use for political parties or unions or country clubs and had only a healthy respect for churches.

He was also not a dresser. He wore serviceable brown pants and rough plaid shirts suitable for crawling around under trailers both because it was a practical thing to do and because he did not want to dress any better than his men. He stuck to that principle even when he called on the CEOs of Fruehauf or John Deere or Caterpillar or even the federal government. He was color blind, which meant he wore socks of different colors unless my mother caught him before he put them on, and he wore the same old brown felt hat to and from work and to church on Sundays. If he went.

Which was why that Christmas his men pitched in and bought him a nice gray suit. He thanked them. Not knowing what else to do, he hung it in the closet in its original zippered bag.

"All hands on deck!" he said one day.

That was how he summoned us when we were about to be loaded into Mr. Brumby's car and carted off to sweep the plant or lick stamps or run errands. We were child labor, unpaid, but we understood: Work was his peculiar and only way of expressing love. His work ethic reached its apogee every Labor Day, which we were informed was a day meant for labor, a day set aside to weed the garden or paint the hall. We painted the hall just about every Labor

Day, but this year we had run out of paint. Not to be discouraged, he piled us all in the car and drove to Sherwin Williams for a can of lead white.

The blue-collared salesman looked over his glasses at my father, who was about his height. In an unpleasantly authoritative voice, the clerk told him he would not sell him any lead white paint.

"What?" demanded my father.

"I'm saying you cannot buy lead paint. The government has outlawed it."

"So what am I supposed to do? Do you have some in the back? Some old stock?"

"I have titanium white." The clerk slammed an unopened can down on the counter and glared at my father, who glared back. My father shook his finger threateningly at him.

"I refuse to use such an inferior product. How can you sell that stuff? It doesn't even cover!" Then he added, "It's not even white."

When he stopped grousing, he made it clear to the clerk that he was unconvinced and extremely unhappy with the government's decision. We took the dreaded titanium white home and painted the blue walls white in two unhappy coats.

Until that very moment, my father explained, he had gladly paid his taxes because the government used that tax money wisely, to take care of the sick and the poor. The government was a benevolent entity, and he its dutiful patriot— until that day.

Our neighbors swore at the government for a different reason. They did not want any kind of taxes, the sick and the poor notwithstanding. That is why they voted Eisenhower into office and why they voted Eisenhower out. This is why they voted anybody in and why they voted anybody out, no matter who.

3. Daphne Du Maurier

My mother's book club met at our house because she did not have a car. She soon became their primary book reviewer. Her assignment for that week was the book on which Hitchcock's new movie was based, Daphne du Maurier's *Rebecca*.

"I have to study," she told us one day after school. We were spread out on the floor reading comics. "How about going outside for me?"

"Why?" I stalled.

"I have to study for my book review. And you two cannot sit still."

Tim, the obedient one, went out. I did not move. To my surprise, I was not immediately banished.

"If you can sit still, I will let you help me practice my review, and perhaps if you do a good job I will take you on the bus down to Woolworth's for a chocolate soda."

"Okay!" I wanted so to be in that room with my mother, but until she tempted me with the soda, I was not sure she wanted me. "What do you want me to do?"

Just listen, she said. That's all. I flopped down on the floor on my stomach with my head in my hands, gazing up at my mother. Her soft brown hair curled close to her ears, flapper style. She could do the Charleston, too, and as she spoke, I truly believed that I was part of her adult life. I wanted to read that book more than anything.

I was not discriminating in what I read. At that moment I was half way through the *Niebelunglied*.

The hero had gone off to war. While he was away, a stranger had come into his wife's bedroom. She mistook him for her husband and let him sleep with her. I had questions about that, but I did not want to interrupt her.

"*Rebecca*, by Daphne du Maurier . . ."

This slim, brilliant, fashionable lady was my mother. I could sit at her feet forever.

"Daphne du Maurier and I were born in the same year."

When she finished, she gave me permission to invite a friend over to make doughnuts. This was even better than going to Woolworth's. I was ecstatic. I asked Harriett—who lived down the hill, Marilyn—whose yard I cut through on the way to school, and Carol—who owned two cocker spaniels.

The four of us trouped into our fashionable black and white kitchen ready to cook. This kitchen had it all: a shiny black ceiling, a black and white linoleum floor and cabinets with built-in flour sifters and cutting boards. Mother was no cook, but you couldn't tell by the kitchen. Aunt Florence was even less a cook than my mother was. Uncle Jenks complained she only knew how to make Jell-O when she married. Their mother fell down on the job, and I think my mother intended to teach me how to cook once she learned how herself.

That afternoon she wore a white organdy apron, by no means a utilitarian apron, tied in a bow behind her back. Pastel flowers, like those that grew in my aunt's garden, were embroidered on its bodice. Utensils and ingredients were assembled, and we soon found ourselves in front of a mountain of rising dough.

It was all ours. We slung fists full of puffy dough onto the cutting board and beat the stuff flat with the rolling pin until the dough was thin enough to cut into shapes. The cutter cut the doughnut and the hole at the same time, and we dropped each piece by itself into the simmering Wesson oil, spattering grease every time. Never mind the damage, the smell of hot oil and melting sugar was heaven come down. We pushed and shoved each other for a better view of the boiling oil, and squealed when the browning doughnuts bubbled their way to the top. My mother took over when it came time to dip the now browned doughnuts out of the oil, but she let us coat them in powdered sugar in brown paper sacks.

We shook those bags as hard as we could, oblivious to burnt fingers and flour in our hair. Powdered sugar dust covered everything, including the black ceiling, where it stuck forever. By the time we were eating our doughnuts, the damage was so severe that clean-up would have to wait until the next day. No party was ever again as good as that one.

My mother woke me early the next morning to come help in the kitchen. As soon as I saw her, I knew something was wrong. She looked pale and leaned against the cabinet, holding tight to the kitchen counter as though she were afraid she might fall.

"Are you sick?" She had never been sick.

"Don't worry. I will be fine." She cleaned some of the grease off the counter. "The ladies will be here soon, and we still have sandwiches to make. And tea."

We cut the crusts off of soft white bread and held the slices together with sweet cream cheese and onion. We built pink layers and green layers, one on top of the other. She asked me to slice down across the layers, so they would become beautiful rainbow sandwiches. I did as she asked, wielding a kitchen knife for the first time, but she did not watch me. She was looking at the oily white stains on the black ceiling.

Finally, she beckoned me over to the sink. "I think you are going to have to do the cleaning up today."

I pulled the metal step-stool over by the sink, climbed up and filled the sink with soapy water. "Okay," I said.

"'Okay' is not the way you talk to grown-ups. Always address a grown-up with 'Yes, ma'am' or 'Yes, sir.'"

"OK. I mean, yes, ma'am."

"That's a good girl." She seemed distant. "I think I will go lie down a minute." She left the kitchen.

I spent hours making rainbow bubbles in the hot soapy water. Soap bubbling was an art, so I took my time. Tim came in with his night clothes on, but he helped me dry. The day wore on and a cloud passed over the sun. We ran out of rainbows.

Finally I took Tim by the hand to get him dressed, but we never made it past my mother's door. A loud thump, like something falling, stopped us. We opened the door to see her lying very still on the floor.

After the ambulance left, some of the ladies who came for the book review herded us children next door. Late that evening, my aunt tried to explain how a surgeon had to cut a dead baby out of my mother's stomach. I never thought until much later to ask how it got there. She told us my mother was still asleep.

When my father came by, I heard him tell Aunt Florence that she was given too much ether, and that she died on the operating table, but only for several minutes. The doctors had coaxed her back to life and had told my father that she needed all her strength to recover, which meant she could not come home to a house full of children.

She moved in with my aunt, and my father was left to run the house in his own way. We ate a lot of canned salmon and green peas. If we had anything left over from dinner, he incorporated it into an omelet the next morning. We learned to eat salmon and pea omelets. If anything was left from breakfast, it was stirred into soup that night. We often had some variety of scrambled egg and oatmeal soup for supper. But on Sundays we had a real meal at my Great Aunt Sue Graham's house, where Bam lived. The Grahams cooked for at least fourteen relatives every Sunday.

In the hours before those dinners, we children watched Hattie catch chickens. She wrung their necks, and the poor disoriented fowls ran in blind circles on the bare earth.

"Come here young 'uns," she called to us. "I want you to pluck these feathers for me. Just rub them with this ice and the feathers just fall out. That's the way."

I watched and thought I understood the secrets of cooking fresh butter beans, fried chicken, mashed potatoes and gravy, fried corn, sweet rolls with butter, fresh figs and fresh churned ice cream made with real cream. There were times I tried to copy what I had seen to avoid salmon and peas, but without much luck.

After those Sunday dinners, the adults excused the children from the table so they could go outside. That part of those Sundays was the best. We waited for four o'clock. At four o'clock things started happening: The gandy dancers churned their stump of a train down the tracks that ran behind Sterling Road at exactly four o'clock, and the four o'clocks bloomed at the same time. We picked the flowers and strung them into necklaces, then chased the gandy dancers as they passed. Once they were out of sight, we slid down the grassy hill to return to our motherless home.

When she finally came home, a nurse came home with her, but the nurse only stayed a short time. My mother looked fine, but she was not the same. She found it harder and harder to do the things she had always done before.

My father encouraged her in his own way: He brought stacks of work home and talked to her about the company, his men, the union. He wanted to see happiness in her eyes when he brought in new business, and he looked for sympathy in his crises. She responded, but barely. Then he told her something he believed would change all that. It called for a celebration.

"We are in the black!" he said.

"I am so glad," she said, but she still didn't seem glad. She appeared mildly interested at best.

He tried again, desperate for her to celebrate with him. Finally, she understood and rose to kiss him. In that rare, conscious moment, she was the first vice-president.

He proposed they take a vacation, but confided in me that he must have been crazy because I knew he never took a day off. He was doing this only to please my mother, he said. But when the time came, I heard him singing *The Road to Mandalay* in the shower and again while he was packing the old Dodge.

Part of his happiness came from the fact that we now owned a new old Dodge—a replacement for Mr. Brumby's car

My father planned a trip to the beach and invited Alec Davies's family along. Alec was his childhood friend whom he consulted on important matters, such as what material to use for roofing, which is why our two families owned the only two steel roofs in Mountain Brook.

We set off down the Florida Short Route in separate cars. I kept my eyes on the road, watching hot tar patches swim on the pavement. When we stopped for necessities along the side of the road, I made tiny tar balls to play with along the way. After one such stop, my father decided that he and Alec should swap cars. Just to try them out.

Alec drove a new Chevrolet that ran well over 50 miles an hour. He reluctantly turned it over to my father. Then he and his wife climbed into the Dodge with us children. The Chevrolet was already disappearing into the horizon.

The new old Dodge was not quite so game: Its door rattled so that Mrs. Davies had to hold it shut, and Mr. Davies cautioned her not to fall out. When he found another place to pull over, he stopped the car and fished around in the trunk. He soon came back with wire and a number of tools, but in the end resorted to wiring the door shut from outside. We rattled on toward Port St. Joe, a peninsula in Florida's Panhandle, on a road that soon became nothing more than a narrow spit of sand with water lapping up over both sides.

We children stayed glued to the window, fascinated that we might drive straight into the sea. But we did not. At the end of the road was a two-story brick house with a nice green lawn, much like houses in Birmingham. The Dodge pulled in beside the Chevy, whose occupants had long since deserted it for the comforts of the house.

An older fellow helped gather the children and belongings. Alec introduced him.

"Kiddos, this gentleman is Sam. He runs the place."

We said how do you do and shook his hand, then followed him inside while our fathers went off to tackle the loose car door. Once luggage and food were deposited, Sam picked up a bucket and some string, and off we went to the shore. Eddies of salt water swirled around our legs as we waded in to the shallows of the Gulf. I fell in love then with everything about those waters—the immenseness of it and the minuteness of it, especially the tiny multicolored shells, the starfish and angel's wings. Those with living creatures inside we threw back to live another day. We filled our bathing suits with sea treasures while Sam busied himself with fish heads and string. It was all excruciatingly beautiful.

"All you chillun, come over here!"

He showed us how to tie a fish head on string and fling it out as far as we could so it would come to rest on a shelf of white sand under the blue water. He told us to hold on to the string until we could see a crab sidle over and grab that head. Sure enough, a crab grabbed hold of my fish head, and with Sam's instructions, I pulled it slowly through the water and hoisted into the bucket. The foolish crab would not let go; Sam had to knock it loose. In very short order, we had a bucket full of fighting crabs that we hauled back to the house.

Sam already had a fire going in a pit he had made in a ring of rocks. He covered it with a metal grate and put a pot of water on to boil. There was a little chill in the air, at least for August, and we huddled close. Then Sam did something that I never forgave him for.

He took my crab out of the bucket and broke its claws off first, then its legs, while it was still living. My gut wrenched with each twist, then he tossed the poor creature's body in the boiling water, where it turned red, its misery at an end. In the end, he taught us how to pick out the meat and eat it.

The next day began gloriously. Standing on the shore, we watched waves form and grow, until they were so large they rolled over and pitched white foam. By afternoon, wind was blowing in such fierce gusts that pine trees bent over, and the rain was stinging our faces. We would have stood on that beach all day if the adults had not called us. They herded us in behind the screen door, which banged crazily in the wind until we hooked it.

From the porch, we watched waves eat up the last bit of beach where we had stood and retreated farther into the bowels of the house, safe. We began an unquiet game of checkers.

That storm swamped us. Electricity went out; the phone made crackling sounds and quit; the road was awash. From the window, we could plainly see that the water no longer lapped the edges of the drive. It had swallowed the road entirely. We were on an island with no way out.

My father paced up and down, seemingly unaware of any danger but mumbling on and on about having to get back to work, more restless than any cat I ever saw. Alec tried to calm him, to seduce him into singing with the others, but he refused. He was inconsolable. He was trapped. And we were having a hurricane.

The adults tried to comfort us, but we didn't need comforting. We loved the ferocity of it. When the wind finally stopped its loudest roaring, we slept soundly, but when the sun came up, the road was still under water and my father was still pacing. My mother said he was *in a state.*

Outside, we children sloshed happily in giant puddles, some of which contained small fish. Sam climbed up a tall ladder to cover gaping holes in the roof with boards. Two days went by before we could tell where the road was, but it was impassable. Another three days and my anxious father told us our vacation was over. Nothing changed his mind. He made it very clear to us that if he could get back to Birmingham, he would never allow himself to be trapped like that again. We climbed into the Dodge, and I kissed my first and last real family vacation goodbye.

Back home, I tossed in my bed in the unfinished attic listening to the living night sounds of katydids and mosquitoes until daybreak. The end of August was brutal, even with windows flung wide. I threw off my covers and rolled up my pajamas to let my legs cool in the breeze. Finally, day began to break. I heard my father downstairs and smelled coffee brewing in the kitchen. Today, he had to take my mother to see Dr. Turlington. She had a lump in her breast.

That day, we learned that my mother, barely over the first surgery, was in for another. She had cancer. Mother was not as afraid of the cancer or the surgery as she was the dreaded anesthesia. But she kept her fears to herself.

The cancer had wrapped itself around so many glands and lymph nodes that Dr. Turlington took everything out. Then, almost immediately, he treated her with radium. Bam came to stay with us while my father and Aunt Florence waited at the hospital. Weeks, then months passed before we saw her.

She showed me then how the radium burnt her from her left arm all across the front of her chest to the right rib cage. I saw her heart beating under her translucent skin, and I saw vacancy in her eyes. By then, her left arm was badly swollen. Once more, she was not to come home until she was stronger.

My father never complained but resumed kitchen duties. Sometimes we ate out. On those occasions he told us we could order anything on the menu, as long as it didn't cost more than a dollar, which was very little.

He practiced his version of medicine on us, too. If any of us dared sneeze, he carted us off to a Mexican restaurant that had jars of datil peppers on each table. One red hot bite of those peppers cured any snot-nosed child instantly. I was living testament that it worked. I never missed a day of school.

Not everything he did was quite so draconian. He invented a special dessert for us, one that required placing a can of unopened sweetened condensed milk in a slow oven to cook all day while he was at work. In the evening, when he came home, he let the can cool. When he cut off both ends of the can, out came his beautifully caramelized dessert.

One evening, as he was hanging his hat in the closet, something exploded in the kitchen: The can was no longer. A sticky white film covered everything, including the newly painted ceiling. After hundreds of delicious, perfectly caramelized treats, one can exploded.

That night we ate egg foo young at Joy Young's behind beaded curtains. Bam said the family needed a real housekeeper, and my father ran an ad the very next day.

Christian woman wanted to cook and care for household with three small children. Room and board plus pay.

Less than a week after the ad appeared, I opened the door to a gracious-sized black woman in a starched blue dress over which was a crisp white apron. She clutched a big navy blue purse in her hand and smiled when she asked me if the lady of the house was in. I explained that the lady of the house was recovering from surgery next door, so I guessed I was the lady of the house.

"Are you coming to take care of my baby brothers?"

"Well, yes'm, and you too." She chuckled. Her laugh cut dimples in her cheeks.

I didn't know I was going to be taken care of, but it was fine with me. I thought even then a chuckle like that, by itself, might lighten all the spirits in the house that so desperately needed lightening.

She wore her hair parted in the middle and combed into a tight dark bun on the back of her neck. She was quick; her arms were constantly in motion, usually hitching up her bosoms—which frequently breached some hidden truss or other. Things that were supposed to keep bosoms in place never worked for Gertrude.

Tim wandered into the living room in short pants with his handkerchief stuck in his pocket. He looked up at Gertrude and asked her who she was, then took out his handkerchief and blew his nose. I told him to stop it because it wasn't polite, but the lady chuckled and told him he had to do what he had to do.

"I'm Gertrude," she said.

I smiled back at her. "Gertrude what?" I asked.

"Just Gertrude."

"It's got to be Gertrude Something. I can't just say *Gertrude*."

"Child, I think it's best if you do," and she broke into another grin that made even her eyes laugh. I invited her in and noticed she hitched up her dress in a different way: one that signified she was ready to go to work. It was her version of rolling up her sleeves. She walked on into the living room, giving it the once over, apparently satisfied. It was I who forgot something.

I forgot Bam was in the house until she came up beside me and touched my shoulder to tell me to move aside. She informed Gertrude that she must wait until my father came home. Then she turned to me and, in this newcomer's presence, explained that I had broken a cardinal rule. I was not to let any colored yard man or colored nurse or colored helper of any kind come in by way of the front door. This time, she said, was an exception because the woman in question probably did not know there was a back door.

I nodded in my discomfort, wanting to say something so as not to hurt this new person who I knew intuitively would join our family, but nothing came to mind. I was never any good at thinking on my feet.

Gertrude did not appear to be offended. She waited by herself in the living room for hours, clutching the purse on her lap. When my father finally came home, he offered her the job, which she accepted. Only then did she retrieve the rest of her belongings that still sat outside the front door.

Like all of our rooms, her room was not quite finished, but she moved in anyway. Her routine included a day off, Thursdays, so my father chose Thursdays to finish painting her room. On the other days, she cooked all our meals. All meals included dessert: a choice of lemon meringue pie, homemade ice cream, pecan pie, blackberry pie, and an occasional apple Brown Betty. Her reputation spread. Children from around the neighborhood showed up on Saturday mornings just to taste her waffles and hear her laugh. She fed stray children like stray cats, and she made sure there was enough.

It was a long, long time before I noticed anything at all odd about her. Tim saw it first, when she was threading a needle to mend his jumpers. The hand doing the threading only had a little finger and part of a thumb on it. I wondered how I could have missed it. She maneuvered pots and pans, irons and ironing boards at lightning speed.

"What happened to your hand?" Tim asked.

"Child, you got more questions!" Gertrude's eyes wrinkled up to laugh.

"So what did happen?" I took up the questioning.

"It was an accident."

"What kind of accident?" I wanted to know everything there was to know. Somehow Gertrude's deformity made her one of those rare and powerful beings who appear in fairy tales, like gnomes or trolls, trying to overcome some witch's curse, although she didn't resemble such creatures in any other way. Gertrude undoubtedly came from some mythic place.

"Well, you see, we lived right near some railroad tracks."

And where was that, I asked. Margaret, she said, then went on.

"One day my baby brother picked up a stick of dynamite and I just reached over and grabbed it out of his hand before it blowed up." She gave us a matter of fact answer, not a bid for sympathy. It was as much information as she ever gave on that subject. She wasn't given to long explanations, but I reckoned she lived through that moment in time and space when nothing and everything happens at once. In a place I could go only in my imagination.

"Oh, I'm sorry," I said. It was not an *I'm sorry* like the kind I said if I broke a vase but the kind of sorry that bubbled up from inside unbidden.

I had questions. Why was dynamite there in the first place? Did somebody want to hurt your baby brother? Why did it explode if you only touched it? Those questions made her sad, so I changed the subject.

"May I see your room sometime?"

"Sure. Soon as I finish flouring this chicken."

She cut that chicken into nine recognizable pieces, wishbone first. I watched entranced as she dredged each piece in a bowl of flour mixed with salt and pepper and set it aside to dry. What just hours before had been a Bantam hen running in and out of our chicken house in the back yard was now nine tidy pieces of floured meat on a dish in the middle of a red Formica table. Gertrude patted the last piece in place and washed her hands. Supper time would be soon, so the visit would be short.

We two went out the back kitchen door and down the concrete steps, through the afternoon shadows cast by a plum tree that was still in full bloom, to her porch. That was Gertrude's plum tree now, just as it was her room.

From the beginning, the architect drew a maid's room with its own entrance on the first floor of the house, but when Gertrude first came it was no more than a shell of raw concrete with a shower where we kept lawnmowers and wheelbarrows. I don't think my father ever fully understood that we might really need a maid's room; he just didn't see things that way.

The architect also drew in wrought iron burglar bars for every window and door. Gertrude's room was no exception, but because she never locked her door, they did her no good. She let me run ahead of her and busied herself taking off her apron. The walls of the room were by now painted eggshell blue; the shower was still raw concrete.

The sun faded as we talked—as I talked, mostly. Just outside her window, plum blossoms turned from daytime pink to sunset rose. A few roses and daffodils bloomed along the bank where my mother had planted them, and the sweet smell of honeysuckle trees and gardenias filled the air. Further down the hill stood my strong old water oak, my climbing tree, my thinking place.

Gertrude sat across from me in a rocking chair by the window. I sat on the edge of her white iron bed, bobbing just enough to make its springs squeak and running my hands over her spread. It was soft blue with a diamond pattern that contained white flowers with pale yellow centers. The diamonds were nappy like rough velvet. Chenille, she told me.

When I asked if she had any brothers and sisters, she rattled off musical names like Eva and Geneva and Jerry who lived in far-off places like Chicago and Margaret.

Then she told me she was descended from an Indian Chief.

"I never saw an Indian chief before," I said.

"Well, they ain't many nowadays." That stopped my questioning, at least for the time being. "Go on, now, get on upstairs. Your momma will be looking for you."

She brought the fried chicken in on a platter, and I counted nine pieces. After dinner I took my plate back to the kitchen and asked what she had for supper, because I had not seen a single piece of chicken left over. She told me in these exact words:

"Don't you worry none. I got plenty to eat."

But I did worry. It wasn't right, I told her.

When school was out and on weekends, Gertrude let us go outside after breakfast. Her only remonstrance was to be back before dark.

School was still in session, but all week long the students at Crestline Heights had been talking about a scientist who was offering fifty cents for every salamander we could catch. Salamanders, we understood, were simple creatures who made excellent subjects in a lab. So when Gertrude turned us out that particular Saturday, Tim and I lit out for the creek.

We were not the only ones. Kids from all over were already there, wading in the shallow rocky waters of the creek that ran through the valley. From what we knew about salamanders, there were plenty for everybody. I held the bucket and made Tim pick them up by their tails and drop them in the bucket. I contented myself with picking watercress for sandwiches. That was as close as I ever wanted to be to a salamander.

In between salamander drops, I asked whoever I could what we were supposed to do with the salamanders after we caught them, but nobody knew. Everybody was guessing. Some said take them to Dr. Ariail's drugstore and give them to him, others said save them until Monday and take them to school. Somebody suggested we ask a policemen. With so many answers and not one worth a damn, it struck me we had been duped. This was a lot of nothing, like eating a mud pie to get into a club with no purpose. We caught a lot of salamanders for nothing. It was time to quit, to turn them loose. Reluctantly we headed back to the headwaters of the creek, which ran across the golf course, to return them to their homes so they could make more salamanders.

Coming toward us from the eighth hole of the golf course was a classmate, Fred Walker, the freckle-faced son of Fred Dixie Walker, pitcher for the

Birmingham Barons baseball team. Fred liked teasing little kids and fighting big ones. I knew by the way he swung his arms this was going to be one of those unpleasant days, and I clenched my fists. But he sidestepped me and zeroed in on Tim, falling into step with him, shoving him as he walked. Tim walked on in silence, regaining his balance each time.

"Oops!" Fred stuck his foot out and tripped Tim hard. The bucket flew. Happy salamanders spilled out onto the green and shimmied through the manicured grass toward the creek, a living tribute to instinct. I held my breath. I was afraid this was just the beginning, and I was right. Fred grabbed a slimy salamander by the tail and hung it over my brother's head.

"Open your mouth, Runt," he said.

Tim held back the tears for a while by sucking in air, then could take it no more. His tears got to me, and as that salamander dangled over my little brother's head, some new kind of rage took strong hold of me. Nobody could do that to my brother. At that moment, I would have died for him if I had to.

I flew at his assailant and hit him as best I could and kept on hitting him until he dropped the salamander and threw up his hands in mock surrender and left. We picked ourselves up, my brother and I, covered with mud and grass stains. Our lace-up shoes were so sopped with creek water that they made sucking sounds as we ran through the back yards and down the alley to our own back door. We stopped only once, to eat a few of the wild cherry tomatoes that sprung up on their own in the alley. We made it to our back steps, leaving wet footprints wherever we stepped. Gertrude stood dead ahead, arms folded.

"Lord, Chile, what you got yourself into?" She wasn't talking to anybody but me, the responsible one, so I told her the whole story. She reached over with a towel and wiped some blood off my hand that I didn't even know was there, then told me I shouldn't fight if I could help it. Maybe this time I couldn't, she said. The quick nod of her head told me that was what she believed.

"Did you hurt *him*?" she asked me.

"Well, I might have knocked out his braces," I ventured, not wanting to elaborate. My bruises spoke volumes.

"Oh, my Lord! Well, don't you worry none because I know what to do. It's this way: If he come around I'll just tell your mama that boy had to have pulled out his own braces because you're just a little girl and he's a big old mean old boy."

I must have looked surprised because the next thing she did was explain that lying was sometimes a necessary thing to do, but not ever a good thing to do.

"Did you ever lie?" I asked her.

"No," she said. "But times I might should have. Bad times when maybe a lie would have kept somebody from getting hurt."

"Bad times before you came to our house?"

"Long time ago. Back when I lived in Margaret.

I wondered what that cost her but didn't ask. We dried out in her kitchen. We never heard any more from Fred.

4. Quonset Huts

I always balked at rising and shining, so my father learned how to lure me into the kitchen with a glass of milk, flavored with coffee and all the sugar I wanted. If this did not work, he was not averse to slapping a cold wet rag on my face.

"Get dressed, Kiddo. You and your brother can make some money by helping me wrap and pack Christmas presents for my clients."

"But I was going to . . . . And why do *I* have to go?"

Whatever it was I was going to do didn't matter. Tim of course, never used the word *but* and never made excuses. My reputation for cooperation had always been less than stellar.

The cold winds of September blew, threatening rain, as we made our way through Crestline up the hill to Key Circle and across the top of Red Mountain and down toward Birmingham. We rolled the windows up to keep out the heavy gray ash and soot that spewed from the city below. Plumes of toxic smoke rose from the steel mills and from Perfection Laundry, and even more from houses that by fall had lit their coal-burning furnaces. Smog filled the hollow that was our city. Birmingham lay below us like a bowl of thick dirty soup held in place by a rim of mountains. Citizens endured the smog and the smell because it meant prosperity.

We drove past the airport, past planes parked haphazardly on the tarmac and huge Quonset huts that looked for all the world like split tin cans lying on their sides. One of these Quonset huts belonged to my father, and it had painted orange letters over the door that spelled out "Birmingham Manufacturing Company."

Inside, boxes lay split open, ready to cough up cargo. Spider webs were everywhere. Rats lived there, too: I knew because I lost many a cat to rat-catching. Whenever a kitten followed me home from school, it would disappear within a few days. My father told me he took them to the airport to catch mice, but I never saw them again.

Daddy handed me a broom to sweep the cobwebs. Although I was not afraid of a single spider, I just did not like lots of them at once. I learned not to swat a spider, ever, because they usually had baby spiders inside. If you swatted one spider, hundreds more would run across the room. I also learned from watching many bugs that they did not usually bite if I held very still and let them crawl in peace. But some bugs were just unpleasant, like spiders and worms.

Before I could put the broom away, we had a visitor. I called to my father.

"Daddy, there's a man here to see you."

"Charlie Phelan?" My father emerged from the back of the plant. I heard caution in his voice. The man nodded at me and came on in.

"Dropped by to see how things are coming along at the new headquarters, George. Good to see the kid working, too. "

"Dropping by" seemed a stretch considering we were in a deserted, remote Quonset hut somewhere outside of Birmingham in the wilderness that was the Birmingham airport. Mr. Phelan caught me staring at him.

"Hello, Kiddo," he said to me. Then he turned back to my father. "Family affair, eh? And hey, it's time for you to take a break. Ok? What's cooking?"

Mr. Phelan moved with lots of energy and smiled a lot. He wore a gray worsted suit and looked exceptionally handsome in it. He had steel gray hair that was combed back from his temples to set off his blue eyes. I wondered if he thought it strange that a girl child was chasing spiders in a metamorphosing Quonset hut.

The two men chatted as they disappeared into the depths of the enclosure. My father showed Mr. Phelan all through the building, pointing out where he planned to put draftsmen, where the hooks and chains for the assembly line would hang, where the office would be and what he planned to use for a paint cubicle. I wondered what this man was doing here.

When they reached the far end of the building, I could no longer hear them. My broom and I worked furiously in their direction to listen. I crowded as close as I could to them without actually making them move their feet, but the swish of the broom drowned out most of what they said. I caught "you need to modernize" and "advertising."

Finally, Phelan slapped my father on the back and told him he really needed to go, but he must remember you had to spend money to make money. Even I knew this was not my father's style, and I said so. Not many more minutes passed before my father escorted Phelan out the door. At the end of the day, I got two new quarters, which was exceptional pay for a day's work.

A few months later, my mother announced that the Phelans were coming to dinner. She summoned me to the dining room to help her add a leaf to the table and set it with silver. She called downstairs to Gertrude.

"Gertrude, are there any clean table cloths down there?"

"No, ma'am, but I'll have one pretty soon."

I went down to watch, fascinated with the linen press, which was a monstrous iron machine hooked up to a gas pipe at the bottom of the basement stairs. It belched every time we fired up its gas jets. Behind its heavy doors hung two long hot rollers into which we fed damp bed sheets and tablecloths. As the linens disappeared, all I could think about was how Israelites fed Baal, a nasty idol I learned about in Sunday school. The linen press ate everything in sight, coughed up steam and spit out pressed tablecloths, sheets and napkins.

Everything in our house ran on gas, and the gas came in handy for blowing up giant weather balloons, too. I loved filling weather balloons with gas and sending them to China, after I attached notes to them bearing my address.

Mrs. Phelan arrived for dinner in a beige silk dress draped fashionably to one side below her slim waist. An elegant woman, she sat very straight. Bam would have approved. She wore her gray hair cropped and tucked behind her ears.

We had roast beef and two kinds of pie plus ice cream that night. As a result, Phelan bought 49 percent of Daddy's stock in the Company, and Daddy made him the Second Vice-President.

This all happened in 1947, the same year the United States decided that even though certain German Nazis were no longer welcome in their own country, they would be welcome in the United States. While the rest of the world spread a wide net to bring Nazi criminals to trial at The Hague, the U.S. Army paid passage for more than 700 Nazis to come to this country. Among these were scientists and engineers like Werner von Braun, who built and tested rockets like the V-2 for Hitler in Hitler's facilities at Peenemünde. President Truman called the immigration "Operation Paperclip."[90] The first wave of Nazi Germans were sent to Fort Bliss, Texas, but most did not remain. More than 200 wound up in Alabama.

Von Braun took the V-2 rocket with him to Detroit and used it to design the first Redstone missile, which he intended to bring to Huntsville, Alabama, for testing. The missile program and Birmingham Manufacturing Company took off at about the same time. Chrysler, which was where the Redstone rocket was being built, contacted my father to see if he could make a trailer to specification for transporting the first Redstone missile from Detroit to Huntsville.

My father was not at all sure he wanted to do anything for a Nazi, ever. He considered it for a long time before he decided Phelan's personality might be just the thing. He had visions of Phelan distracting the famous German so he could work with the men actually building the rocket.

That was the first time Phelan ever went with him on that long drive to Detroit. In the end, he was right. Phelan entertained Werner by himself, royally. Von Braun turned my father over to the engineers assigned to the actual rocket building: von Braun's brother and a young fellow named Brosco. Together they produced the trailer that hauled the first missile from the Chrysler plant in Detroit to the NASA facility in Huntsville, Alabama.

That next dry summer, I spent one Saturday wandering alone in the browning woods, where I found a nest of tiny white eggs, no bigger than half the tip of my little finger. I scooped them up in a big oak leaf and carried them home in my pocket. I left them on the side porch so Gertrude and I could research them in the encyclopedia. Then I went inside for supper.

The next morning I woke before anybody else and tiptoed down the stairs and waited for Gertrude to come upstairs. I tried not to wake my mother because she was having very rough nights. Finally, I could wait no longer and ran barefoot downstairs to find Gertrude. Her face lit up when she saw me, but her smile faded when I told her what was on the porch. I wanted to show them to her so she could tell me what kind of bird could lay such small eggs.

As Gertrude and I stepped out onto the porch, a tiny black snake, way thinner than a pencil, was scurrying across the tiles just an inch away. Gertrude saw it before I did. All I saw was the last of a thin black tail disappearing through the bricks and another snake wriggling out of its egg. We watched spellbound until the last little black snake hatched. Gertrude used her dust pan to catch as many as she could and tossed each newborn out into the bushes to fend for itself.

"How come you aren't afraid of snakes?" I asked her.

"Huh! They's lots of things worse," she said. "We won't tell your parents."

I asked her what was worse, but she didn't tell me. I reckoned if she remained a mystery forever I guessed it was because she had to.

1950. World War II still loomed large in my father's mind. To him, Nazis and the KKK were one and the same, and both had a presence in Alabama. He never doubted he might have to face them one day. But on that summer day, nothing was further from his mind. He had more pressing issues.

Plain and simple, production was up. The Company had long ago outgrown the Quonset hut and traded it in for a building in Woodlawn. The building desperately needed a railroad spur.

Tomorrow, my father told Ed Vickery. Tomorrow he would go see the mayor. Ed was the most important man in the company now; he ran the company when my father wasn't there and ran it well. When tomorrow came, my father wore his new gray suit for the first time.

The men on the first shift clocked in, expecting to see their boss already there, crawling under a trailer. They looked around for evidence of a rusty shirt sleeve or a leg in tan trousers visible around a corner. They stopped at the threshold of the plant and looked at each other, shocked. The boss was dressed snappily in his Over-The-Mountain clothes. They chuckled because they had speculated for months whether or not they would ever see the boss in the famous gray suit.

"Well, wonders never cease!" Richard Smith grinned. He was the shop supervisor—a tall, lanky, soft-spoken man they called "Smitty."

Charlie Barksdale popped out from Engineering when he heard the chatter and gave my father a thumbs up. Then he retreated into his drafting department.

"We're growing," said my father to his audience, as though he needed to explain his unusual appearance. "We've got to. We can't move trailers out fast enough, and we can't even park those we have already." Shiny orange flatbed trailers were parked up and down the street on unused space begged from friendly merchants in Woodlawn.

"So I'm going to talk to the mayor." He finished on his way out.

As he parked his car on 20th Street in downtown Birmingham my father paid no attention to the soot settling on his collar. He was deep in thought. Morning was the best time for business because the air seemed cleaner and heads were clearer. Even though black smog always burbled up in black clouds from smoke stacks all over Birmingham, it was worse in the afternoon. This time he didn't mind. He had much to be thankful for: He lived in a town he loved, and he had met payroll! He hummed to himself as he walked down the street toward the courthouse.

Among the cities in the nation hit hardest by the end of World War II, cities with men no longer needed for war, like Birmingham, were the hardest hit of all. Hundreds of rolling mills and mines, thousands of miles of railways shut down. Men, many of them veterans, still these many years later roamed the streets looking for work. My father set out confidently to tell the city's commissioners how he could put dozens to work now and many more later. He offered them not just any work but good productive work. He had always in the past had the backing of the union men, too. Now the men had more work than they could handle and had even stopped asking for advances in pay—even Moseley and Mims. Speculation in the office was that Mrs. Moseley and Mrs. Mims had slowed down in the baby-making department.

His father and grandfather had a part in building Birmingham's railroad bridges, lakes and mines, so he took his responsibility to his city seriously. He wasn't asking the Big Guys for much. He wasn't even asking for the kind of stuff the Big Guys expected him to ask for: no free buildings, no political favors. All he wanted was a little more of Birmingham's labor force and the right zoning for a piece of rail, although he wouldn't turn down a few tax breaks.

He bounded up the wide courthouse stairs, his arms pumping with each step, hardly slowing down as he pushed open the oversized glass-and-brass doors. Inside, he checked the roster to make sure nothing had changed. It had been a while. Then he proceeded happily down the long hall to Mayor Cooper Green's office.

Mayor Green was well into his tenth year in office, and it was no surprise to find some of the mayor's cronies standing around drinking coffee in the mayor's office. But my father had an appointment and would not be deterred. When the other men turned from their conversations and acknowledged his presence, he stood with restless feet, turning his hat in his hands and waiting for them to leave him alone with the mayor. He took a quick inventory.

Sims was a leftover from the last administration, thinning black hair combed in oily strands away from his forehead. Carter was a gent he knew from the sign shop, the one who always wore a pinstripe suit. He knew who Cummings was because of his monotonous diatribes against "Commie Pinkos" and for his part in the recent tarring and feathering of a union organizer. Cummings gave my father a grin made entirely of upper teeth. They were not leaving.

"Hear you done unionized," said Cummings. "Got any blacks in your shop?"

My father ignored the man and spoke directly to the mayor, asking for permission to speak to him privately.

Behind his back he heard one of the other men tell another "We don't want any of them companies with them damn commie unions." And came the expected reply, "Atlanta can have them if they want, but we don't want them here in Birmingham."

"Well, Cummings, George and I have some talking to do. Do you suppose you fellows can leave us alone here?" The mayor was uncomfortable, embarrassed by the man.

My father waited for the last man to close the door behind him, then made his case. Had the mayor already read his letter?

"George," said the mayor, clasping his hands behind his head and leaning back in his chair. "You see, I understand the situation you're in, but the commission and really, the city fathers, don't want any more plants downtown with unions. We don't want trouble. Unions means integration these days, and integration means trouble. You can understand that can't you?"

So it had been decided before he ever got there. The mayor could have saved George the trip.

"Now don't misunderstand me, I don't support these naysayers all the way, but the way the Commission sees it, looks like you only have two choices: throw out the union and enjoy the support of the commission or move to another town."

Alabama workers everywhere had begun to shun their dying locals because of this kind of talk. Control over the unions was a simple matter of crying "your daughter is going to marry a Negro" or that local union members were "God Damn Commie Pinkos." To hear them tell it, Russians lived incognito in every neighborhood in Birmingham and stood behind every door in every local union shop with sickles in their hands. It was killing made easy. Birmingham Manufacturing was denied not only easier access but all the perks other companies got—like tax breaks, free paving or railroad siding—as a matter of course.

But to Phelan, my father's problem was not the Commissioners or the union or the communists or the Negroes. Phelan told him the problem was his image, and he doubled his efforts to change my father's image. He applied for membership in organizations like the Truck Trailer Manufacturers Association and the National Association of Manufacturers. Then he dragged my father in behind him, protesting.

During that era my father did learn to respect these huge organizations. He became accustomed to acting on recommendations from the TTMAs and NAMs of the world, and his company profited. He drove to Miami or Washington or Wilkes Barre to listen to chairmen of boards talk, to hear their propositions for better production. But what he heard most was about communism and how communists had infiltrated all the institutions in the United States, including the unions. He heard it so much, he figured he must be behind the times: He was still trying to digest the fact that part of Nazi Germany now inhabited Alabama, even though only a few years before Nazis had been the greatest enemy of all, the people who killed Cy and all the Jews and so many of his other friends.

The National Association of Manufacturers supported an anti-communist outfit called the John Birch Society. Its claim to legitimacy, as far as my father was concerned, was that it named itself for a missionary, John Birch. The Birchers bandied about the word *communist* whenever it suited their purpose, painting everybody they disliked with the communist brush until their rants took on the shape of a crusade. Nobody could escape: rock musicians, classical musicians, teenagers, teachers, black citizens, Italian and Greek citizens, Catholics and other people who misguidedly attended the church down the street. Nazis went under the radar as communists multiplied. My father had yet to meet one, though.

Many years later, after I finished college and was settling in to a summer job in the office at BIRMCO, I watched a driver park an unfinished flatbed less than ten feet from my window. Men gathered around it, resting elbows and feet on the unpainted steel carriage, puffing away on cigarettes and stubbing them out on the bed of the trailer. I asked my father who they were.

"They're union men talking to my men."

I was definitely nearsighted. "Which ones are union men?"

"Actually, they all are. It's a union shop now, so all the men are union men. Their contract with the union is about to expire, and they have a chance to vote on whether to keep the union or not."

"Will they? Vote to keep it, I mean?"

"Well, Kiddo, actually I don't think they will, but we will just have to wait and see." We walked out to the shop together.

Kids' drawings lined the walls of the shop, cartoons of stick figures in sundry dangerous situations bearing messages like "Wear your helmet" or "Pick up your tools." Union and management both agreed upon these safety rules years ago and had offered prizes to kids who could illustrate them.

One of the Negro men walked over to my father.

"Mr. Stafford, they done told us our union is going to charge us hundreds more dollars in dues. It ain't true, is it?"

"That's just a bad rumor."

"And they told the whites that us blacks are going to strike to get paid as much as they are. I know that ain't true. We'd be in a heap of trouble if we made as much money as they did."

"Who's telling you all this?"

"Union busters I guess," said the man, looking embarrassed.

"Well, they certainly have their reasons, but that's the very reason you shouldn't believe everything they say," said my father. After the man left, my father turned to me.

"Correction. They are not my union men after all." He reckoned a vote against renewing the contract could be good or bad. Good not to have to bargain with them. Bad if a union worse than the old CIO local took over. The Klan was known to want to oust the CIO.

The men voted the union out. When Phelan saw that BIRMCO no longer had a union shop, he figured the time was right to put the Company on the map. He took it as a signal to begin an ever more expensive round of plane trips, dinners, and advertising.

The Company rocked along a few years without a union and even added more men, most of them very young. My father found it harder and harder to keep up with them all. One morning as he walked around the plant, one man in particular stood out because he was older.

"Good morning. You're new, aren't you?" He was not sure, but he introduced himself anyway. "I'm George Stafford."

"Wayne Caswell, Sir. Yessir I am."

"You live close by?" The name sounded familiar.

"Yessir, I live with my mother Alma up in Irondale."

"Alma Caswell? My grandmother knew an Alma Caswell. Was your father Joseph Caswell?"

"He was." Wayne smiled broadly.

"If I remember, he helped my grandfather." Recognition set in. "I am so happy to meet you."

"Yessir, I'm glad to make your acquaintance, too, Sir." Wayne shook his hand. "That was a terrible accident."

"Do you remember much about it? The accident at Margaret, I mean. Of course, I don't imagine you were around then. It wasn't named Margaret at the time."

"Not that much, Sir, except that they named it Margaret right after."

"Are you a union man, too?" asked my father.

"Yessir, I sure am. But it ain't the same union. Not the same at all. They don't want blacks and whites mixing no more like they did back then, you know. Kind of a shame."

My father let his eyes wander around the shop. He didn't see a single black face, not even Henry's. He turned back to Wayne.

"How is your mother?" asked my father.

"She's fine, Sir. I would like you to meet her some day, but she's confused sometimes. She used to tell me your grandfather saved my dad's life."

"How was that?"

"Not real sure, Sir."

The tram cars! William's warning to the family not to talk about it. "You think they thought my grandfather was your father?"

"It was what she thought. But in the long run they got my dad anyway."

"And you're still a union man?"

"Yessir. Couldn't not be I guess."

"A union man without a union?"

"Yessir. I guess that's true. But maybe it's for the best with unions what they are now."

"Still, I am proud to meet you Wayne. And yes I would like to meet your mother." The two men chatted a bit longer.

He went back in to the office to speak with Phelan, who had paged him while he was outside talking to Wayne. Phelan loved to fly, and now insisted my father take the plane with him to the convention. My father thought flying extravagant and had just never felt the need.

"Time is money," Phelan said. "No need to spend time and money calling on Fruehauf. We'll see them at the convention."

I heard the conversation and was amazed when my father agreed. If he flew from now on, it would mean we would not be included in his trips. As children, we always went along with him, never minding the long hot afternoons in the sweltering back seat of the Dodge because at the end, we always went somewhere exciting, like the swamps in Louisiana and abandoned mansions in Mississippi.

I took my father to the airport and watched him wave goodbye from the window of the plane. Phelan had given him the window seat for that first trip.

Once they were in the air, my father told me later, he watched wistfully below as all the highways he had driven from Mississippi to Texas scrolled rapidly underneath. Then the plane flew across the desert, and the Rockies came in sight.

He did not become alarmed until the mountains began to approach the plane. The pilot came on then, to assure the passengers that the plane was indeed climbing, but by now my father could see nothing but rocky cliffs approaching his window at breakneck speed.

They made it over the mountain just in time, but by the time the plane landed, my father was shaking.

"How was it?" asked Phelan.

"Well," he said. "I will never fly again unless I'm in a hurry. And I can fairly well guarantee you I will never be in a hurry again."

In spite of all the conventions and road trips, the orders Phelan promised did not materialize. After one particularly long drive across the vastness that was Arkansas, because he only went on road trips now, my father returned to his office to find a note on his desk.

"SEE THE SAFE." He often found such notes on his desk, especially on Mondays. In the safe was another note:

"SEE THE CHECKBOOK." The checkbook showed all the checks Phelan had written that week. It also showed that all the company had left was $200. The next note was in the checkbook

"PLEASE GO TO THE BANK AND COVER CHECKS." My father closed the checkbook and took off to see Dozier Arnold, PA, the company's auditor. Arnold saw him coming and put his pen down to look up at my father. Dozier rarely said much, but when he did speak it was right to the point.

"Did you know you were broke?"

"I do now!" my father said. "What do we do about it?"

"Nothing. It's too late. You should have seen me about six months ago."

"I have fifty men out there who need paychecks. It's never too late. We will make it work."

The two men worked on into the afternoon, determined to find a solution. When they finished, my father asked Dozier to call the bank and tell them exactly what he had just told him.

The bank worked by lending money to BIRMCO based on Accounts Receivables, which meant trailers built and delivered but not paid for. The men would be paid with this loan, and when payment for the trailer came, he would cancel the loan. The system had worked for years, but as my father put it, Phelan short-sheeted the system: he took out loans on work the company never had. Phelan's "orders" never happened.

My father waited about 20 minutes after Dozier called the bank, then left. As soon as he walked in the front door of the bank, vice-presidents abandoned their offices and walked with him the length of the bank to the president's office. They sat down. The president looked at my father.

"We understand from Dozier Arnold that you are broke." My father turned to the officer he did business with and said:

"I have been trying to tell you that for six months. I want you to cancel all of those loans!"

Their jaws dropped, but it was clear what had happened. They spent the rest of the day coming up with a plan to keep BIRMCO afloat.

After much discussion, the bankers themselves called Phelan in. The bankers imposed a budget on him of something like $100 a month for travel and $25 for advertising. Phelan managed for about a week, but by the second week was badly over budget. By the third week, he was three times over budget. The bank put even more pressure on him.

By the end of the third week, Phelan showed up in my father's office carrying every record the company had. He dropped them all on my father's desk.

"Here," he said. "You can have all the books because you know so much about them." He had a flair for the dramatic and stalked out. He then went on vacation and stayed for two weeks.

While he was away, my father consulted his attorney, Ormond Somerville who helped him restructure. The restructuring went this way: My father sold one share of stock to one of the company's long-time shareholders, Harry Ross. Mr. Somerville then made Ross an official director of the company so that he and my father together made up the majority. Then the two directors called their own meeting and made a motion to stop Phelan from writing any more checks. Lastly, they hired John Muir, who had been the auditor for Alabama Power Company, to look at the books.

"All I have to say is that Mr. Phelan is certainly creative. He has invented the one-legged journal entry. When something doesn't balance, he just adds something in until it does!"

When Phelan returned, they called the required directors meeting to vote on the check-writing motion. It passed two to one.

"I can't believe you are doing this to me. Don't you know how many thousands of miles I have traveled? Do you know how many places I have been? I do not feel appreciated." It was a passionate speech.

The next morning, Ronnie Brasher, the office manager, greeted him.

"Mr. Stafford, I believe you were planning to buy some more file drawers? Well, you won't need them now. Mr. Phelan took all the files."

Even then, even after that, the three parties managed to muster an amazing amount of good will and agreed to part. My mother's medical bills were put on hold until my father could secure a brand new gargantuan mortgage on us, the house and the office. Thanks to the bank, things began to be put right.

At home, my mother depended more and more on me for everyday tasks, like grocery shopping. Right after Phelan left, she came out to the car wearing her old pale blue skirt with a white blouse for a trip to the grocery store. She still looked beautiful, in spite of her swollen arm. We wandered the aisles calculating how many servings a roast would yield and how many potatoes were necessary for six people.

Within a month, much of what went in the basket had to be put back on the shelf. My mother kept her sense of humor and commented she planned to honor the Catholic tradition of fish on Friday from then on, in the form of canned salmon.

During one such Friday supper, we heard a knock on the front door, which turned out to be Jack Davis, the Company's accountant, the least likely person to show up on a Friday night we could imagine. My father invited him to join us. After dinner the two men retired to the living room. My father sat on the non-allergenic Naugahyde sofa, and Jack sat on the non-allergenic Naugahyde chair. Jack was long-faced.

"George, I had to come talk to you. I've been working on the books." He was empty-handed, not even a briefcase nearby.

"Is there something wrong with the books again?" George looked hard at Jack's face, trying to read it.

"Well, yes and no," he hesitated. "According to the books we are missing about a dozen tires . . ." His voice trailed off.

My father said he had been afraid of that because the Company had nowhere to store them.

". . . and two trailers," finished Jack.

My father looked stunned. Picking up his coat and hat he drove with Jack out to the plant to see for himself. He confirmed Jack's story. How could he handle any more irretrievable losses? That was the moment he turned to religion. My mother already had.

5. Springville

The decision to inject religion into the equation meant instituting Wednesday morning Bible studies at the Company in Woodlawn. The pastor of the Jimmy Hale Mission, Leo Shepura, held prayer meetings, too. No matter whether the men and women were Baptists, Presbyterians, Seventh Day Adventists, or Catholics, Mormons and Jews, they were required to attend. My father figured this was the best way to counteract whatever evil was lurking around out there.

We did a lot of discussing though, me and my father. I had to say I thought all that enforced religion might not turn out as well as he hoped and perhaps he might consider taking an interest in some other subject, like music or politics. He did not hear me. Gertrude and I talked about it.

"Sometimes I think he really does hear me, you know.'

"He does sometimes," she said, not taking sides.

"But once he makes up his mind. . . ." I knew it didn't matter what I said.

"Yes'm, there's a big difference between hearing and listening all right."

We all had our hands full, especially when my mother lay in bed with fever. Her swollen arm and the consequent fevers came as a result of too few lymph nodes, and the fevers lasted for days, in spite of massive doses of penicillin. Gertrude tried to ease my father's burden.

"Now Mr. Stafford don't you worry none. I can take care of Mrs. Stafford and the kids, too."

He talked to her just as he talked to me. But just as he ran ideas by me and did not expect a response, he talked to her the same way, not really expecting an answer. We both heard him out, though, every time, which meant we were both privy to his thoughts.

1958. In spite of the prayer sessions, a new union came into the lives of the men who worked in the shop at BIRMCO—a local of the Steel Workers Union, not the old CIO. Surprisingly, the workers voted unanimously to accept it.

Wayne was right. This union was different. One of the union organizers was a man named Cummings, a friend of some powerful men who, they said, wore sheets. Nobody took Cummings seriously, but they did take the new union seriously because it had been injected with a Ku Klux Klan faction that had its own agenda. The KKK marched again. It had a presence downtown and even burned a cross in the Jewish neighborhood across the street from my house. They planted fear like seeds, then disappeared.

At home, we heard no more banter around the table, no more garbled poetry or songs. Table conversation, in fact all conversation, turned serious. Too serious. My mother had begun to see everything under a Biblical microscope. She objected to Episcopalians in general, but made an exception for Aunt Florence. She gave her a pass only when her Episcopalian sister found a single objection to the Episcopal faith, which was that she couldn't quite go along with *apostolic succession.* I looked that up. When I was a child, I had to look up *predestination* because we were Presbyterians. Discussions over whether I, in particular, believed in the Trinity or apostolic succession or predestination became a source of much concern among the rest of the family. The implications were gargantuan, and potentially fatal apparently.

Gertrude made her Thursday night visits to the Jackson Street Baptist church, so such conversations were not news to her. But when the pilloryings began, she always muttered under her breath and left the room. I asked her what she said once.

"Just don't get me started," she said.

Bam came over on Sundays. By now, Sunday dinners had moved from the house with the four o'clocks to our house. As we were clearing the table after one Sunday dinner, Bam was waiting in the doorway for one of us to take her home. I was gathering dishes to take to the kitchen. Gertrude came in to clear the table, and I picked up another plate. Bam held her hand out as though to stop me.

"I don't want you to do that," she said to me.

"I am clearing the table," I said, puzzled.

"You have a servant for that. In my family, they used to say, 'Why have a dog and wag your own tail!'"

What I said that day cost me dearly. I did a bad job of it.

"She's not a servant. She's Gertrude!" And I added lamely, "Besides, I *want* to clear the table."

I thought we had left that kind of attitude behind years ago, but it had resurfaced. I heard Bam loud and clear, and so did Gertrude. My cheeks burned, but I picked up another dish. Bam *had* been raised that way; she *was* old; she deserved respect because she was my grandmother, but I knew that for Gertrude, Bam had crossed a line. That line was part of a much larger line that had been a long time in the making. In the kitchen, Gertrude banged pots around, letting off steam in her own way.

Bam heard the noise. She looked at me, puzzled, and too old to understand what it was she had actually said or why I even bothered to answer her.

The next morning as we came down for breakfast, I heard Gertrude's determined footsteps climb the stairs up from her room. She stood there not in her uniform but dressed in her navy blue Sunday go-to-meeting suit, wearing a simple hat decorated with a cluster of tiny purple berries and a touch of veiling. This bit of finery signaled her intentions. She put her suitcase down and looked at me.

"Y'all be good now, you hear?" Her words rang with finality.

"Are you leaving?" I asked

"Yes, ma'am," she said. She only said yes ma'am to me when she was put off. I tried to think of something to say, but my head had something wrong with it.

I didn't even ask about breakfast. Gertrude knocked on my mother's bedroom door.

"Mrs. Stafford," she called gently through the closed door.

"Come on in," said my mother.

Gertrude opened the door a crack. The penicillin had kicked in and she was sitting up.

"I'm going to have to leave. You all will be all right with Mrs. Stafford Senior here, and I just want you and Mr. Stafford to know I will miss all of you."

My mother sat up straighter. She did not ask why. She wouldn't, even though she had no idea. She accepted the information and left it at that.

"Where are you going?"

"Chicago," Gertrude said. And she was gone.

Civil and union unrest were only two of a whole raft of bad things going on in Birmingham in the early 1960s. My father and his Company were so distracted they did not see them coming.

He did know he was through with Birmingham politics and talked about nothing but moving out to Springville. He found a piece of land there, next to a railroad, that he could buy for very little. Besides, taxes in St. Clair County were low.

"I wonder if my men will come with me if I move the plant way out to St. Clair County?" he asked me. "You know what Gertrude said. We talked about this before she left, and she told me there were plenty of men out in the County who needed jobs. Wayne said the same thing. But I don't want to lose the men I have, either."

He took the chance and bought 180 acres of vacant land in the town of Springville, much of which had been sold years ago for pennies on the dollar because the owners could not give clear title to it.[91] He announced the move to the Company. To his delight, St. Clair County gave him a railroad spur and he built his factory. That piece of land and my father were off to a new start.

Wayne stayed on. So did Smitty and the rest of the office. Many of the old men left, though, after the second union came in. Among the newcomers were some of the same men who were evicted from company housing back in 1935, the same ones who had worked at the docks during the war. They had come home to Margaret and St. Clair County. They, too, were off to a new start.

My father drove an hour to Springville every day. He did it with renewed energy, arriving before his men and staying long after they left in the afternoons. He was more the way he had been, trying to find out if a man had problems like caring for elderly parents or having a third or fourth child, except that he no longer shunned suits or crawled under trailers. He tried, but he missed some things.

He drove past signs and never saw them. Those posted along Highway 11, which was how he drove to the plant, said "Welcome to St. Clair County" and were signed "Ku Klux Klan."[92] The KKK was alive in his own back yard and he had not even noticed.[93]

6. The Armor of God

At some point, while I was in high school and not paying attention, my parents succumbed entirely to their new interest: church. We observed new rituals at home. My mother had always heard us say our prayers when we were small, but now I said my own, partly because it was the grown-up thing to do and partly because my prayers were that she would leave Tim alone. I did not want her to hear me say it.

Every night at bedtime I heard Tim's voice from across the hall, saying his part of the prayer, blessing everybody and praying the lord his soul to keep. When my mother took over, she prayed the more complicated parts and ended by petitioning God to put some armor on Tim. I conceded silently that was probably a good thing, because Tim was always a hair's breadth away from being beaten up and I might not always be there to protect him.

There was another, more public religious ritual that began in our living room about that time. It cut into my mother's grocery shopping time and caused us to have to forage at the end of the day for something to cook for supper.

In the early days after her several recoveries, she tried to write again. When I heard her clattering away on her Royal, it made me happy, optimistic even. But she soon found out that even the physical act of typing was too much and caused her arm to swell. Almost everything she had enjoyed in days past became nearly impossible for her to do later.

In September 1946, strangers, ladies from the church, came to call, gloved and hatted. My mother smiled graciously, welcomed the ladies in, and made them ribbon sandwiches and iced tea. By 1947 they expected more food and more from my mother, who was not well in the first place and had a lot on her plate already with children to feed and a house to run.

The ladies' message was a one-liner: The healing oil of Jesus was only available to those who gave up.

Evelyn, they said to her, you most likely won't be able to give up unless you accept your condition and not question it. Then they set about praying that she might have the courage to do just that. The more the ladies came, the longer the prayers.

I was never sure what time the Bible crowd arrived, although they certainly came in time for lunch. They were always still in session when I arrived home from school, even though I took my time walking with the other fourth graders from Crestline down Fairway Drive through the neighbors' yards across the alley and up the hill to my house. It was no fun coming home to a darkened living room. My eyes always had to adjust before I could make out the ladies laying hands on one another and praying, my mother in their midst, her swollen left arm propped up on a pillow in a vain attempt to drain it and lessen the swelling.

Emma's lonely old piano sat in the corner, out of tune. A hymnal lay open on its music rack. Once in a while my mother played it. She could read music, which I could not, even though I loved that piano. I picked out tunes, but the written notes meant nothing to me. On prayer days I tiptoed regretfully past the piano to my room.

I never questioned their intentions. Clearly, they knew something I didn't. Perhaps their prayers might heal my mother after all.

But nothing happened. As time went on, she declined from so much missing tissue and so many inactive lymph nodes. With only about half of her chest left, her body could not rid itself of toxins. Her fevers sent her to bed every few weeks, and the episodes came closer together. Penicillin stopped working.

Between her fevers and with Gertrude gone, the house fell ill with black holes into which freshly ironed shirts, fresh pies and fried chicken fell. Mostly it was lonesome.

Minor chaos returned, as did pea omelets and oatmeal soup. My mother struggled to keep up, and Bam moved in with us permanently. But Bam was no consolation. She never acquired the skills that came with running a house. She saw her role as being there in case of emergency, otherwise she sat quietly working crossword puzzles. Tim and I came home from school to nobody in particular or everybody in particular and went to our own rooms to read. The ladies came and went undisturbed.

An extraordinary thing happened a few years later, though. One Sunday afternoon, I opened the door to find Gertrude standing there in the same navy blue outfit and veiled hat she wore the day she left.

"Wow!" was all I could say.

Gertrude just stood there grinning for a minute, then she came on in. I yelled out to the rest of the family "Guess who on earth is here?"

My brother came running just in time to see her put her apron on. With no more than a nod to us, she went into the kitchen and back to work. So much had changed during the time she was gone it would take ages to tell her. We were in some kind of deep pit we could not climb out of, and I didn't think Gertrude was prepared.

She saw the changes, though. The garden that my mother had once banked with azaleas and iris and daffodils was plowed under and replanted. Where flowers once flourished, rows of bean stalks grew, sending out tendrils to cling desperately to improvised chicken wire. Scraggly tomato plants climbed V-shaped stakes, and miracle of miracles, corn grew in Mountain Brook.

"You can't eat flowers," my father said the day he took his tractor to the plot.

The next morning, Gertrude hummed away at us as she made pancakes, trying to cheer us up. She stared at my wrinkled skirt, which was way too big for me. I pinned it up at the waist, waiting to grow into it, and I had tried to iron it

215

with the pins in place. She threw up her hands when Tim arrived in similar condition, wrinkled all over. She stood by the back door and looked out at the stump of her plum tree that had once bloomed so beautifully in the spring.

"Who cut down the plum tree?" she asked.

"Well, it quit producing plums," I answered. Blessing of blessings, she laughed with us, and we thought for a brief moment that all would be right with the world.

After breakfast she set up her ironing board right under the window. We still had one tree that bloomed—a mimosa tree whose branches reached all the way up to my window on the second floor of the house. A summer breeze ruffled its pink puffs as though to say, "We're still here!"

A few hours later, just before lunch, the doorbell rang. Gertrude beat me to it and opened the door. I had forgotten for a minute they would come. There stood that gaggle of ladies holding Bibles and sandwiches. None of us said a word, but then neither did they. They just walked right past us, making themselves at home.

I tried to explain to Gertrude that they were regular visitors and invite them in at the same time. What I did not say was that they were more at home in our house than my own father, who was constantly on the road trying to drum up business, or that I spent most of my afternoons in my room.

We regained our composure. During the years she was gone, my life took place mostly in the back of the house, but now that she was back, I haunted her kitchen.

Sometimes we still read aloud, and sometimes she wrote notes for my father to read when he came home. Her spelling was not so good, but it definitely had improved. In the days before she left for Chicago, when we had the whole living room to ourselves, we would sit cross-legged on the floor and pick out books to read, mostly the *World Book Encyclopaedia*. We read through it indiscriminately. We read so many volumes that she told me I ought to enter myself on the quiz show, "The $64,000 Question." This was the greatest thing playing on our new television. But she was wrong: I would have frozen in fear and would never have been able to answer even a single question.

She was right about one thing, though: I did store a huge amount of information in my head in those days, stuff that really served no purpose whatsoever. I memorized the letters on the spines of the encyclopaedias: "A-Are. Are-Beh, Beh-Bur, Bur-Cha, Cha-Con . . . " and other nonsense. No telling what she learned. The only tradition left from the time before Chicago was the game of Monopoly that Tim and I played every day. It still began on the first day of school in September and ended on the last day of school in June.

This was the last week of school. Tim and I agreed to play to the finish. No kindnesses allowed—no loans to each other, no mortgages, no looking the other way when an opponent landed on your hotel. This was for real. We threw the dice and began.

By Wednesday we only had two more days and two tests to go before school let out for summer. The game was over. I let Tim win anyway.

That Thursday at school, we students clamored to go out on the playground, even if it meant having to listen to Mrs. Snellgrove give orders. Mrs. Snellgrove was a skinny, rather sour older teacher with blondined hair that curled below her ears. If I thought about her at all when I was not on the playground, I imagined her fixing breakfast with a head full of rollers, her mouth painted bright red and set in a hard straight line. In my imagination, she looked back over her shoulder and barked instructions to some very small children who stood timidly in line behind her, looking terrified.

When the bell rang for recess, we spilled out onto the one corner of the playground where clover blossoms grew, where the sun shone brightest. It was a child's haven of living green in an otherwise dirt-scuffed schoolyard. Those of us who never made cheerleading took refuge in the clover patch, where we sat quietly like Ferdinand the Bull and admired those who *were* chosen. I never resented not being chosen. I could never do the splits anyway.

This day would have been a wonderful nearly last day of school except for Mrs. Snellgrove. She forbade moping about making daisy chains and beat her baton on the ground—the one with the red ribbons on the top—which meant she intended to organize us into a competition. She used that baton to tap the team's leaders, the school's star runners, on the shoulders and to draw lines in the sand so she could divide us into teams. We were about to race.

Each leader she chose already knew which students she wanted on her team. The leaders took turns calling names. Duds were called last.

"I need not tell you," Mrs. Snellgrove emphasized, looking as though it pained her to say it. "But you leaders must choose every single girl." Then she added "even the slow ones."

The teams were chosen, the girls in line behind the leaders. Mrs. Snellgrove gave the signal for the first two girls to run. "Go!" She whacked her baton on the ground.

I told myself I could run, that today I would complete the race. I would keep going and show her I could do it even if I *was* chosen last. Each girl reached the finish line and took her place at the back of the line. Each girl brushed the dust out of her eyes, and each girl smelled of the effort put forth in her last celebratory burst of energy at the end of a year of grammar school.

My turn finally came. Mrs. Snellgrove looked grimly at me, then back at her stopwatch and signaled. I ran like the wind, exuberant and expectant. It was my best start ever. I could feel it.

Then I crumpled. It never failed, and it never failed to surprise me. My in-breath caught somewhere halfway to my lungs, and I could not suck it in any further. I slowed, bent over, trying to expel enough air to inhale another breath. My legs turned to lead pipes. My shameful world slowed to a crawl.

Mrs. Snellgrove did not look at me, but concentrated on the watch on her skinny wrinkled wrist. I longed to turn and run, but I was spent. I walked to the finish.

She formed us into a tight regiment and marched us back into the building for lunch. She looked so much like the way she looked in my dreams that I had to look twice to be sure she was not wearing hair curlers.

At Crestline School every child, except a few special kids who had inexplicably serious disorders that required special diets, had to buy a lunch ticket. No ticket no lunch, and my ticket was used up. The lunchroom teacher punched its last hole on Wednesday and reminded me to bring more lunch money.

My mother was supposed to leave a dollar by the front door, but as I expected she would, she forgot. She didn't mean to; she just forgot. After my performance on the playground, I could not bring myself to make this dilemma public, so I spent lunch period hiding in the bathroom.

By the final bell I was hungry and more than ready to bolt. Even though I ached for the loving company of friends who rode bicycles with me or floated leaves down the ditch on Fairway Drive with me, I left with no goodbyes. I did not even stop to clean out my locker. I walked slowly until I rounded the corner out of sight of the others. Then I ran.

I outpaced them all then, jogging left and right, crossing narrow streets until I reached my cut-through up the hill. With my last large gulp of air, I dove into a dense tangle of privet hedge that stood between me and home, tears streaming down my cheeks. Scratchy branches of privet tore at my sweater and pulled my hair. Once out of the densest, thickest part of the privet, I brushed away spider webs and leaves. I looked down at myself to take stock of the damage, but what I saw struck horror deep within my very being.

Tent worms, tiny white humping things, miniature disgusting aliens, covered my dark blue sweater. Of all the creatures in the world I hated most and could not bring myself to touch, slimy worms topped the list. I preferred snakes or cockroaches or even scorpions to worms. At that moment, a bad day turned into a monumentally unforgettably bad day. The nasty things crawled all over me from the top of my head to the waist. I screamed and cried, brushed at the crown of my hair, tore at it trying to rid myself of my tormenters, far too many to brush off. Picking them off one by one was out of the question. Terror cost me my common sense. I stripped off my sweater, pulled it over my head, threw it down in the alley and ran.

I arrived home raking my fingers through my hair, naked to the waist and crying so hard I knew the neighbors were looking out their windows at a girl gone crazy. I imagined the disgusting things still touching me, crawling on me. I arrived at the front door exhausted and gasping for air.

I forgot everything else as I threw the door open. Only after the door banged loudly against the wall and after my eyes began to adjust to the dark, did I realize I had burst in on the ladies. I stood there, shirtless.

One of the women shrieked. I had no escape.

"The hedge . . ." I tried to explain. "I cut through the hedge. It was full of worms."

Most of the ladies kept their eyes cast down until the final *Amen*. Then they all looked at me at once.

"Where *are* your clothes?" I could not see who was doing the asking.

"I had to. I had to take my sweater off," I was making no sense and I knew it.

"Are you hurt?" I heard my mother ask. I had to admit that no I was not.

"Then go to your room, please, Dear." The *Dear* part really got to me. "And put your clothes on."

As I turned to leave, I heard whispering accusations and saw women staring over their glasses at me. As I tried to make my way to the kitchen, Mrs. Simons's voice trumpeted clear over the others. She was talking about Herod.

"You know, Herod refused to give praise to God so the angel of the Lord had Herod eaten by worms." Mrs. Simons always introduced herself by saying "And you understand, that's *Simons* with only one *M*."

"Jesus, drive the evil one away from this precious child," she concluded after the Herod quote.

Hold it! She was talking about me as though I weren't there. You would think I had some kind of cancer, which I did not. My mother looked pale and frail, which she was. I felt sick inside and quietly closed the door behind me so they would not know I had heard, although I was certain they intended me to.

By the time I reached the kitchen my eyes were so clouded by tears I could not see, but when I blinked, Gertrude stood there as always, finishing up her ironing. She set the iron upright on its stand at the end of the ironing board and turned to me. I swallowed hard, trying to find my voice. What I had done would make no sense to anybody, I was sure. I felt irreparably foolish.

"What happened to your clothes, Child?"

"I can't go back through there! I can't get to my room, and I don't have my sweater."

Even in my confusion I knew she understood. Funny enough, I knew she knew I understood, too.

"You ain't done nothing now. You just sit there and I'll go get you a top."

At that moment, what I could never say out loud was more than anything I wanted my mother back and my house back. I wanted to turn on the lights and open up the windows and sit on the floor with Gertrude and read the encyclopaedia. I knew my mother was afraid of illness, and she was afraid of bills. She was afraid we might not be perfect or acceptable in the eyes of the Lord, and she would be to blame. That was the fear that overwhelmed her then. She had forgotten everything except the fear.

That night, after supper, when I was putting on my pajamas, Tim brought in one of his balsa wood airplanes for me to look at. He built balsa wood planes out of balsa wood kits with decals all the time. He had replicas of every plane ever flown in any war. Planes hung from his ceiling and sat on his dresser, finished and unfinished, painted and not painted. He was half dressed for bed, toothbrush in hand, between bath and lights-out. I stood in the middle of my room already in my pajamas, *Wonder Woman* comic book in my hand, ready to hide under the covers with a flashlight and read without being caught with the lights on and told to cut it out.

Tim stared, which was not polite. In a few minutes, he walked right up to me and touched my pajama shirt—just about where my pajama pocket was—with his index finger. I looked down, curious to see what it was he was looking at.

"What's that?" he asked. I really didn't know what he was talking about.

"What?" I asked back. He acted annoyed and gave me a serious punch in the chest, right where my skin was beginning to bulge.

"*That,*" he said, punching again. Then it dawned. He saw something I had not seen, something my body was doing that had nothing to do with me, was separate from me. I never thought about my body at all before this, but now somebody else thought about it and found it wrong. I took a second look. How I had managed to never notice that part of my anatomy I will never know, but my brother noticed. I was as fascinated as he was.

"I think they're bosoms," I said, surprised. I hunched my shoulders over then to make them disappear. "Go to bed," I said.

Tim and I took off straight after breakfast the next day, cutting through the back yard across the alley to retrieve the never-to-be-worn-again contaminated blue sweater. Tim brushed off the few dry leaves that still clung to it and handed it back to me, but I refused to touch it. He tucked it in his belt and off we went to pick watercress out of the creek.

On Saturday, my mother woke with another high fever. My father had already called the doctor and was about to go pick up some new antibiotic.

"Daddy, let me ride with you."

"Okay. Get a move on." I could tell he had a thousand things on his mind, and I was not one of them. "See if you can find Harry. We will have to take him with us, too."

I found my youngest brother watching Howdy Doody. He was none too happy when I pulled him away and dragged him out to the car. It occurred to me Daddy had no idea what was going on right under his nose, and I should let him know.

"Daddy, do you know Mrs. Simons?"

"No. Who is Mrs. Simons?" my father asked. Harry was squirming in his seat, wanting to go back to Howdy Doody.

"The lady that stopped you in the hall yesterday, says she just has one *M* in her name."

I wanted to ask what he thought about her. I wanted to say something was not right, but my father just told me to hurry up.

We picked up the prescription and brought it home. Tim was back in his room working on model airplanes. Mother raised her head enough to take her pills with a sip of water, and I slipped out quietly to let her sleep. By late afternoon she was up and drinking a cup of coffee. The new drug worked.

"George," she was saying to my father. "She is not saved. She would never have these problems if she had taken Jesus for her Savior."

I was the only "she" around that my mother could be talking about. How did my mother even know what my problems were? Or even if I had any? She never asked. And how did she know whether or not I was saved for that matter? She hadn't asked that either.

"Evelyn," my father was standing up for me, I thought. "I think you are making this into something it is not. It's just a stage."

This was even worse, I was evidently nothing more than a stage. It was not the cancer that took my mother down, it was me. I was the cancer. Gertrude told me not to bother my head about it.

The church women found so many demons under the cushions and in the corners that my mother did not have the time or the strength to believe in herself any more, much less me. As she grew weaker, I grieved over what was happening to her. I had to concede that Mrs. Simons may have been right. Maybe some devil had taken up residence. But somebody else would have to fight that devil for my mother.

1953. We girls were sixteen. We had the radio up as high as it would go and all the windows open. It was the middle of July—me in my old white shorts and my new blue and white striped shirt, Ellen letting her dark curls fly, Jeanne holding onto her hat and Martha with curlers on just in case we ran into somebody we knew. Just a bunch of girls out driving.

"Did you hear they kicked the new girl out of school?" Jeanne drove the Chevy with one hand. In our town, nobody had ever been kicked out of school, so it was big news. Jeanne was always the first to break a story.

"Jillian? I don't know her last name. What happened?" asked Ellen

"She was pregnant, that's what happened." Jeanne said it bluntly, waiting for the shock value.

"Hush," said Martha. "Do *not* say that word."

"Oh, come on. That's what it is: *pregnant.*" Jeanne gave it emphasis this time. "And it's against the law to go to high school if you're pregnant."

"You're so dumb, Jeanne. It's not the law. It's school rules."

"I wonder why she didn't call Dr. Cloud . . ." Martha flicked her cigarette out the window.

"Who's Dr. Cloud?" Ellen always asked questions. You would think she did not know anything at all.

"Well, silly, he is the doctor who makes house calls if a girl in Mountain Brook gets pregnant." Martha knew everything about everything. "Yup. Drives right up to her front door, puts her in the car, and presto a few hours later, she is back home."

"How do you know?" I asked.

"Just do." I believed her.

It had not rained in months. Overton Road was dry as an ant bed. The wind filled our blouses and we let our arms drift across the car's window ledge to catch the air. We were sixteen and we were flying. Somebody suggested earlier that we drive over the mountain and ride down Overton Road because we had never been there. Overton Road had a reputation for undesirables who fought on Saturday nights. The area was forbidden and irresistible.

We drank our cokes as we drove along, then turned off the paved road onto Overton, which was nothing more than an uneven bed of ugly red clay that wound through pine trees and scrub, not a house or a person in sight. Ellen wanted to turn back, but we had come this far. We had to see what was so bad at the end, and we won.

The Chevy bounced in and out of jagged ruts, throwing us from side to side. Jeanne was smoking a Kool and flicked her ashes out into the road. Somebody said "end of road or bust," which was exactly what we intended to do—until we saw the police car parked just ahead of us. Its lights and sirens were off. One policeman sat in his patrol car making a call; the other was focused on something in a ditch.

We slowed way down, trying to see what the cop was doing. None of us ever expected to see a body, but we did. With horror, we watched as the cop pulled a body out of the ditch. It looked like a thin man with dark hair combed straight back from his forehead. We drew closer then. The body was that of a girl, probably not much older than we were. She wore a sort of gray uniform that looked way too big for her and was partially covered with a small flowered blanket like a baby blanket.

The policeman in the squad car waved angrily at us, shouting at us to get out of there as his radio blared.

"Get them out of there, *now*," said the radio. The cop spoke back into the microphone.

"Can't you get us some help out here?" The response was unintelligible.

Nobody wanted to leave more than I did, and nobody had to tell us twice, but we had to turn around. We turned, upsetting coke bottles and losing lit cigarettes in the upholstery. Before we reached the highway, we were a mass of hysteria, coke, ashes, smoke and dust. We never said a word, but we heard each other thinking.

"It was not her . . . Jillian I mean," said Jeanne. She turned back onto the Florida Short Route and drove us all home in silence.

That night, an article in the paper read: "Woman found dead on Overton Road." My father sat on the far end of the Naugahyde sofa under the one standing lamp. "She was married," he said. "She died of a back room abortion. Her name was Mrs. Pilgrim."

"Hush, George," said my mother. "We don't talk about such things."

"They ought to make it legal," continued my father. "Something that dangerous needs to be done in a hospital. Any doctor who does these things in his kitchen should be locked up."

"It might not have been a doctor," I said. "Could have been anybody. They found her a long way out there on Overton, didn't they? Nobody lives on Overton."

My parents discussed briefly that God must have had a purpose even if we could not understand it. The poor girl was predestined to die.

I could not, no matter how hard I tried, see God sitting by, letting a demonic doctor carry this out. I could only imagine a sad and frightened woman in the hands of somebody who probably believed he or she could do what he or she could not. I knew that somebody botched the job and butchered the patient—somebody without training and without sterile equipment and without a back-up emergency system if something went wrong. Mrs. Pilgrim did not know Dr. Cloud. She did not live in Mountain Brook. She had no surgeon, no nurse and no hospital, nobody to save her.

I took my bath, put on my pajamas and went out to the kitchen to talk to Gertrude about what we had just read in the paper. She knew all about things like that and let me talk on and on.

"I was pregnant once, too."

"I guess you never told anybody," was all I could think to say.

7. A Homecoming

Funny I don't remember anything about the events that led up to that day. No discussion, no sharing around brochures, not even a hint out of my brother Tim, who would turn thirteen that fall, that my parents were making plans for him. But then, I wasn't very astute in those teenage years. My life spun as wildly as any other teen's.

The night of the announcement, my father sat in the driveway waiting for the church ladies to leave. He sat so long he had to honk. One by one the ladies donned hats and gloves, took up their matching handbags, kissed my mother on the cheek and held her hand momentously before they said their goodbyes.

`Mrs. Simons hung back to speak to me. "Faith alone cures," she told me, as though her words might chop me in two.

I didn't know either what she was trying to tell me or how to respond. Since I didn't say anything, she repeated it.

"Yes, ma'am," I said this time, still perplexed.

"Your mother worries about you," she said pointedly to me. She took forever to leave.

"Yes, ma'am." I said again, no more enlightened. I kept the door open for my father.

"The Lord is leading you both, I know," she said to my father as he came up the walk.

"We will certainly give that some thought." It was one of his stock phrases, his tongue-in-cheek one.

Relieved of my duty, I disappeared to my room to finish my book. I chose books alphabetically by author, because that is the way our library arranged them. Beginning on the top shelf, left hand corner, with *A*, I had long ago finished Charles Dickens and George Elliott. I had reached *S*, and my current read, James Street, was the sexiest book I had ever read.

Gertrude announced dinner the way she always did: "Y'all come and get it before I throw it away," but this time without the accompanying grin. It was Thursday night, Jackson Street Baptist Church night, and she was already late.

Tim took forever coming downstairs and my mother took forever saying the blessing, but we finally began. Tim heaped his plate and Daddy called him a bottomless pit. Gertrude left for the bus, and my parents began to discuss some religious school I had never heard of.

I thought briefly about bringing up the subject of the prom or even broaching the issue of James Street, but thought better of that, too. I briefly contemplated saying I had smallpox or planned to leave for Paris on the next flight. In utter despair I suggested we discuss Shakespeare or the elections, but I was met with silence. My few attempts to divert table conversations away from the Bible always failed.

"Well, Lyn, if you don't want to be a part of this family, then we understand. You are in our prayers. Maybe it's better if you go to your room and think about it."

I could not believe I was hearing this from my father. It confused me. His words were not unkind, really, but not kind either. I excused myself from the table and retreated in tears to another long silent evening in my room.

During that particularly grim evening meal, my mother made an announcement even as I made my retreat.

"Tim is going away to boarding school to become a missionary," she called out to me. I expected her to add something, some kind of explanation, but she did not.

"Boarding school?" I asked. I turned and looked back at Tim, but he sat in abject silence.

"This is not just any boarding school. It is for missionaries," she finished.

"He's not even thirteen—he is just beginning high school," I began. "Why?"

My father tried to save the day by launching into a glowing description, saying what a beautiful campus it had among the palm trees in Florida. He lost me somewhere about the time he said it had tennis courts. It was all irrelevant.

How had I been so distracted by my own life that I didn't even know this was being considered? I waited for some word from Tim, but he only looked at his plate. After dinner, I tried again to talk to him, but this time he looked down at the floor. He mumbled something I could not understand. In my room, I dissolved in tears, wrestling with a deeper kind of sadness.

In a bit, through the closed door, I heard Gertrude talking to my mother.

"Mrs. Stafford, go see 'bout your daughter. You go on up to her. She's crying."

I waited quietly for my mother after that. Finally, before lights out, I heard her walking across the hall toward my room. She didn't knock and she didn't come in; she spoke to me through the closed door.

"Are you all right, Dear?" It was something. I said yes, and she went away.

My brother left not long after that. His absence was unreal and unnecessary. All I could do was wait for him to come home.

The night he left, Gertrude missed church, even though she made it to the bus stop on time. The bus driver drove right past her. He had done it before. Sometimes he even picked up speed, as though he thought it funny. The same bus driver had been with Birmingham Transit for years. He was the one who drove us kids downtown to the YWCA or to the movies.

"It's church night," Gertrude muttered as she returned from the bus stop. "And he knows it."

That was enough for me. I reported the incident to the Transit System.

The next night as I lay tossing in my bed, I heard male voices in the yard behind Gertrude's room. Her door was immediately under my window, so I could hear everything clearly. I rose and stood by the window to listen.

Whoever they were, they spoke in muted tones, threateningly. For once I was glad we all had burglar bars on our windows.

I made out two voices but could not see the speakers, because they stood under the porch, trying to coerce Gertrude into opening her door. The tones was more sinister than shouts and epithets. Although I had my hand on the phone's receiver, something told me it would do no good to call the police. My parents slept soundly on the other side of the house. I waited and listened, hyper alert, fingernails digging into my palms.

My throat was so dry, I doubted I could talk to the police even if I did call. Finally, I heard the intruders knock on her door a time or two. When the knocking stopped, I picked up the phone, but they had apparently given up. I saw them walk away. I stayed awake the rest of that night. The next morning I told her I heard everything and that I had my hands on the phone the whole time.

"And I was on the other side of that door with a brick." She figured out what I had done and begged me not to call the Transit Authority again. The peacefulness between us stretched again. It was I who had caused these men to come knocking on her door in the middle of the night. I had no doubt caused her other anguish just by being born where I was, who I was. It did not matter that I had not chosen to be white or live in Mountain Brook, but I would have given anything to have had it otherwise.

"Ain't no need to be afraid," she said. "It won't do you no good."

"But I am afraid." I wanted to add "for you" but I did not. Suddenly it became clear to me that my actions did bring on consequences for other people. My life *was* wrapped up in theirs, and something inside me grew up, not necessarily happily.

After Tim left, so much happened that Christmas came before I knew it. My parents drove all the way to Florida to bring Tim home for the holidays, and I waited. After forever, my father pulled in the drive.

Tim looked wonderful. He had an actual jacket on, a navy blue one. I ran up to him to hug him. To my astonishment, his neck was stiff as a board, he did not respond. Something was very wrong. I wanted to know what they had done to him, but all I could think to do now was to try to cheer him up.

"How about a game of Monopoly?" I offered. He told me no.

"Okay," I said. "I'll go get the comics and you can read them first."

"No, no, I can't." I let it lie for a little while, but no matter what I suggested all he would say was "No, no, I can't."

Thinking he just needed time to readjust, I waited a day and tried again.

"Let's go to a movie." Nothing. "New Superman comic?"

"No, no, I can't go to movies. I can't read comics," Tim said, "and I can't ride in cars."

To say I was stunned would not do justice to what I felt. Nothing satisfied him. "It's a Superman comic, stupid! How many thousand times have we read Superman together? Or Archie or Wonder Woman or Veronica for that matter?"

"I can't. I can't. I can't." Tim hung his head. When he finally looked up I saw he, too, was dismayed. "I took a pledge at school."

Then he launched into how he now loathed and feared the things of this world, but he failed to convince me. He was taller than he had been, but not as tall as I was, and his hair had lost its childish softness. It was thick and dark like our father's.

"What else can't you do?" My words had no joy in them.

"Listen to the radio."

"Listen to the radio? You're kidding. What about Amos and Andy? What about the Green Hornet?"

"No, I took a pledge."

"Who made you take that pledge?"

"I wanted to."

"Tim. No. Surely it doesn't apply when you're not at school." I was reduced to pleading.

"Yes it does. I can't serve the Lord and listen to the radio or go to dances or ride in cars or read comic books or play cards or talk to atheists."

"Baloney," I said. My father's handiest word. "You can't ride in cars? So tell me how you got home?"

"That's different. It's Christmas and I had to come home. Daddy brought me."

"Okay, so you're home. That makes it okay, you see? Those are school rules and you're at home. We don't have those rules. You want those stupid rules to spoil Christmas?"

I looked from then on for the kid who helped me hunt salamanders, the brother I fought for, defended, loved, and waited after school for. But what I saw was a disoriented soul. "What have they done to you?" I did not expect an answer and he did not give one.

My heart hurt for him in a terrible, profound way. I had failed him, too.

When it came time for him to graduate, I was away at college. When that school year ended, my parents drove me to South Florida for his graduation. There was no "Land of Hope and Glory." They marched my brother out on a stage with a lit candle to hold while he gave what they called a testimony. He was dressed in white like the sacrificial lamb he was.

In 1958, at twenty-one, I returned to Birmingham to register to vote. I paid my poll tax and waited in line to take the test now required by the state of Alabama. They called it a "literacy test," and everyone had to pass it in order to vote. Ahead of me in line was a nice looking, gray-haired African-American in a tan suit. When he was called up to the table, he held his hat in his hands as he came forward. The official, in an accountant's vest, squinted at a paper before him but pushed it aside. He needed no help.

"Name Woodrow Wilson's running mate and tell me what platform he ran on."[94]

The older man spoke politely to his interrogator.

"The answer to that question is that no Negro is going to vote in Jefferson County this year." The elderly gentleman turned and left the courthouse.

"Next." I was next in line. "Who was the first president of the United States?" he asked, full of self-satisfaction.

I wanted to hit him. Was this what Alabama had done to democracy? I had gotten to know a few African-American students from Howard University in Washington DC when they joined us for events at Hollins. The college in Roanoke, Virginia prided itself on producing musicals like the *Mikado* and hosting conferences. It occurred to me that those Howard Students must be registering to vote for the first time, too. I had high hopes they would not have to undergo the kind of treatment I witnessed in Birmingham.

I learned later from these committed students that they gave up their holidays to attend workshops on how to get out the vote. They still believed our democracy would work. They did not believe in demonstrations and certainly not in violence, but a rumor was spreading among them that if all else failed, they would consider a march on Washington. I even heard the words "peaceful demonstration" for the first time in my life from them.

I told my father the story of my day at the polls but could not bring myself to tell Gertrude. Instead, I asked her what she thought about demonstrations.

"My church says if we want to fix something, we have to go through the courts. They say demonstrating is wrong and so do I. Do that make sense?"

"I think so." Actually, I felt a little relieved. My feelings were in the peace-at-all-costs category.

"Rev. Jackson [95] thinks it's only low class Negroes who want to demonstrate." She added under her breath "And I don't want nothing to do with them."

"What do you mean *low class*?" I never dreamed African-Americans used those words to describe their own. Not that it mattered, but in my particular white world, we used the word *common*.

"Like some of those Negroes that came to Margaret after I grew up. They were trouble. I wouldn't have left Margaret if they hadn't come."

She was right about the trouble, but it was not just in Margaret. The South had been courting trouble all along. I just had not seen it until that day. She changed the subject.

"Now tell me about Mr. Burns," she said.

She was talking about Burns Johns, whom I was dating at the time, a senior at the University of Alabama in Tuscaloosa. She knew I thought I was in love, but she had not yet passed judgment on my choice of men.

My mother had. If she thought I was serious about a young man, she sometimes took him aside and quizzed him to find out whether or not he was saved. Not until she had treated three or four boys this way did one of them have the courage to tell me what was going on. I despaired of ever knowing what she thought about them as human beings, so I turned to my father for his opinion, but he left such opinions to my mother. I had little to go on.

Both of my parents were wrapped up in the "Christian war on communism." Our mailbox filled to overflowing with sleazy pamphlets, magazines, flyers, tracts and booklets containing supposed threats and ugly cartoons. Nikita Khrushchev had indeed banged his shoe on the table in a fit of rage at the United States and had said he was going to bury us. That one temper tantrum led to a no longer subtle, righteous frenzy of anti-communism everywhere I turned. Communists were taking over our government, poisoning our water with fluoride, corrupting our children and about to bomb us with secret stockpiles of atomic weapons. The public bought it. School children drilled for it and hid under their desks.[96] President Truman even established the Federal Civil Defense Administration to build bomb shelters, and these bomb shelters were endorsed by the John Birch Society.

Better to be safe than sorry, my father said. He designed his own bomb shelter.

By this time, I had marriage on my mind, certainly not communists. Burns approached my father to ask him to give us our blessing as he should have, but he refused to comment and sent him on to speak to my mother. In those days I did not know what was going on in those interviews. Somehow, Burns survived the quiz. Looking back, I believe Daddy was against the marriage. But at the time I thought he really did not care, that he was just too busy building bunkers.

The next day my father woke me early to ask me if I wanted to go to Europe, which was astonishing. He had always drilled it into us that there was nothing in Europe we could not find in the United States. I took him up on it, of course.

By the time I returned from Europe, he had built a bomb shelter fortified on every side by twelve inches of concrete, lead, dirt, sand, and bricks. When it was finished, he and my mother stocked it with canned foods. Eventually he invited me out to see his handiwork.

Burns came along with me. I was going to marry him anyway.

"Daddy, what on earth are you thinking? Do you really believe communists are going to bomb us? Look at Russia, Daddy, all they have is a ballet!"

"Well, you never know. Just look at this gem! It took some real engineering, don't you think?" He ignored my question.

"Is that what you're doing? Engineering?"

"You bet. And if BIRMCO can't build them, nobody can." He was not joking.

"You really think the communists are going to bomb us?"

"Well, maybe not the communists in Birmingham."

"What?" I said. "Who do you know who is a communist?"

"Well, I heard the communists want to build a soviet Negro republic right here in Birmingham." He thought a minute and added, "I don't think that makes much sense."[97]

I thanked God for this small concession, but he went on to destroy his credibility completely.

"But it seems that the communists have infiltrated your high school.[98] Furthermore, the Kremlin has taken over the CIO. I am sorry about that; I always respected the CIO."[99]

"And which newspaper is that?"

He produced a copy of the *Birmingham Independent*, a badly typeset weekly. He nodded his head sadly. He believed it, but he was prepared. He had built a solid, functional bomb shelter, approved by the government of the United States.

Burns pointed at the mound of dirt. "And you think we might have to move in there some day?"

"You never know," said my father.

"In that case, how on earth will I ever find it?" It wasn't near anything I knew.

"I'll draw you a map," he told us. And he did.

Like many young people, Burns and I married a year after we graduated, according to custom. I thought him very handsome: Six-foot-two with dark brown hair, he wore horn-rimmed glasses, which I interpreted to mean he was studious. Besides, he was a good dancer. By then he was stationed at Fort Jackson, South Carolina, for his six-month tour of duty and missed most of the pre-wedding festivities.

We married in May and drove to Fort Jackson, where we began life in a cottage on Blossom Street, right off Divine. Fort Jackson, I learned, was not named for the infamous Confederate general but for the ignominious president who massacred Creeks at Horseshoe Bend and passed the Indian Removal Act of 1830.

We drove straight from the church to the base, foregoing a honeymoon. The troops told me my new husband "could sure shoot the bull." For some reason I thought that was a compliment. I learned mostly that what he intended to make of this marriage had nothing to do with what we had promised each other.

After Fort Jackson, I dreamed we might move to New York or Washington DC, where I could work in an art gallery. Instead, we returned to Birmingham because, Burns reasoned, that was where he was more likely to find a good job. But when we actually made the move and were in our first apartment, my new husband decided he needed a sabbatical and put his feet up until the next year, which was 1962.

I returned to work at the University of Alabama Medical School as a lab tech in the Pathology Department, not necessarily a job for an Art History major. My first responsibility was the care and feeding of a thousand white mice. The second was helping in the lab. The lab was Dr. Sidney P. Kent's invention, and research was his life. It became mine, too. Everything about it was exciting: tubes running in every direction, contraptions for freeze drying hanging from the ceiling and coils of metal tubing running from floor to ceiling. This was a lab Rube Goldberg could love.

Usually Dr. Kent sent me to the morgue for specimens, but there were times he went alone. When he was on his way back to the lab with a particularly intriguing organ or bit of tissue, I could hear him coming. He always shouted "Eureka" at the top of his lungs as he approached with whatever it was on a cafeteria tray. We cut slices of whatever it was with a freezing microtome, then examined it under his electron microscope, which was one of the first. I stained slides and sometimes helped write his presentations, which may or may not have turned out well.

I was tired a lot and learned how to prop myself up on a stool with my back against the swinging door and sleep. Dr. Kent woke me when he opened the door and knocked me off the stool.

I never really knew what Burns did that year. When I asked, he took offense, so I let it drop. But we had a baby coming. Just before the baby came, in May 1962, he took a job in a furniture store.

We named the baby Keith after nobody in particular. Because I entered motherhood with as little preparation as I had entered marriage, everyone including my husband thought it best if I spent the first few days at my parents' house. I was not so sure. Gertrude reassured me and said she would be there.

My husband drove us from the hospital. The family gathered to cuddle my baby and praise him as intelligent and good looking. Once I had my own child in my arms, Burns left for our rental house, a cottage on the edge of the zoo. My mother, Gertrude and I were left to fend for ourselves.

"He is just beautiful," said Gertrude who seemed to be taking charge. She cuddled him close until he all but disappeared in her aproned bosom. She felt his bottom.

"Mrs. Johns, I think he's wet!"

I cringed when she called me that. I wanted her to call me by my first name again, but she would not. I unpinned the offending diaper, and my mother took one look at the stump of cord on his belly and pointed. "What is that?"

Of course, I thought, she had never seen one before. A nurse came with her every time she had a baby. We pulled a diaper out of the blue diaper bag hanging on the crib, which was nothing more than a large piece of gauze that unfolded and unfolded again until it seemed as big as a table cloth. Nobody moved.

"Do you know how to fold it?" I asked my mother. She looked at me terrified. Somebody else folded those diapers, too. I turned to Gertrude.

"No, ma'am. Our diapers didn't look anything like that."

We were good at admiring babies but slow in the care-of department. Neither babies nor diapers came with instructions. Together, through halving and thirding and quartering and again in reverse order, we hit upon a design to swaddle him in that made him look like a poorly constructed turnover.

Then I curled his tiny hand around my finger and laid him down beside me. In that rare, unbelievable moment, I experienced something mothers all over the world experience when they look deeply into their child's questioning eyes for the first time and fall forever in love.

My mother looked proud and uncomplicated for a change. Gertrude looked wistful. I had never seen a wistful Gertrude before.

"How was your trip to Chicago? Did you love it?" I asked her then.

"Well, I did and I still do." She smiled. "My sister is there."

"Then what brought you back?"

"Well, I had to see that baby!"

I could tell she considered him hers, too. I slept then.

My husband dropped by after work but found me in bed. He meant to be clever of course, but it set me off on the wrong foot.

"Women have babies in the cotton fields all the time. They don't even stop working. They just have their babies and get up and go right on picking cotton."

"Huh! I ain't never seen no such thing," said Gertrude.

"Did you ever pick cotton?" Burns asked Gertrude. I couldn't believe he actually asked her that. I was grateful that he at least didn't ask if she ever had a baby.

"No, Sir, I never did," she said as she drew herself up indignantly.

Those rocky first days passed, and my husband took us home. I struggled, not just because my pains seemed worse but because everything was new and strange. Then came the first crisis. I was washing diapers by hand and hanging them outside to dry. The rains came, and there was not a single dry diaper in the house. I didn't have a car. All I had was the telephone, so I called my husband, but he was less than happy to hear from me.

"Can't you see I'm working? What do you want me to do?"

"Please, could you pick up a few more diapers for me?" I knew it sounded lame.

"Call your mother." That was all. He hung up. The elephant was in the room.

In June, I went back to work, but not back to the lab. I took a lowly copy editing job with Birmingham Publishing Company. My job was to ready an author's manuscript for publication, and I could not have loved it more.

Many well-known and lesser-known authors passed through those doors. To me, the most compelling were our local African-American authors like Geraldine Moore, who wrote the society column for the African-American community, Dr. John Nixon who wrote his memoir, *Stepping Stones,* and the wealthy entrepreneur, A. G. Gaston who named his book *Green Power.* Whenever I worked with these wonderful authors, I learned a little more about Birmingham and how completely ignorant I had been about this side of Birmingham. By 1963 I was hooked.

That Sunday in September, a tragedy occurred in the African-American community in Birmingham that changed everything forever, for all of us. Somebody blew up the 16th Street Baptist Church, and four beautiful little girls were killed. I drove over to see Gertrude. For the first time, I put my arms around her and wept. We had nothing we could possibly say to each other that made any sense. The horror of that bombing and especially its aftermath haunts me today.

On Monday morning as I drove to the Publishing Company, I took the road that went past the bombed-out church. An old green Chevrolet cruised slowly in front of me, almost stopping in front of the blackened hole in the church. Four men hung out of the windows waving Confederate flags.

My whole being exploded then, as much as if I, too, had felt the blast, which in one sense I had. I pulled up beside that car, rolled down the driver's window in my car and shouted through my tears at them—ugly words I never knew I knew. I could not find words nasty enough to tell the bastards how disgusting they were. Finally, they pulled their flags in and drove off. By then, my heart was pounding so I could hardly drive. By the time I reached the office, I walked straight through to the ladies' room, hot tears streaming down my face, where I could do nothing but beat on the walls. I was glad Gertrude had not been with me.

Gertrude no longer came to my house or my mother's on a regular basis. She sometimes worked in an orphanage across town then, but during those happy months when Keith was a baby, she occasionally came to my house on Mondays. By the time of that bombing, Keith could sit up.

I could tell Gertrude was restless. She had something on her mind other than taking care of small children, and she finally got it out.

"I can't stay no more now, Mrs. Johns. I've got things I need to do in this life, and if I don't do them now, I won't never get them done."

"I knew it," I said. "Gertrude, even I can tell when your mind is somewhere else. I think my mind has been somewhere else, too."

She picked Keith up and held him on her shoulder.

"How come you know that?" she asked.

"Well, when you stopped having to fold diapers, I saw relief in your eyes! No. I know that's not all of it, is it? You have something important to do, don't you?"

She laughed out loud, deep and hearty.

I had been right. "So where is it this time? Where are you going?"

"Washington."

"The state?"

"No, ma'am. DC."

"And what is in DC?"

"Well, it's a march. I'm going to march."

"I thought Reverend Jackson was against marches."

"He is, but he is not me. I am going to Washington to march with the women. We think maybe it is not enough to vote; maybe the law doesn't work so good any more. Maybe a demonstration might help. I have to go. It is about all I can do to help us get some civil rights."

"And your children?" She called the orphans her children. They would be all right, she said, at least while she was gone.

I took Keith from her and put him in his white plastic high chair with a handful of crackers to push around with a spoon. Supper was cooking in the oven, so I dished up a jar of beans and wrapped a thigh and drumstick for her to take along. Then I looked around for a sweet and added two cupcakes to the bag. I was a little embarrassed about my cooking.

"It's not much. I'll be thinking about you."

Before my husband came home, she was gone. I did not discuss it with him because I knew he would not want to hear it. I looked in the papers for days, to see if the women's march actually happened, but could not find a thing. Life went on. I felt for all of those women, but it was still not my fight.

On the outside, I lived like the working mother I was, taking a free-lance job when I could and volunteering here and there as though nothing else was going on. But it was. Huge things were going on, and everything was in flux.

8. Affirmative Action

Nineteen sixty-four brought us the Civil Rights Act, some of which governed hiring practices. Lyndon B. Johnson signed Title VII into law, and the government declared Affirmative Action applied to all companies with more than 25 employees.

A Compliance Examiner wrote my father that the government was coming to scrutinize his hiring practices. The Company must prove it did not discriminate, especially on the basis of race.[100]

The Company readied itself as best it could, but when Jack Davis handed over the list of all the employees in the plant, my father's eyebrows shot up. Only one African-American on the list: the janitor, Henry Sims. He told me he had no idea, and I believed him. The year before, he and Smitty had talked about bringing on more African-American workers, and Smitty was supposed to look into it, but with all that was going on, nothing came of it.

In spite of all the Civil Rights efforts going on around us, in spite of more and more calls for justice, the KKK was still in control. They pulled everything they had out of their bag of tricks: telling white workers that black workers wanted their jobs, threatening African-Americans who tried to help themselves, nullifying everything that might have helped. African-American men and women were afraid to ask for a job, much less run for office or join a union.

Henry was singularly not afraid, but then he was not a threat to anybody. The day the inspectors came, Henry appeared wearing brand new corduroys and a starched blue shirt. It was his idea. My father was overjoyed and surprised. He asked Henry to walk with him and the inspectors, which he did—every step of the way. When the officials questioned Henry about how well he was treated, he had an answer.

"Well, you see, Gentlemen, it's like this. I have my own bathroom." He pointed to a door that had a sign over it that still read "colored." My father smiled a little. I think the inspectors got the point.

Henry also brought his blue '52 Dodge along with him. It was old, but polished until it shone like a mirror. Henry parked it in front of the office, and everyone breathed a sigh of relief. Everybody thought BIRMCO just might have passed the test. Everybody thanked Henry, and my father gave him a much-deserved raise. Then my father set out to make some changes in personnel, even before they learned for sure that the company definitely did not pass muster.

Once again our government offered its own form of encouragement. It offered to pay the Company to train minority workers in relevant fields, specifically to train new hires for BIRMCO. My father approved. It was an excellent idea and the times were right.

Birmingham's hated white supremacist, Bull Connor, was no longer Commissioner of Public Safety. He was no longer the most powerful man in the city and he was no longer able to flim-flam the public into hiding bombings and beatings and castrations. [101] He had done such crazy things as blaming the bombing of the 16th Avenue Baptist Church on the church itself, saying the African-American community did it to raise sympathy for itself. With Connor gone, citizens believed the South would rise again, in a better way.

BIRMCO happily invited the Pipefitters Union to train new welders. The Pipefitters boasted it had the best training program in town, and twenty-seven men from all around St. Clair County showed up at the plant that very first day, most of them African-American. The mood in the yard was festive—for a week.

At the end of that week, my father wanted to show me how the training was going. We bypassed the office and went straight out to his beloved shop, where he greeted those on the night shift as though he had not seen them for years. Two welders in training, unidentifiable under their helmets, concentrated on their work.

Suited in goggles and gloves, they had their brown boots planted firmly in the flux and gravel, steadying themselves as they welded two layers of steel together, one brad at a time. The noise was deafening, but to us it was heaven.

Together, we watched the welders' throwers shoot blue flames from their torches. Showers of white-hot sparks flew in the air above as steel plates aligned and melted together, almost seamlessly, in the hottest part of the flame. These new men were good, precise. They had already learned just the right motion and the exact amount of heat so no steel was wasted. Men in other parts of the shop still slugged bolts down by hand.

One young man came up to my father and shook his hand and thanked him for the opportunity. He told us he had come early the evening before and was about to leave: The night had been a good one. The newbie went home whistling.

Then, as the second week progressed, the potential hirees dropped out, one by one. Men with such promise, even the most ambitious and most talented, left without telling anybody they were not coming back or where they could be reached. People talked of course. Just another group of lazy, shiftless good-for-nothings abusing the system. What else could you expect? My father had pinned his hopes on another group of no-goods. How else could he explain their attrition? He groused on about their ingratitude, forgetting the lessons learned during War Production Board days. Had he forgotten how white workers resented trainees of color, and the fights and killings and strikes that threatened to shut down the war effort? Or how the president of the United States finally had to intervene?

That kind of lazy-shiftless talk had conveniently absolved almost everybody for as long as he could remember, and he did not stop it. He was wrong, of course, but his immediate concern was time and money, losses sustained in the training venture. He had lost face. So when the government seemed satisfied that he had made the effort, he vowed not to do it again. It was not worth the battle.

1974. The plant in Springville had grown, my children were in school and I was once more helping out at Birmingham Manufacturing. My father gave me the title of "accounting coordinator" and a desk near Jack Davis.

We drove the forty-five minutes from Birmingham to Springville every day because it gave him time to think as well as a chance to unburden himself, especially about my mother. My work day began after I drove each of my three children to his or her respective school. Keith was twelve, Susan was ten, and Walter was five, and all were in different schools. My job, once again at the medical school, was only part time.

Jack's dark brown hair was trimmed neatly around a bald spot on the top of his head, just the way monks wore it. He never seemed flustered, always spoke softly. I set up my typewriter and opened the ledgers. At intervals, Jack looked up at me over his spectacles and asked if I was doing all right, which was his way of asking if I understood which figures went in which column or how to take inventory.

It was only bookkeeping, but I took it as a good puzzle waiting for me to solve. I would never ask Jack unless I absolutely could not figure it out by myself. For reasons unfathomable to me, my father gave me tasks way beyond my competency, such as finding a picture of a "removable gooseneck drawbar" or "instructions to permit the forward end of the trailer bed to engage the ground or other supporting surface." When one day he asked me to find instructions for "quick actuating means for holding the forward end of the trailer bed at selected elevations," I went crying to Jack.

Jack knew all along how frustrated I was, but he had no idea how truly desperate I was to hide my incurable ignorance of mechanics. He stepped in to help; he found pictures and instructions. After each crisis, I dug gratefully and wholeheartedly into the ledgers, lettering as precisely as any monk. Surely my father would appreciate such artistic ledger entries, so much so that he would never again assign me a task beyond my competency. But that was not what he intended to do.

"Jack," I asked, as the light began to dawn. "Which file do *you* look in for these things? Show me."

He took me to the back room to a drawer labeled "Patents." My father invented things. I had always known that, but I had never put two and two together. This was how he chose to let me know what his inventions were. He wanted me to find out for myself. Finally, I stopped acting as though I had it all together. We had a new understanding, my father and I, a new kinship.

A housekeeper stayed with my mother now. My husband was away, as he was so much of the time, and I was once more a passenger in my father's car on the way to the plant, a much wiser employee and a more sympathetic daughter. We talked as we rolled along. The ride had been otherwise uneventful.

Until I looked up. Ahead of us on the overpass stood an odd gathering of men that, in that brief second, appeared to be hanging over the guard rail, waiting for something. Even though the cars ahead of us passed under without incident, the scene felt oddly menacing. I asked my father to slow down so I could get a better look.

I was right about it being menacing, but I was very wrong about slowing down. A shout went up from the men on the bridge as they sent a barrage of rocks down on us. The rocks hit their mark, and a crack appeared in the windshield. We tried to dodge more of them by speeding up under the bridge for protection, but we had to come out eventually, one way or another. My father thought fast and spun the car 180 degrees back the way we had come, and drove until we were out of range. We slowed down, looking for any patrolman that might be cruising the highway.

"It's not the union. The union is not striking," he told me. "It's a wildcat strike, but I never thought this would happen."

The Springville police told us they could not do a thing unless either my father or I could identify the perpetrators and press charges, which of course we could not. Their faces had been in silhouette, the sun behind them. The chief of police looked directly at my father with an expressionless face and shrugged his shoulders. He clearly planned to take no action. My father was as angry as he was the day the paint store clerk refused to sell him lead paint—probably angrier. I had never heard him raise his voice, but he did this time.

"I will not tolerate a shrug from an officer of the law! You are a policeman and you have a *duty* to control mobs."

I tried to control my father. The Klan had close ties with the law, even in Springville, and we had reason to be uneasy. We were not hurt, but I had no idea what else might be in store. We took the back way to the plant, even though the chief assured us nobody would be hanging over the bridge. The perpetrators were long gone.

In the yard, the whole staff as well as a few workmen wandered around outside, seemingly lost, moving among indeterminate scatterings of metal objects. I first recognized Jack's head in the crowd, then Smitty's tall frame towering over the others. As Smitty walked toward us, the little congregation of people formed a path to let him through. Behind him came Fayme George from the office, Wayne, Ed Vickery, one of the engineers and one or two men from the shop.

Unopened containers of grease and gallons of paint, loose tires and other equipment littered the grounds. Wayne and others moved swiftly, picking up the flotsam and jetsam, and Jack plopped himself down in the dirt to help mount tires.

"Thanks everybody. Can't deliver them unless we finish them. But seems they could figure out that this is where their money comes from." Smitty seemed as confused as my father.

Inside the shop, the machines were deathly quiet. The last of the men who were departing to join the strike walked past us. They averted their eyes and walked unimpeded right past Smitty, down the road toward Margaret.

A short distance away, strikers chanted "Strike. Strike. Strike," while they beat on tin cans and fence posts. I heard sounds like baseball bats on metal, and loud noises like comealongs breaking into something.

"What do they want?" my father asked Wayne.

The Company had met with the union three or four times already. Promises had been made; demands had been met. Wayne looked up from the water cooler where he was splashing water on his face, ready to respond, but it was Jack who answered.

"Trouble," he said.

Those who stayed to help clean up the mess tried to decide what to do next. Smitty spoke with authority.

"Thanks, everybody. Thanks for your help. We cannot finish everything right this minute, and we do not know what else might happen. Even though the sheriff is on his way to keep his eye on things, I think we will close the shop and let all of you go on home. I know what you might be up against: Just look at that car. But we hear those men have gone home."

Wayne and the other two took off. They sent me home, too.

By that Saturday, violence had erupted all over the State of Alabama, violence especially against picket lines. Strikes and fights broke out at American Cast Iron Pipe, at Stockham Valve and Fitting and at just about every major manufacturing plant in Birmingham.

This time, the war raged within the unions. Union members lashed out at their non-union coworkers. In the shooting and bombing rampages that followed, nobody was sure who was responsible for the violence. Shouts of "Scab" and "Commie Pinko" and "Nigger Lover" seemed to be aimed at the older locals mostly, but the shouts came from strikers and non-strikers alike.

Smitty called my father at home that Sunday. He never called except in an emergency and never, since my father had become a religious man, on Sunday. Smitty had more bad news.

"They burned my barn down."

"Who did? Are you hurt? Did you see them?"

"No, I wasn't hurt and no I didn't see them. The union's not talking, either—we still don't know what they want."

I looked down at my hands: My fists were permanently clenched. When strangers fell in step with me at the grocery store, or if I thought I saw cars following me, I tensed. Several times I pulled into my own driveway and saw a car with two men in it parked across the street. I held my children tight in front of me and hurried them into the house. Each time it was the same car, and each time the same men flicked cigarette ashes out of the car windows.

I wished briefly for my brother, but I was the only family member around, and it could not be helped. My parents were old and my children young, and I was the responsible one. I stayed close by and answered the phone. Too often, nobody was there.

My father asked why, even after all the prayers and Bible studies, the men had struck. The strike was going into its twelfth week, and the demands were growing more and more bizarre.

Union Hall. The day came for independents to make their final decision. Downtown, men crowded into the hall.

Jerry Bradford and the other African-American members moved instinctively to the rear of the assembly room. After the Pledge of Allegiance and an opening prayer, the meeting began. Both union and non-union were present, and the president stepped in to make his plea.

"We are here today because of men like William Mitch and Samuel Gompers. Before we had leaders like that, workers were so bad off they had nothing to lose. They risked everything to fight for their rights. Because we have unions, we now have rules: Owners can't discharge a man any more just because he's a union man. Owners have to provide safety measures and time off, insurance and all those benefits we never had before.

"Today some of us find ourselves outside the unions, with new problems. Alabama some time ago declared itself a right to work state. This is so, and you not only do not have to belong to a union, but you do not have to abide by a union's agreements with management. I think we hurt ourselves this way.

"You independent truckers can strike on your own. The law will uphold your right to do so, but we have to stick up for each other." He paused letting his words take effect. "And I understand that you have grievances that you believe only the federal government can address. You may be right that the union is not ready to take these things on."

He opened the papers he had folded in his hand and read from the top of the stack.

"Oil prices are at an all-time high, so high a trucker cannot make a living. How can we make the government stop this profit gouging by the oil companies? I don't think we can. Will they put price caps on our diesel fuel? I doubt it. Will they put an end to the 55-mile-an-hour speed limit? You tell me."

The union leader slammed the palm of his hand on the table. "The real question is will they listen. Unless we stop transporting goods right here, right now, we will never get anybody's attention."

Cummings, the rabble rouser from Cooper Green's old office, sat on the front row and rose to speak. "To hell with whatever the union has agreed to. We start here. We stop Birmingham Manufacturing from turning out lowbeds."

A tall trucker named Theo, in jeans and a plaid shirt, stood then. He had his own list.

"Item One. Birmingham Manufacturing Company, Springville, Alabama. We can only support our independent truckers by shutting down the company that makes the trucks. All of us in this room are reasonable men who want to end this strike, but we are also committed men. The independent trucking industry is at stake, and if they can't make a living then we can't either."

"First demand: The Company must use the democratic method to decide who has seniority." Nods of approval went around the room. The only "no" came from Wayne, who was the most highly skilled welder and had seniority. Clement was new. He worked in the paint booth but had influence. With a change like this in place, Clement's job would take precedence over Wayne's.

"Second. We want a cost-of-living raise of 5 percent." Somebody in the audience said the company had already okayed that, but nobody had removed it from the list.

"That was a union concession. Third. We want an hour and a half for lunch."

"When did they put that in? Nobody in St. Clair County gets more than 45 minutes." Wayne spoke up again. He was not inclined to veto anything, but he could at least give them something to think about.

Even Clement said it made no sense. "Where do you think we can go for an hour and a half? We are miles away from anything out here in Springville," he said. "Anyway fuck that! If we take a longer lunch hour we will be late getting home." He had one foot out the door, ready to go home even then.

It had been a long, long twelve weeks and it was not over. Wayne moved they table the motion. The motion was tabled.

"Four. We will not be required to wear hard hats in the shop."

"That makes no sense. That's an OSHA requirement." Jerry said from way in the back, but nobody paid any attention. The demand stood.

"And Five. A worker can have somebody punch the time clock for him." This was a new item altogether

Clement moved they approve the truckers' recommendations. Those present approved the list except for the lunch break.

When the formal meeting adjourned, men hung around smoking cigarettes and talking politics. Cummings, who had been fairly quiet, decided to toss out one more thing for the men to think about. He looked toward the back of the room where Jerry and his friends stood.

"I say we stick with the union. If the unions don't represent the white race, then who will?"

"Well, unions ain't just white, you know. That's your Klan talking." Wayne spoke up just as his father had spoken up in the old days, against discrimination, but Wayne was no longer sure if it would do any good. He added, "Furthermore, the Attorney General says the Klan is a *subversive agent.*"

"That's a lie. I ain't no subversive agent." Cummings looked threateningly at Wayne. He would take care of Wayne later. "I ain't no subversive agent. I'm a goddam *patriot.*"

"I ain't no subversive agent, neither," yelled out a tall yellow-haired man close to the back. Murmuring and bitching began to take hold of the rest of the men.

"Well, if you ain't white you're probably a communist," a third man hollered. He was a big man with heavy shoulders and a narrow waist, so narrow his jeans were about to fall off.

While everybody was talking, Clement managed to slip out the door and head home, as had most of the African-Americans who had been in attendance. The whites turned their attention to Jerry, by now the only Negro there. Jerry was left to defend himself.

"He's one of them goddamn commie pinkos that want your little white kids to go to school with Niggers. Do you want your daughter to marry one of them Niggers?" It was the same third man, the one with the yellow hair.

Jerry took one step forward.

"What you got to say, boy?" The third man stood in front of the exit now, to block anybody who wanted to get past him. Nobody called the man out, nobody tried to counter this ugly side, not even men who had always called their Negro counterparts "brother."

"Just a minute," said Wayne. "We ain't the Teamsters, Boys. We ain't run by gangsters and Mafia. We don't have to act like them. We treat each other with respect."

"You telling me you want your daughter to go to school with black kids?" Fists shook. A real fight was brewing. Such a fight could go only one way.

Jerry thought out what he would say before he spoke. It was hard to give up the fight before it began.

"We don't want that no more than you do," he said. The once hot-headed son of the Black Mason was tamed. He was a minority of one with only one thing in mind, to save himself by keeping the peace. This was not an issue they had to decide today, he told them. It had nothing to do with the management contract. He kept talking and defused the powder keg.

The strike at Birmingham Manufacturing ended after fourteen weeks, but the unions were never the same again. Union members split into two camps, one against discrimination and one not. The scene repeated itself one strike after another from town to town. Managerial conglomerates across the nation winked and encouraged the division. In no time at all, these great divides brought down the whole union movement. And it came down hard.

9. We Meet Again

Nobody heard from Gertrude either during or after the strike. I called her on the phone once or twice in the years that followed, but she was busy with "her children." We had all but lost touch.

Then one day in 1978, when I was shopping downtown, I ducked into the old Woolworth's where the sit-ins had occurred during the 1960s. The soda fountain at Woolworth's still made chocolate sodas, which brought back memories that had nothing to do with the '60s. My mother always took me there for a chocolate soda after a visit to the doctor or a trip to buy school books or go Christmas shopping. Nobody sat at the counter that day, so I eased onto one of the stools and ordered a soda.

It brought back sadness, too, and I told myself I would not do it again. With good doctors and therapy, my mother had survived all these years, but she only survived. Her surgeries had limited her; she never left home now unless my father or I took her, and she was not there with me.

I drank half of my soda and was soon back out in the broiling June sun. My eyes adjusted slowly to the brightness. I thought my short-sightedness was playing tricks on me, but I was sure I saw a familiar shape coming toward me, arms outstretched. It was Gertrude indeed.

She looked wonderful, younger. She wore a tailored navy blue dress with a broad white collar that made her look almost slim, and she stood in comfortable brown shoes with a little heel that made her seem taller. She no longer carried the dark blue purse in both hands in front of her skirt but hung it fashionably from her shoulders. For just a fleeting moment I saw the new Gertrude: A real

253

woman who had gone to Washington and returned with a new purpose in life, a new resolve. But as we clung to each other, she was the old Gertrude and I was still the child. I fought back tears and just looked at her, still hesitant to ask too many questions.

"Where are you headed?" I finally asked. Her expression changed.

"I'm headed for the bus stop. Headed for West Blocton."

"Are you going to see your father?" I knew Bradford had moved there after they shut Margaret down.

"No, ma'am. He died last night. I'm going to meet Jerry, and we're going to the funeral home." That was all she said. She did not say how upset she was that her father had spent most of his life in the mines and had died with nothing to show for it. She only said she missed him.

"I'm so sorry," was all I could say.

"How are the children?" She changed the subject.

"Well, doing just fine," I said.

"You still working at the Company?" I was not sure which company she meant, but took it she meant Birmingham Publishing Company.

"Well, no. I'm working at UAB most of the time—and sometimes for my father."

"Well, that's just fine. That's just fine."

"Enough of that," I said. "Tell me how you are." She still wore her hair straight back in its neat bun, but the dark was streaked with gray. "And what are you doing these days, anyway?"

"I just stopped off at Pensions and Securities.[102] They send us little ones to take care of, you know." She smiled at nothing in particular on the sidewalk, as though she were looking at a little child.

"Are you ever going to stop working?" I wondered if she could, even if she wanted to. Then I surprised even myself, saying something that had been on my mind a long time.

"You know, if you ever want to retire, you could come live with me. I mean it," I said. "Now, I don't mean work for me. I mean come *live* with me. I have room, and I would like that very much." I knew I was overstepping my bounds. Her dimples fled, and she looked startled.

"No, ma'am, I can't." Then by way of explaining herself: "I have my own place, you know, out in Springville. And they still need me . . . the children, that is."

"Promise me you will let me know what you are doing and where you are, will you?"

"Well, yes'm, I will." She nodded hesitantly, as though she had more to say.

"You think I don't know anything about what's going on about Civil Rights, don't you? Well, that's not quite true. I cannot know all of it, but I know enough to worry about what might happen to you, being by yourself and all."

We talked a while longer. When we parted, we exchanged telephone numbers and I promised to come visit.

My first two children were almost grown now—about to go off to college, another finishing high school. The youngest was still a happy kid. I had done all I knew how to do to make sure they knew people of other races and creeds, but it was hard to figure out then, in Birmingham. I took them with me whenever I did volunteer work in African-American communities; I enlisted their help when I could in any neighborhood other than their own; and I looked but found pitiful few chances for them to play with children of other races.

It seemed beyond trivial to say these other children did not have the same opportunities as mine. But until that moment, standing next to Gertrude, it had never occurred to me that I, too, had been fighting that battle, although not very effectively. It was a lonely job, but I should have done better.

Five years passed before I received another of Gertrude's rare phone calls. She invited me to come see her. I had her address tucked inside my address book.

As a white girl driving out the Springville road and up the hill into the African-American neighborhood, even in the 1980s, I was still uncomfortable.

The laws had changed, and the bombings had ceased, but we still never knew what to expect.

I left Highway 11 for the old Margaret Road. White children still stood in tight knots on the sidewalk, and black children played in the red dirt near the train tracks. The old pump house stood nearby. I turned onto the gravel road and crossed the tracks to head up the hill. I drove past a few trailers, then counted off house numbers, which were badly out of order. Where I thought her house should have been there was nothing, only a vacant lot full of weeds.

I parked the car beside the field and ventured across it. The path led to a dense patch of trees. It looked familiar, somehow, but it had been so long. I could be wrong. I cut through a path in the trees. I recognized a sunlit clearing where the old wooden cabin used to be, but it was gone. In its place was a well-kept single wide trailer, decorated with potted begonias.

She stood at the top of the stoop, waving at me and making her way down the steps not too easily, holding on to the hand rail. In the tidy yard, two pine bark rockers with flowery ruffled cushions sat facing each other. Scattered around the entry were Impatiens in full bloom. Just beyond the trailer stood Gertrude's blue and white Oldsmobile, parked under a shade tree as though resting from a very long drive. Only then did I see the driveway that came up from the other side of the hill.

We spent the afternoon rocking, talking about little things. She owned the trailer, she said. She really did not know her neighbors and was not sure she wanted to. She still drove to work at the orphanage, and her sister was coming to visit.

I told her my mother needed more help dressing now and was not eating properly. She had lived longer than anybody ever thought she would, I said. She had beaten the odds, I said, even though anesthetics and cancer had taken their toll.

Gertrude listened quietly for a while then told me how she loved this part of St. Clair County. She loved watching green things grow. Her eyes lit up at the thought, and she smiled.

I thought she was okay, but I had not heard her chuckle. This left me thinking she had left something unsaid. I thought about quizzing her, but the day was so lovely I did not want anything to spoil it. When we said our goodbyes, she said something that I'm sure she thought I understood. I supposed it had to do with my mother.

"Don't be afraid of losing anything," she said.

"Unless it's your soul" I quipped, finding relief in my lame joke. She smiled again, her old curiosity smile I knew from encyclopedia days.

Late that evening, I wrote her another letter just for the heck of it, putting in writing what I had told her before about coming to live with me and saying I wasn't kidding when I said I would take care of her. I was hesitant to write it. I didn't want to embarrass her or put pressure on her. I dropped it in the mail.

She never wrote me back. But then I guess I had not really expected her to.

When the phone rang that next February, I was certain I was about to have at least a short chat with my dearest friend, but the voice on the other end was not hers. It was her sister's.

The sister's words entered my consciousness only in bits and snatches. Gertrude at home all that time, breast cancer like my mother's, funeral next week. Her passing was a blessing, the voice said.

I hung on to that voice on the other end of the phone, listening hard for details, not wanting to let go, not wanting to hang up. But no more details came.

On the day of the funeral I drove over to pick up my mother. I dressed her in a new cream-colored pants outfit I had bought her, and I helped her with her lipstick. I boosted her into the front seat of the station wagon, where she sat silently, not really understanding where we were going. I drove her down Montevallo Road toward Oporto Avenue.

As the white steeple of the Jackson Street Baptist Church appeared over the rooftops and the clapboard building hove into view, I could see that it, too, had aged. The siding sparkled with a new layer of whitewash, but the window panes needed caulking. Some of the panes had cracks in them, and gaps between the risers and the stairs confirmed that the ground had settled.

This was where Gertrude had felt most at home, where she went all those Thursday evenings for so many years. She had been in charge of the altar and had friends there, people she knew and cared about. And I did not know them.

We pulled into the parking lot. I held my mother's purse and helped her out of the car. We walked around to the front of the church. I put my arm under hers as we climbed slowly up the stairs and through the double doors of the sanctuary. Just inside, men in undertaker suits presented me with a fan and a printed program honoring Gertrude. All her kin were listed there. All those names I had heard about for so many years were real people.

One of the ushers accompanied us to the second row on the right hand side of the tiny chapel. I helped my mother slide into the pew ahead of me. She looked lost, small, and confused, but she was the survivor sitting beside me. Gertrude lay in a box at the end of the aisle, dressed in her blue dress with the wide collar and would never be sitting beside me.

The times, the chances, had passed. I felt foolish and incompetent and white. More than that, I felt tears welling up inside me and knew I could not stop them.

All Gertrude's friends and relations sat in the front pews on the left side of the aisle. Where her sisters and brothers sat was no more than a watery blur of hats and veils and handkerchiefs. When I tried to concentrate on what the minister was saying, I missed most of it. Finally the minister said "Amen," and the singing ended. Eulogies began in earnest. A few ladies stationed themselves near the exits to assist anyone who might faint.

But the eulogy stopped in mid-sentence. Something stirred in the back of the church. Everybody turned in unison to look, and I turned to look, too. Someone opened the main doors, and a ray of light slid across the floor halfway up the aisle. The church ladies and the choir members abandoned their posts and returned quietly to their seats.

A young woman with a dimple much like Gertrude's stood silhouetted in the doorway, shepherding about a dozen stair-step children. Boys and girls of all colors and sizes and shapes assembled themselves into a small straggly line and began a little procession toward the front of the church. They nudged and punched each other, but made a hesitant parade that moved slowly down the center aisle. Each child held a drawing or a few flowers or a paper cut-out. Each child, too small to see over the sides of the coffin, walked solemnly in front of the altar and turned past the table where the coffin lay, and each child laid his or her treasure gently beside the coffin. These were Gertrude's babies.

Empty handed, the children turned to go back down the aisle. Their teacher gathered them to her, one by one, as they reached the door and before they left the sanctuary to go back out into the sunshine. The eulogies took up where they left off. I do not remember much of anything else.

My father missed the ceremony. He had been away on a business trip, trying to shore up a floundering sales report. His days had not varied much in the past few years. He still went to work every day. My caregiver tasks had eased a little, although I was still on call in emergencies. Emergencies occurred regularly enough and usually meant a ride to the doctor or a trip to pick up medicine or groceries or what have you. It also meant real emergencies, like falling on ice.

The week after the funeral, my mother landed in the hospital once again, where she stayed for days. Some nights when I stayed with her, she did not sleep. I do not know what they were giving her, but she saw things in the corners, up on the ceiling and at the foot of her bed. She tried to tell me what she saw, but I never saw it. When the apparitions kept her awake, my heart went out to her, but they kept me awake, too. When the fever subsided, so did the shadows.

My father came to fetch her on a Saturday. He took her home and helped her into the living room chair. She still looked confused, and he left her in my charge. He disappeared behind the piano, and I heard him fiddling around with wires and plugs.

"We're home, Mom," I said. It was a Saturday, so I took her back to her bedroom and helped her change her clothes. I thought a loose jacket and matching pants with an elastic waist might help her feel better. She was still pretty even if she was just out of the hospital.

From the living room I heard static from the old radio as my father scrolled through the stations. In a little while, I heard the *Voice of Firestone* going full blast with Richard Tucker singing *Faust*. I could not believe what I was hearing.

After the piano had lain dormant all those years, after even the hymns had ceased, we were all listening to real music! We three listened together for that lovely hour. Then my father shut off the music and looked me in the eye.

"Some things just are not that important anymore," he said. "I've sold the bomb shelter."

"Good," I said. "It was too much like asking for something terrible to happen."

"Well, it still might, but mostly it's a bunch of hooey."

The only words I could think of were his: "The marines have landed" and "War Eagle!"

We sat quietly for a while, then he began to hum. My mother looked over at him, a rare moment of recognition lighting her face. In a minute he walked over to the sofa and took her hand to help her stand. Then he held her around the waist and lifted her just off the floor until her feet came to rest on his own. He began a slow two-step and began to sing. He forgot I was even there.

"When I'm calling you Oo-Oo-Oo, Oo-Oo-Oo."

The Indian Love Call. My mother chimed in, but so faintly the words were lost. They made it together at least across to the dining room. A little wobbly, but who was watching?

ACKNOWLEDGMENTS

I want to thank Constance Adler, my editor, for encouraging me to finish this work. I am especially grateful to her, to Hollins University and to all those who participated in her creative nonfiction workshop for their invaluable feedback and advice. The others I want to mention are the special angels in the sundry libraries I consulted as well as my friends and family, Johnnie Riley White and Bruce Fort who made comments and suggestions, and Bill Brosco who shared with me his experiences in this country's very first missile program, building the Redstone missile that was modeled after the German V-2 rocket. I wish I could thank those who are no longer with us: Gertrude Bradford and my grandmother, Margaret Berry Stafford, who shared their stories with me so many years ago, or my father George Stafford and his sister Marjorie Branscomb, who together recorded their memories of these people and events. I hope I have been faithful to what they told me and have done justice to their stories.

END NOTES

[1] Zukoski, Charles. The Button Gwinnett Columns. Lyn Stafford Brown, ed. 1990.

[2] McWhorter, Diane. Carry Me Home: The Climactic Battle of the Civil Rights Revolution (New York: Simon & Schuster, 2001).

[3] Frommeyer, D. W., II. Shoe History: Reflections on Polished Leather. A History of the Western Boot, http://www.shoeinfonet.com, accessed 22 May 2012.

[4] City of Leicester. Footwear Manufacture, A History of the County of Leicester: Vol. 4. (City of Leicester. 1958) pp 314-326.

[5] From Lithuania to the Chicago Stockyards -An Autobiography: Antanas Kaztauskis. Independent LVII (Aug. 4 1904)241 48. http://www.digitalhistory.uh.edu/social_history/10stockyards.cfm accessed May 8, 2012.

[6] The College of Engineering Library, University of Cincinnati, accessed May 8, 2012 http://www.libraries.uc.edu/libraries/ceas/about/history/index.html.

[7] McKenny, Thomas, James Hall, Hatherly Godd, Joseph Godd. History of the Indian Tribes of North America: with biographical sketches and anecdotes of the principal chiefs. (Philadelphia: D. Rice & Co., 1872) www. Accessgenealogy.com/opothle-yoholo-speaker-of-the-councils.htm accessed March 14, 2014.

[8] Ibid. Opothle Yoholo negotiated these terms in this secret treaty before he, too, left during the Civil War at the insistence of Abraham Lincoln.

[9] Frankovic, Joseph and Jeremy Lynch. Friendly and Brotherly: Letters of 1826 from the Department of War. From the Fort Smith Historical Journal. Vol. 31, No. 2. September 2007. http://library.uafs.edu/fshsj/31- 02_Complete_Issue.pdf accessed March 14, 2014.

[10] The Story of Jonathan and Pleasant in "Coal Mining," Encyclopaedia of Alabama. http://www.encyclopediaofalabama.org/face/Article.jsp?id=h-1473, accessed February 2013."

[11] The Abhika Tribe: Creek Nation History. Handbook of American Indians, 1906. http://www.accessgenealogy.com/native/tribes/creek/creektowns.htm accessed January 2012.

[12] Armes, Ethel. The story of coal and iron in Alabama (Birmingham, Alabama: The Bienville Publishing Co., 1910) 47. Before Alabama even became a state, entrepreneurs acquired the four coal fields that lay within Alabama's borders.

[13] Lafferty, RA. *Okla Hannaii*. Garden City, New York: Doubleday & Company, Inc. (1972) p. 145.

[14] Rev. W. C. Bradford, Pastor, First Baptist Church, Tuscaloosa, Alabama (photo in author's photo files).

[15] "The Abhika Tribe, from Creek Nation History, http://www.accessgenealogy.com/native/creek/early-history/Abhika_tribe.htm.

[16] Malvinia's grave marker at Oak Wood Cemetery in Waukegan, Illinois shows she died on February 20, 1862. The records at Oak Wood may reflect a re-burial or may be otherwise incorrect.

[17] Melsheimer, Frederick Valentine. Studied at Holzminden, ordained as a clergyman in the Lutheran church in 1775 at the University of Helmstaedt, and served as chaplain of the Brunswick Dragoons before coming to the United States.

[18] Avenue E, or 5th Avenue South, between 10th and 11th Streets in Birmingham, Alabama. See also "Concordia Club: Germans in Birmingham" in the Birmingham Public Library, Department of Archives and History, Birmingham, AL.

[19] Corley, Robert G. and Marvin Yeomans Whiting, editors (July 1979). Dedication. Journal of the Birmingham Historical Society. Vol. 6, No. 2.

[20] 1901 Alabama Constitutional Convention Official Proceedings. Forty First Day, Montgomery, Alabama, Wednesday, July 10, 1901. Speech by Mr. Heflin of Randolph County, p 1028 of 4450. http://www.legislature.state.al.us/misc/History/constitutions/1901/proceedings /1901_proceedings_vol1/day41.html.

[21] From http://www.worldwar1.com/biokais.htm May 7, 2012. The Kaiser said this to troops heading for the Boxer Rebellion in China.

[22] Armes, 335.

[23] Edwin Grant Stafford born 12 March 1870, Alice Mary or "Allie" born 31 August 1873, George Timothy 27 October 1875, and Cyrus Winfield Black Stafford born 7 July 1878.

[24] Taft, Phillip. Research Notes on Alabama Labor History, 1902-1977. Report: Johnathan Grossman. William Sylvis, Pioneer of American Labor (New York: Columbia University Press, 1945) 180. Taft Collection, Birmingham Public Library, Birmingham, Alabama. 1-75

[25] Taft Collection folio 49.1.1.1.3. Birmingham Labor Advocate, 56.

[26] Armes, 433.

[27] Taft Collection, folio 49.1.1.1.3. Samuel Gompers wants his union, the Alabama State Federation of Labor, to be a "model of fair behavior" with both blacks and whites. Selma refused to allow Samuel Gompers to hold its 1900 convention in its hall unless it was all white.

[28] Taft Collection, folio 49.1.1.1.3. Birmingham Labor Advocate. As quoted in the *Birmingham Age-Herald*. 26 April 1902. Commander Craight of the United Confederate Veterans offered a hall to the union "without regard to the color line."

[29]http://www.brainyquote.com/quotes/authors/s/samuel_gompers.html#lyc MRzQXps8fOH5a.99 accessed 19 June 2012.

[30] Edwin married an Alabama girl, Alline Deas, on New Year's Eve 1893 at Grace Episcopal Church. The couple lived briefly at 7321 First Avenue, East Lake then moved westward to 6011 First Avenue South, Birmingham.

[31] Armes, 109.

[32] Massilon Bridge Company built railroad bridges in Gadsden in the 1800s, before it merged with the Canton Bridge Company. Canton Bridge built through truss bridges in Jefferson County and later, an iron one. Engineers were hired for a variety of reasons: to harness the power of water, to build recreational lakes, to assess seams of ore and to shore up mines. Historic American Engineering Record in HABS/HAER. Collection found in the online catalog of the Library of Congress.

[33] Conference for Education in the South: Proceedings of the first Capon Springs Conference for Christian Education in the South. General Collection, State Library of North Carolina. Published by the Conference, 1898.

[34] James D. Anderson, contributor. The Education of Blacks in the South, 1860-1935. (Chapel Hill, North Carolina: University of North Carolina Press, 1989) pp 80 ffd. Alabama law, from 1832 until the 5th Amendment, provided fines of up to $500 for anyone who tried to educate a slave. The master punished the slave at his discretion. African Americans were forbidden from congregating unless an approved entity oversaw the meeting. That entity was either five slave owners or a Negro minister, but that Negro minister had to have been licensed by an approved church beforehand. In 1901, Alabama's Constitution was designed to limit education and disenfranchise Negroes, poor whites and citizens of foreign descent.

---

35 Woodson, C.G. The Education of the Negro Prior to 1861: A History of the Education of the Colored People of the United States from the Beginning of Slavery to the Civil War.(New York: G.P. Putnam's Sons, 1915) p.565.

36 Anderson, 82 ffd.

37 *The Southern Aegis*, August 17, 1934. Vol. 61, No. 33. Copy in the Pell City Library, St. Clair County, Alabama, accessed November 2013. Joseph Caswell is based on the story of union organizer, John Dean, kidnapped from his room in a Huntsville hotel. Union organizers were often kidnapped, tarred and feathered or even killed. Unions did not survive after World War I.

38 Taft Collection. folio 49.1.1.1.2. Convict revenue 1880s.

39 Ibid.

40 Alabama Fuel and Iron Company collection found in the Hoole Special Collections Library, Tuscaloosa, Alabama. Gandrud Reading Room, Mary Harmon Bryant Hall. Resolution of the Board of Directors, June 17, 1937, File 4643/2.

41 Ibid.

42 Taft Collection. Folio 49.1.1.1.3. Lists of ongoing strikes and lockouts.

43 Taft Collection. Folio 49.1.1.1.3. 1900 convention of the Alabama State Federation of Labor.

44 Taft Collection. Folio 49.1.1.1.2. Evans, Frank. Column in the *Birmingham Age-Herald*.

45 *The Southern Aegis*, August 17, 1934.

46 1901 Constitutional Convention: Official Proceedings, page 2097 Accessed June 2012 at http://www.legislature.state.al.us/misc/History/constitutions/1901/proceedings/1901_proceedings_vol1/day41.html.

47 1901 Constitutional Convention, pages 2070-2072.

48 Armes, 40, 42. In 1920, the trail went through Woodlawn.

[49] Armes, 144.

[50] Armes, 25.

[51] Alabama Fuel and Iron. 1928 Annual Report. Folio 4643/1.

[52] Taft Collection. Folio 49.1.1.1.2. "Coal and Coke Mines."

[53] Alabama Fuel and Iron. 1931 Annual Report of the President. File 4643/1.

[54] Alabama Fuel and Iron. 1934 Annual Report of the President. File 4643/2 and 1932 Board of Directors Minutes, Vol. 4, pp 51-118.

[55] Ibid.

[56] *The Southern Aegis*, August 31, 1934. Vol. 61, No. 35. Pell City Library, Pell City, AL.

[57] Ibid.

[58] Alabama Fuel and Iron. 1934 Board of Directors Minutes, 51-118.

[59] Taft, Philip and Gary M. Fink. Organizing Dixie: Alabama workers in the industrial era. (Tuscaloosa: The University Press. 1981). 112-115. Intimidation at the church in Brown's Station.

[60] McWhorter, 118.

[61] McWhorter, 52, 118.

[62] Windham, Margaret Foreman, compiler. History of Springville: Including the 1969 Edition and revisions and additions by Donna Cole Davis and Virginia Cole Taylor, p. 142. 1993. Copy in the Southern History Department, Birmingham Public Library.

[63] Taft. Organizing Dixie, 91-95 Story of Overton.

[64] Alabama Fuel and Iron. Annual Report of the President 1934. File 4643/2.

[65] Ibid.

[66] Alabama Fuel and Iron. Board of Directors Minutes of 15 June 1927. Vol. 4, pp 2-50. File #4643/1.

[67] Alabama Fuel and Iron. Annual Report of the President 1932. File 4643/2.

68 Taft. Organizing Dixie, 104, 111. J. L. Perry of TCI, one of the employers who formed the American Iron and Steel Institute, was successful in getting a cost of living wage increase for the men without the unions. He also squelched rumors that the employees would lose their jobs if the union gained recognition. Employers routinely discriminated against union members and shot roving pickets. In 1934 Union members reported they were shot by company-employed deputy sheriffs carrying machine guns.

69 Taft Collection. Folio 49.1.2.1.16 handwritten note from Borden Burr to Paul Pinkard.

70 Windham, 142.

71 *The Southern Aegis*, Vol. 61, No. 32, Ashville, Alabama. Friday, August 10, 1934 and Vol. 64, No. 16, 16 April, 1937.

72 *Birmingham News*, Wednesday, August 9, 1934. Microfilm Room, Birmingham Public Library, Birmingham, Alabama.

73 Alabama Fuel and Iron. Annual Report. 14 January 1933. Hoole Special Collection Library, Tuscaloosa, Alabama. Gandrud Reading Room, Mary Harmon Bryant Hall.

74 *Alabama: The News Magazine of the Deep South*, Hoole Special Collection Library, Tuscaloosa, Alabama. Gandrud Reading Room, Mary Harmon Bryant Hall.

75 Alabama Fuel and Iron. Annual Report of the President 1934. File 4643/2

76 *The Southern Aegis*. Vol. 61, No. 33, Friday, August 17, 1934. The kidnapping of John Dean.

77 Taft Collection. Folio 49.1.2.1.16 letter from William Mitch to Hugh L. Kerwin dated August 8, 1933.

78 Taft Collection. Folio 49.1.2.1.16 contains a typed note of a conversation between J. D. Acuff, Chairman of the Bituminous Coal Labor Board, and Charles B. Barnes dated April 6, 1934 stating that Acuff had gone to the operators to ask them to agree to a checkoff but was refused by DeBardeleben Coal Company.

[79] Taft Collection. Folio 49.1.2.1.16 Handwritten note from Borden Burr to Paul Pinkard, manager of Western Union, dated September 18, 1936 disclosing the contents of a telegram sent by William Mitch, then president of District 20, United Mine Workers of America to Hugh L. Kerwin, Director U.S. Department of Labor telling him of dynamite and machine gun nests planted on the DeBardeleben property. A similar telegram from William Mitch to Frances Perkins dated March 21, 1934 is also in this file.

[80] *St. Clair Aegis,* 15 November, 1935. p.5. "At Margaret, witnesses said that 25 cars and two trucks full of miners were turned back ater [sic] an explosion of dynamite in front of the lead car and after being fired on. . . .Whether or not the killing happened on company property or on a public highway will hinge much of the legal action. The union miners maintain that the killing happened on a public highway, while the officials of the Alabama Fuel and Iron Company maintain that Thomas was shot to death while trespassing on its property near Acmar. . . . Coroner Gray stated emphatically that the killing occurred on a public highway."

[81] *Pell City News,* October 31, 1935. According to officials of the United Mine Workers of America, union miners went to Margaret and Acmar to try to organize the miners of the Alabama Fuel and Iron Company. Officials and employees [sic] of the mine company said that the men invaded the company property to force the men working to quit and join the general coal strike.

[82] Alabama Fuel and Iron Company. Meeting of November 2, 1935.

[83] *Pell City News,* November 7, 1935, p 1.

[84] *Pell City News,* November 14, 1935, p 1.

[85] *St. Clair Aegis,* November 15, 1935, p 5.

[86] Taft Collection. Folio 49.1.1.1.2. Coal and Coke. Amalgamated Association of Railroad Employers and Birmingham Railway, Light and Power Co. locks out 300 of its workers. Others who locked out workers included L&N and Railway Power & Light, because workers said they would join the Amalgamated Association of Street Railway Employees of America. Furnace operators unite in Birmingham, oust the unions and reduce wages. Yellow Dog contract ends the unions until WWI.

[87] *Pell City News*, December 12, 1935, 1.

[88] Alabama Fuel and Iron. Resolution of the Board of Directors, June 17, 1937, File 4643/2.

[89] McWhorter, 61.

[90]Called "Operation Paperclip." More than 760 Germans, including many engineers and scientists, were shipped to Ft. Bliss, Texas. These lists are on Ancestry.com. New York, Passenger Lists, 1820-1957 [database on-line] Provo, UT, USA: 1947. http://interactive.ancestry.com/7488/NYT715_7509-0606.

[91] DeBardeleben sold parcels for $10 per acre because he could not give clear title to them.

[92] McWhorter, p. 138.

[93] George Thayer. The farther shores of politics: the American political fringe today (Simon and Schuster, 1967) "At the same time the KKK was courting the pro-Nazi German-American Bund, the two orgainzations held a joint rally in New Jersey's 'Camp Nordlund.'"

[94] In 1912, Woodrow Wilson ran against Theodore Roosevelt and William Howard Taft on an anti-monopoly policy among other things.

[95] Ed., *Birmingham World* article on the Veterans of World War II. Rev. Henry Jackson called King and Shuttlesworth 'upside-downers' and tried to dissuade them from demonstrating. He held the middle class view, which was that they should work only through the courts.

⁹⁶ *Birmingham Independent: Dedicated to a free America*. Birmingham, Alabama. Copies in Birmingham Public Library, Southern History Room.

⁹⁷ Don Terry. Bringing back Birch. *Intelligence Report* (Spring 2013, No. 149) accessed 11 December 2013,
http://www.splcenter.org/home/2012/spring/bringing-back-birch.

⁹⁸ Jimmy Jones. Radical Left organizes in Birmingham. *Birmingham Independent: Dedicated to a free America*. (Birmingham, Alabama, October 19-26, 1966).

⁹⁹ McWhorter, 71. Quote from Gerald L. K. Smith of the Christian Nationalist Crusade.

¹⁰⁰ Letter from Joseph L. Spencer, Contract Compliance Examiner, Post Office Department Correspondence dated November 4, 1968 referring to previous action. Birmingham Manufacturing Company papers in the offices of Adams and Reese Law Firm, Birmingham, Alabama. Accessed November 2013.

¹⁰¹ An African-American named Judge Edward Aaron was castrated by the original Ku Klux Klan of the Confederacy on September 2, 1957. Forster, Arnold and Epstein, Benjamin R. *Report on the Ku Klux Klan*. New York: Anti-Defamation League of B'nai B'rith, 1965, p 20.

¹⁰² The orphanage that once served primarily orphans and small children, the old Mercy Home, was taken over by the Department of Pensions and Securities in 1974.

75075975R00157

Made in the USA
Columbia, SC
12 August 2017